Donated by
Msgr. Owen F. Campion

D1154675

WITHOUT EQUAL

H. M. QUEEN ELIZABETH, THE QUEEN MOTHER

ANN MORROW

HOUSE OF
STRATUS

Acknowledgements

Over the years I have been grateful for help from many people close to the Queen Mother who have been supportive in different ways. To respect the wishes of those who do not wish to be identified, some names have been withheld.

It is a sad fact that many of those in the Queen Mother's charmed circle have not survived to meet the new century. All the same the contributions of those late advisers and friends who were so much part of her life make a valuable basis for this celebratory portrait. They include Sir Martin Gilliat, her Private Secretary; Lord Charteris; Group-Captain Peter Townsend; Lord Drogheda; Lord Boothby; Commander Vyner; Sir Frederick Ashton; Sir Hugh Casson; Sir Peter Pears; Lord Home, and Lord Thurso, on all of whose memories and first-hand observation this biography is founded.

I am also indebted for background material and brief quotes to the following: *The Journals of Woodrow Wyatt*; *Battle Royal* by Kirsty McLeod; *Queen Elizabeth the Queen Mother at Clarence House* by John Cornforth; *Secret Muses, the Life of Frederick Ashton*, by Julie Kavanagh; Andrew Roberts in conversation with Sir Isaiah Berlin, the *Evening Standard*; *George VI* by Sarah Bradford; *My Darling Buffy* by Grania Forbes; *The Roy Strong Diaries*; *Class: Knowing Your Place in Modern Britain* by Stephen Brook; *Mrs Keppel and Her Daughter* by Diana Souhami; *George V* by Kenneth Rose; *The Royal Jewels* by Suzy Menkes; *Life Regained* by Frances Partridge.

In addition my thanks again to the Dowager Countess of Strathmore at Glamis; to Lady Bowes-Lyon at The Bury, Hertfordshire; Dame Frances Campbell-Preston, and Lady Elizabeth Bassett at Clarence House.

My thanks to my publisher David Lane, to Mike Shaw, an agent without equal, and Jonathan Pegg, his assistant at Curtis Brown.

My appreciation is as always of editor Janice Robertson for the graceful touch of her pen to the manuscript and Marianne Taylor-Seymour for her fresh, designer approach to the selection of photographs. Thank you to the House of Stratus team in London and Yorkshire, especially Mark Bollon, Emma Drew, Tim Forrester, Sasha Morton and Lorraine Saunders for their contribution in bringing this book together.

To my husband I owe most, for his special understanding, guidance and the entertaining flavour of his contributions. This book is for him, for our families and friends, here and in Australia, America, Ireland and India.

Sir Ralph Anstruther: former Treasurer and good friend who lives near the Castle of Mey.

Mrs Lilian Bailey: a psychic who helped the Queen Mother after the King's death.

Stanley Baldwin: Prime Minister at the time of the Abdication.

Cecilia Cavendish-Bentinck, Countess of Strathmore: The Queen mother's mother.

Lord Charteris of Amisfield: distinguished courtier and friend, Private Secretary to the Queen and later Provost at Eton.

Ruth, Lady Fermoy: good friend to the Queen Mother and grandmother of Diana, late Princess of Wales.

Janet Fox: maid at Glamis and one of the first to hear the news that Elizabeth was engaged to the Duke of York.

Sir Martin Gilliat: The Queen Mother's Private Secretary and friend who shared her love of the turf.

Norman Hartnell: The Queen Mother's dress designer.

Seamus Heaney and Ted Hughes: Poet Laureates.

Marie-Luce Jamagne: the Belgian woman married by Group Peter Townsend after separation from Princess Margaret.

Mrs Alice Keppel: mistress of King Edward VII and great grandmother of Mrs Camilla Parker-Bowles. Mrs Keppel had two daughters. One was Violet Trefusis who had a romance with Vita Sackville-West. The other daughter, Sonia, married Roland Cubbitt. Their daughter, Rosalind, married Major Bruce Shand and had three children, Mark, an explorer, Annabel, and Camilla, who later married Andrew Parker-Bowles and then fell in love with Prince Charles.

Dr Cosmo Lang: Archbishop of Canterbury.

Lionel Logue: speech therapist who helped the Duke of York get over his stutter.

Monster of Glamis: [allegedly] Thomas, 12th Earl of Glamis.

Haakon, King of Norway: in love with the Queen Mother for years and hoped she would marry him.

Joy Quested Nowell: The Queen Mother's milliner.

Mrs Caroline Scott: [maternal grandmother], shaped the Queen Mother's artistic taste in Italy when she visited Villa Capponi as a child.

Commander Clare Vyner: valued friend who assisted the Queen Mother's purchase of the Castle of Mey when she was newly widowed.

List of Illustrations

Contents

The Royal Family

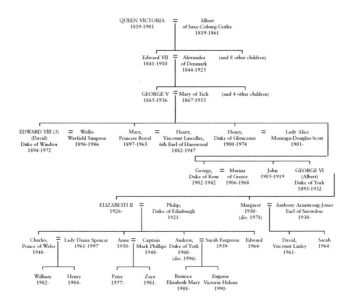

QUEEN VICTORIA = Albert
1819-1901   of Saxe-Coburg-Gotha
               1819-1861

Edward VII = Alexandra   (and 8 other children)
1841-1910   of Denmark
             1844-1925

GEORGE V = Mary of Teck   (and 4 other children)
1865-1936 1867-1953

EDWARD VIII (3) = Wallis   Mary, = Henry,   Henry, = Lady Alice
(David)   Warfield   Princess Viscount Lascelles, Duke of Gloucester Montagu-Douglas-Scott
Duke of Windsor Simpson   Royal   6th Earl of Harewood 1900-1974   1901-
1894-1972   1896-1986   1897-1965 1882-1947

George, = Marina   John   GEORGE VI
Duke of Kent of Greece 1905-1919 (Albert)
1902-1942   1906-1968   Duke of York
                                   1895-1952

ELIZABETH II = Philip,   Margaret = Anthony Armstrong-Jones
1926-   Duke of Edinburgh   1930-   Earl of Snowdon
               1921-   (div. 1978) 1930-

Charles, = Lady Diana Spencer Anne = Captain   Andrew, = Sarah Ferguson Edward   David, = Sarah
Prince of Wales 1961-1997   1950- Mark Phillips Duke of York 1959-   1964-   Viscount Linley 1964-
1948-   1948-   1960-   1961-
                                                     (div. 1996)

William   Henry   Peter   Zara   Beatrice   Eugenie
1982-   1984-   1977-   1981-   Elizabeth Mary   Victoria Helena
                                        1988-   1990-

Earls of Strathmore and Kinghorne

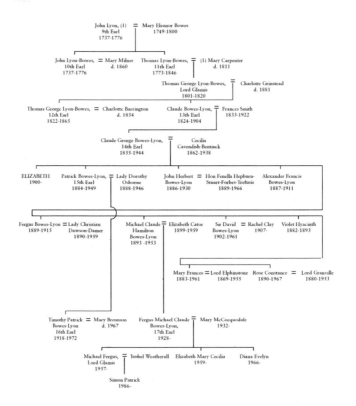

John Lyon, (1) = Mary Eleanor Bowes
9th Earl   1749-1800
1737-1776

John Lyon-Bowes, = Mary Milner   Thomas Lyon-Bowes, = (1) Mary Carpenter
10th Earl   d. 1860   11th Earl   d. 1811
1737-1776   1773-1846

Thomas George Lyon-Bowes, = Charlotte Grinstead
Lord Glamis   d. 1881
1801-1820

Thomas George Lyon-Bowes, = Charlotte Barrington   Claude Bowes-Lyon, = Frances Smith
12th Earl   d. 1854   13th Earl   1833-1922
1822-1865   1824-1904

Claude George Bowes-Lyon, = Cecilia
14th Earl   Cavendish-Bentinck
1855-1944   1862-1938

ELIZABETH   Patrick Bowes-Lyon, = Lady Dorothy   John Herbert = Hon Fenella Hepburn-   Alexander Francis
1900-   15th Earl   Osborne   Bowes-Lyon   Stuart-Forbes-Trefusis Bowes-Lyon
             1884-1949   1888-1946   1886-1930   1889-1966   1887-1911

Fergus Bowes-Lyon = Lady Christian   Michael Claude = Elizabeth Cator   Sir David = Rachel Clay   Violet Hyacinth
1889-1915   Dawson-Damer   Hamilton   1899-1959   Bowes-Lyon 1907-   1882-1893
                    1890-1959   Bowes-Lyon   1902-1961
                                     1893-1953

Mary Frances = Lord Elphinstone   Rose Constance = Lord Granville
1883-1961   1869-1955   1890-1967   1880-1953

Timothy Patrick = Mary Brennam   Fergus Michael Claude = Mary McCorquodale
Bowes-Lyon   d. 1967   Bowes-Lyon,   1932-
16th Earl   17th Earl
1918-1972   1928-

Michael Fergus, = Isobel Weatherall   Elizabeth Mary Cecilia   Diana Evelyn
Lord Glamis   1959-   1966-
1957-

Simon Patrick
1986-

FOREWORD

A Golden Harvest

The world looks at her with an indulgent smile, this eminent Victorian who has inspired more affection than almost anyone else in 20th-century Britain. Her style is unique. Without any hint of switched-on charm, she brings the best out in people.

Queen Elizabeth the Queen Mother is without equal. Whether dressed in layers of chiffon and ostrich feathers, or reflective in black with diamond clip and poppies, people love the way she looks. Faces in a crowd light up when they see her.

Her warmth and grace in old age cheers us all. Still there is that zest for life which once revitalised a stuffy, inflexible monarchy. Keeping her place as the most popular royal, she has seen off competition by being 'herself', yet she remains unimpeachably blue-blooded.

But Elizabeth never wished to be royal. Twice she refused Prince Albert's proposals. When eventually she accepted the King's second son, she came to embody the best of the British monarchy. Queen Marie of Romania thought her 'one of the dearest, sweetest women in the world'.

Few people have enjoyed so many titles in a lifetime: born Lady Elizabeth Bowes-Lyon, she became Duchess of York when she married in 1923, then Queen, Empress of India, and finally Queen Mother. Her Household still refers to her as Her Majesty, Queen Elizabeth, and thinks of her daughter as 'the young Queen', down the road at Buckingham Palace.

The peaceful family life enjoyed by the Duke and Duchess of York, and it was an exceptionally happy royal marriage, was shattered thirteen years after the wedding by the Abdication.

'Bertie', as Elizabeth always called her husband, was catapulted onto the throne, forced to become King.

Fond of her brother-in-law, Edward VIII, Elizabeth made allowances for him and put the blame for the Abdication squarely on the taut shoulders of the American divorcee, Mrs Wallis Simpson, the woman he loved.

The stress of being King, the Queen Mother believed, shortened George VI's life. When the King died in 1952, Mrs Simpson was referred to as 'the woman who killed my husband'.

There was granite beneath the charm, a friend said of the Queen Mother ... although hers was 'the nicest form of granite'. Even when they were both elderly widows, the hand of friendship was never extended to the Duchess of Windsor. This has proved to be one of the few areas where she has shown real bitterness. In the Queen Mother's company, you mention Mrs Simpson's name at your peril.

The first wholly British Consort since Tudor times, Elizabeth set an enviably high standard for any future king's wife. As Queen she had an almost Diana-like effect.

Doyenne of the royal family, her courage and compassion during the Second World War have never been forgotten. In a Herculean task which surprised the gloomy prophets, George VI, with her support, restored the monarchy to a level of almost unprecedented popularity. The King spoke of his wife as 'my helpmeet and my joy'.

After his death, overcome by depression, she was tempted to retire to the peaceful seclusion of her Scottish castle. But Sir Winston Churchill told her, 'The people need you,' and persuaded her to return to public life. Dedicated, philosophical and rarely fretful, she carved out a singularly successful solo role as Queen Mother. 'A very strong personality', Lord David Cecil said, 'for someone so unaggressive'.

Her faith, her stamina and her willpower sustained her through long years of widowhood, enabling her to create a remarkable public life for herself. Before she changed the rules, widows of kings were expected to be discreet dowager figures in quiet subfusc clothes, hovering unobtrusively in the Palace shadows.

Then along came the Queen Mother with her love of bright colours and sheer enjoyment of the public eye. Surprisingly modern, she used helicopters like taxis. The 'chopper,' she says, 'changed my life as conclusively as that of Anne Boleyn.'

Yet she would treasure her beloved Edwardian standards. She never drove a car, rarely wore trousers except to go fishing, and was hardly ever seen without a hat even on picnics. 'Holding hands in a boat was her idea of courting,' a friend said, summing up the appeal of this gentle woman who captivated kings.

Strong, brave and original, believing the best of people, she was not often disappointed. Astronauts, ballet dancers, world leaders, opera singers, war heroes, rock musicians, stable lads, scientists, ghillies and gondoliers, all were touched by her magnetic quality, something in that faintly rolling walk, the slow smile and genuine solicitude.

Her 'salad days' charm meant she never had to assert herself. It was rare to hear her slightly high cut-glass voice in public, and then it was a reminder of old-fashioned values, summer afternoons, cricket, Pimms on the lawn and full-blown tea roses. With her round face, even in old age, she rarely looked cross or haggard. She smiles a lot.

Harbouring reserves of energy remarkable for someone half her age, she sailed through two hip replacements, one at the age of ninety-eight, and then a cataract operation so she need never be seen wearing her tortoiseshell spectacles in public.

In her ninety-ninth year she was still carrying out engagements. Whether at the Blue Cross Animal Hospital, the Citizens Advice Bureau or the London Gardens Society, her commitment was always seamless. When the Queen was in South Africa in November 1999, the Queen Mother stood in for her and gave a bravura performance leading the nation in two minutes' silence for the war dead of the century. Afterwards she met veterans outside Westminster Abbey and stood in the cold for over an hour, swopping memories of the Blitz as if with old friends.

There was genuine surprise that anyone should turn out to see her, that murmured, appreciative 'Oh, thank you for coming,' and if it was raining or windy, 'and on such a dreadful day ...' When her horse Laffy won the Ulster Grand

National in 1962, a woman in the crowd called out, 'Would you bless us Your Majesty?' Such was her ability to generate enthusiasm. In spite of this affection bordering on adulation, the Queen Mother remained an unassuming person, with time only for 'real people'.

She was born at the beginning of the century. The year 1900 was an auspicious one. Britain was the world's most industrialised country; the first Zeppelin took off; the French Impressionists defied the critics and held their first grand scale exhibition in Paris. The life expectancy of a woman was then sixty-seven. Having lived to such a great age, the Queen Mother attributes her longevity to her Scottish genes and her Leo star sign. Proud of her Scottish ancestry, she watched the Queen in Edinburgh, in June 1999, opening the first Scottish Parliament in 300 years.

The death of Diana, Princess of Wales in 1997 inspired a new public sentimentality in Britain and, in the emotional heat of the moment, a brief hostility to her husband's family. Illusions were stripped away faster than you could say 'Republic'. In this critical mood the Queen Mother feared briefly for the monarchy's survival.

As a devoted wife, she had been dismayed by the unseemly divorces of three of her grandchildren and the avalanche of trouble which followed for the royal family. Appalled by the massive fire at Windsor Castle and, worse, the taxpayers' refusal to pay the restoration bill, she agreed with the Queen's description of 1992 as an *annus horribilis*.

But grievances were aired and the result has been a warmer and less distant monarchy. After living through a more dramatic royal crisis in 1937, the Queen Mother was delighted to see the Queen looking happier and enjoying more popularity in 1999 than at any time during her reign. Now she can look forward to the Golden Jubilee in 2002 and to celebrating her daughter's fifty steadfast years on the throne.

Her politics have been straightforward. A fan of Lady Thatcher, her unwavering belief has been in a 'good old Tory government with a strong Labour opposition'. Aristocrats turned Socialist are seen as 'traitors'. A glass would be raised in mock toast to Mr Anthony Wedgwood Benn, who abandoned his title. African dictator Idi Amin and Jimmy

Carter have also been toasted – the former American President gave her a syrupy kiss and was never forgiven: 'the only man since my dear husband died to kiss me on the lips'.

Changes she has not liked have included removing 750 hereditary peers from the House of Lords; the proposed ban on fox hunting, and the loss of British identity as we all become more European. She has never warmed to Germany. Worst of all for her has been the fast disappearing British Empire. When asked what being Empress of India felt like, she replied, 'It was very nice while it lasted.' Luckily this was not being said about the British monarchy.

At heart a natural sybarite, she has always enjoyed music, walking, gardening, old churches, traditional cottage flowers, couture clothes, feathery hats, landscapes, dancing and entertaining.

Indeed, her love of dancing has been legendary. Highland lairds, who think nothing of having two Barnsley chops for breakfast, got winded as they partnered her in the 'Dashing White Sergeant'. 'Perhaps Ma'am would like to rest?' The answer was 'Certainly not', and that has been her attitude to life. It is her platinum rule never to show tiredness but to walk head up and smile. Lord Wyatt of Weeford thought the Queen Mother had the heart of a young girl.

There are a million things about her that are special: breaking up afternoon tea at Clarence House with a gentle hint, 'Oh my dears, we all have to go,' or 'No, not another drink; I mustn't be tiddly at the Palace'. Leavetaking has been one of her gifts.

Lord Charteris of Amisfield said, 'She had a magical ability to make one feel witty and deeply interesting.' Hers is an authentic interest; a plump small hand with pink varnished nails pats a sofa inviting you to sit beside her, making all nervousness disappear. 'Do you like these cushions? My daughters had them redone.' Adored by both her children, the Queen Mother has always given them graceful, unquestioning support.

At weekends at The Royal Lodge, Windsor, it was not unusual to see the Queen on her hands and knees in the garden weeding her mother's flower beds, explaining as she came in, brushing a twig from her hair: 'Mummie couldn't find a gardener.' 'Oh darling, can you stay for a drink?' the Queen Mother would ask. 'Sorry ... can't stop,' the Queen would reply, giving a light kiss to that comforting cheek before rushing back to the Castle to entertain a clutch of advisers, and talk about Prince William's training as future King William V, the possibility of Australia without the monarchy, or the Commonwealth in the 21st century.

'The most marvellous mother one could have,' the Queen says, and salutes the Queen Mother at every Birthday Parade. Mother and daughter speak every day. 'Your Majesty? Her Majesty, Your Majesty' – a happy task for the Buckingham Palace telephone operator. On 4th August 2000 there will be a birthday telegram from Buckingham Palace.

The Queen Mother was the first member of the royal family to smile in public, to fly round the world, and to enter a crowd with outstretched hand. Her mellow experience, her kindness, her wisdom and those impeccably high standards have all left a golden harvest being enjoyed by the Queen and generations of young royals today. Her values have touched us all.

CHAPTER 1

A Honeyed Childhood

The Queen Mother had an Edwardian childhood of privilege and cosseting, and would always acknowledge this sunny start to a remarkable life: 'I realise more and more the wonderful sense of security and happiness which comes from a beloved home.'

Even by Victorian standards of winsome little girls with perfect manners, Lady Elizabeth Bowes-Lyon was exceptional with her 'infectious ease' and voice of 'drowsy sweetness'.

Born in London on a muggy, damp Saturday, 4th August 1900, the Strathmore's ninth baby, Elizabeth, was a 'bundle of prettiness' with tufts of dark hair, and was admired in the pram embossed with the family crest.

Her mother, the capable Lady Cecilia, was thirty-eight, a Cavendish-Bentinck, and great-granddaughter of the 3rd Duke of Portland, who had been Prime Minister twice and Home Secretary under Pitt.

Upright and god-fearing, the daughter of a clergyman, she expected women guests to wear white veils crocheted like mantillas and laid out in their bedrooms for morning family prayers. This tall, slightly angular woman, her lacy collars softening a tendency to beakiness, 'definitely wore the trousers' but had 'a genius for family life'.

Elizabeth's father 'Claudie', forty-five year old Lord Glamis, later the 14th Earl of Strathmore, had estates in Durham, Hertfordshire and Scotland. This meticulously correct figure prided himself on being a descendant of Robert II, the first of Scotland's Stuart Kings. So he was not impressed when ten year old Elizabeth was told by a palmist at a garden party, 'You will be a Queen when you grow up.' Proud of a lineage going back to the Middle Ages, he said: 'If there is one thing I have determined for my children, it is that they shall not have any post about the Court.'

He was tall with white whiskers and military bearing, and had a known weakness for 'Shooting pudding', a version of Christmas plum pudding served when out on the grouse moor. He also enjoyed flicking oranges at his wife in the dining room, a pastime at odds with his dignified appearance. Lady Cecilia usually caught these fruit missiles and would be rewarded with a hug by her husband, who would go to sit on the edge of her chair and put an arm around her.

He was descended from hard-drinking Scottish stock. In the old days it was not unusual when the Strathmore bucks dined for a pageboy to lurk beneath the table, ready to leap up and loosen the men's collars as they fell inebriated from their chairs.

Elizabeth, the second youngest of ten children, was born in a summer marked by several important events: another election victory for the Tories and their Prime Minister the Marquis of Salisbury, the death of Oscar Wilde in Paris, the first flight of the Count Zeppelin airship, and the last months of Queen Victoria's reign. Victoria died on 22nd January 1901.

For some reason, Lord Glamis showed an uncharacteristic woolliness and failed to register the birth of this most important baby, leaving it until 21st September and then incorrectly as having taken place at St Paul's, Walden Bury, Hertfordshire. This Queen Anne House, which had been in the Bowes-Lyon family for two centuries, was their weekend country home. Called 'the Bury' by the Queen Mother, it was a place she would always associate with extraordinary happiness.

There would always be an endearing mystery about exactly where in London she was born. Sharing her parents' Victorian reticence about health, nobody was quite sure whether the birth had been at the family home at 20 St James' Square (a Regency house in Mayfair with graceful windows), in a hansom cab, in an ambulance on the way to a hospital, or a house somewhere else in London. Nobody knew. Lord Glamis would uncomplainingly pay his fine of seven shillings and sixpence for being four days late registering the birth.

Her passport, No. 380040, states that she was born in London, as indeed did the Queen Mother herself in an unsolicited statement in the 1980s, an attempt to stop any more prurient speculation.

A simpler explanation for the oversight was that August was traditionally a dead month in London, and Lord Glamis (family motto: 'In thee O Lord, have I put my trust') had fled on the 12th with the annual grouse exodus to Scotland to take part in the Dalhousie, Bute and Douglas shoots. His wife, not feeling up to the journey, stayed behind.

Hardly a slapdash couple, Sir Claude and Lady Cecilia had been oddly absent-minded about the formalities, which could scarcely have been new to them. Each of the other children had been registered speedily and correctly. In the column marked 'Occupation', Sir Claude always wrote 'Peer's eldest son'.

The eldest child, Violet Hyacinth, born in 1882, died of diphtheria when she was eleven. Lady Strathmore designed a tablet for her with two cherubs holding a wreath, which hangs above the eau-de-nil chancel in All Saints, the family church near the Bury.

This medieval church, high on a hill and adorned with tapestried kneelers of snowy doves and sheaves of wheat, has a plaque to the Queen Mother and a memorial window to her brother David Bowes-Lyon. David was a churchwarden and Lord Lieutenant of the county, and a merchant banker with Morgan Grenfell. He lived at St Paul's until his death in 1961.

The other Strathmore children were close in age: Mary Frances May, born 1883, who married Sidney, Baron Elphinstone; Patrick, Lord Glamis, 1884, who married Lady Dorothy Osborn; John, 1886, who married the Hon. Fenella Hepburn-Stuart-Forbes-Trefusis; Alexander, 1887, who died of a brain tumour when he was 24; Fergus, 1889, married Lady Christian Dawson-Damer, killed in action in 1915; Rose, born 1890, married to Rear-Admiral William 'Wisp' Leveson-Gower, later 4th Earl Granville; Michael, born 1893, married Elizabeth Cator.

Lady Elizabeth was christened on Sunday, 23rd September 1900, after Matins. Lord Glamis thought his youngest daughter looked like a cherub and insisted her second name should be Angela.

David was born on 2nd May 1902. He and Lady Elizabeth were occasionally mistaken for the Countess' grandchildren. This would airily be passed off with a biblical reference to my 'two Benjamins', Benjamin being the youngest of Jacob's twelve sons.

At thirteen months, Lady Elizabeth was running about; at three she was self-possessed enough to ask the factor at Glamis, 'How do you do, Mr Ralston? I haven't seen you look so well, not for years and years, but I am sure you will be sorry to know that Lord Glamis has got the toothache.' At four she was enjoying her copy of 'Little Folks' magazine. A guest who arrived early thought her 'the most astonishing child for knowing the right thing to say', as she suggested: 'Shall us sit and chat?'

Lord Gorell, Secretary for Air in Lloyd George's coalition government, was struck by how Lady Elizabeth was 'responsive as a harp, wistful and appealing one moment, bright eyed and eager the next ... quick of intelligence and alive with humour'.

David, who would later refer quietly to 'my little sister who has married rather well', called her 'Elizabuff'. This became 'Buffy' and, as a sobriquet, easier to live with than most. When he was beaten with a hunting crop she wept. The bond between them lasted all their lives.

After his death, his widow Lady Bowes-Lyon, a niece of Lord Astor's and formerly Rachel Spender-Clay, continued living at the Bury. A happy house with yellow and white Adam ceilings, in the village of Walden, it still has charm though now industrial traffic roars past on the A1. In the hall, scribbles on the wall show the heights of Bowes-Lyon children – Elizabeth, October 1902, aged two. Her bedroom with pink chintz rosebud wallpaper remains unaltered.

In the family album, one photograph shows David, two, and Elizabeth, four, with her large eyes, curling hair, demure in tussore smocks and white ankle socks. But as Lady Bowes-Lyon pointed out, there was a steely determination about young 'Buffy', who can be seen hanging on firmly to the handles of a wheelbarrow. She looked sweetly at the photographer under his black sheet while David tugged unsuccessfully to regain control of his favourite garden toy. He got his own back later by pushing his sister out of an apple tree, which left her with a small permanent scar on her leg.

As adults they remained close. When President of the Royal Horticultural Show he inspired her with a love of gardening and she became an authority on roses. Every summer, long after his death, the Queen Mother would go back to the Bury and its mellow memories. She would walk in the rose garden where once her husband had proposed.

The younger Bowes-Lyon generation would organise jolly picnics to distract the two elderly widows from too much introspection, as they sat on a seat looking out across the lake at a white temple created in 1961 and decorated with the initials D and R entwined.

The Strathmore children were considered 'a good looking lot', a bit 'wild,' but well mannered. Glamis could be spartan; the children were quite accustomed to gathering up old newspapers to keep warm in bed. Lady Strathmore believed in thrift and parsimony. But there was intangible warmth and love for all the children in the family.

'We haven't had no presents lately,' David remarked meaningfully to his sister, as Lady Nina Balfour arrived in the drawing room of their town house. 'No,' replied Lady Elizabeth, 'but perhaps we shall have some big ones now Nina has come to London.'

The need for economy that was instilled into Elizabeth prompted her to appear once in the still room (the housemaid's pantry) at Glamis, suggesting: 'If you could make the pats of butter a little smaller it would be much better. Persons leave some of the big pats on their plates and that is very wasteful.' Their sensible, practical parents taught the children simple virtues.

'Nobody is boring,' Lady Strathmore told Elizabeth; 'and if you find somebody or something a bore, the fault lies in you.' The Queen Mother never forgot her mother's invaluable maxim.

Elizabeth's nickname was 'Merry Mischief' and she had a 'certain roguish quality'. An unusual child, Lord David Cecil noticed her in Hyde Park with her nursemaid, remarking on her 'small charming rosy face, around which twined and strayed rings and tendrils of silken hair'. She learnt to ride at the age of three, and later would follow the hounds of the Berwickshire Hunt.

Though sweet and appealing, Elizabeth was not always a paragon. She confessed one day when she was six, 'I have been so naughty … I have just taken the pair of scissors Mother has given me and cut up all my new sheets in strips.'

Until the age of four, home life was mainly in London and Hertfordshire. The Queen Mother thought of St Paul's as 'that dear friendly old house' with its mature red stone, scent of magnolia outside the large Queen Anne windows and pot-pourri in the drawing room, where she would try and lead in Bobs, her Shetland pony.

There were Persian kittens and ring doves called Caroline Curly-Love and Rhoda Wriggley-Worm. 'Here,' the Queen Mother liked to tell her daughters, 'were all the things that children could desire, dogs and tortoises … and on wet days books that are best read on the floor in front of the fire.' It was a honeyed childhood. She would try to recapture some of this enchantment for the two princesses, but the Abdication would cleave through the fantasy. There was nothing 'cosy', a favourite Queen Mother word, about Buckingham Palace.

Life for Elizabeth at the Bury was idyllic. Her memories were of summer days, often up at six for haymaking, then scampering along alleys of intertwining lime trees and past high, topiaried mulberry hedges shaped like peacocks and classical urns. The oak wood created by the French architect Le Nôtre, shaped like a starfish, was 'the haunt of fairies, with its anemones and ponds and moss-grown statues'. Here Elizabeth and her brother David chased each other round statues of Diana the goddess and the discus thrower – nicknamed 'the Bounding Butler'. They would pause only to pick wild strawberries.

In spring, the two would jump the Zambesi, their name for a stream running between banks covered in primroses. They sat under an oak tree and read, nibbling from their store of dark Meunier chocolate. They hid cigarettes in the Flea House reached by a shaky ladder from the Brew House.

A pleasing task was checking the fruit harvest with the gardeners. The 'two Benjamins' liked to go ahead to the red-walled kitchen garden to test for themselves the ripeness of the espaliered pears, peaches and plums.

It was not all unqualified bliss however. There was an unsuccessful attempt to save Lucifer, the pet pig, from being raffled in a local fête; Bobby the bullfinch, who had often hopped onto Lady Elizabeth's plate for titbits, was killed by the cat and buried in a pencil box.

At the end of the day, there was warm milk by the brass fender, as Clara Knight, known as 'Alla' to the children, only seventeen but already sensible and motherly, darned faded cotton dresses and ankle socks. One of twelve children, this willing girl came from the nearby village of Whitwell and was helped by Catherine 'Catta' McLean from Glamis. 'Alla' was single minded in her devotion. One day she would be photographed in all the newspapers – not for her pretty clothes, for she always wore a chamber pot hat and stout shoes – but because the Queen invited her to the Palace to look after her own children, Princess Elizabeth and Princess Margaret.

To the busy staff in both houses, the two youngest children were 'the dearest little couple'. Lady Elizabeth always seemed to take the lead, one housekeeper recalled. She would appear tripping down the stairs while her brother always hung back. 'David is rather shy,' his sister would explain, then artfully open a kitchen cupboard and help herself to some more of 'those nice creams'.

In London they went to the Constance Goff Kindergarten in Marylebone High Street and the Matilde Verne Pianoforte School in Cromwell Road, which in those days was a pleasant run in a horse-drawn carriage from Mayfair. Years later the Duchess of York invited Madame Verne to tea and asked if she would help the Duke of York to learn to play the piano. 'Oh Madame, you must give the Duke of York some lessons, I have already begun to teach him his notes and he knows three!'

Occasional treats included a visit to the theatre to see a J M Barrie play or some Shakespeare. Weddings and parties were excuses for new clothes for Elizabeth, pale pink or ivory satin frocks dotted with roses, her hair held back in a bow. Shortage of pocket money was not unusual though and the children's tennis racquets were frequently full of holes.

The Earl of Strathmore, by the standards of the day, was wealthy, inheriting £250,000 in 1904 when his father died. But he was alarmed when he got a telegram out of the blue in 1907; often in those days they heralded bad news. This one made him smile. It was a simple request: 'SOS. £.s.d. RSVP. Elizabeth.'

When Patrick Bowes-Lyon married the Duke of Leeds' third daughter Lady Dorothy Osborn in 1908, Elizabeth was a bridesmaid, a serene little figure in muslin and lace. At another wedding, she was a Romney heroine, with flowing sashes and a big hat. Hats always suited her. The Queen Mother adored clothes and could never resist new confections – 'delicious', 'such fun'.

Even such a charmed childhood had unhappy, bewildering spells. When David was sent to prep school at Broadstairs, he was miserable at first, and lost weight, while his sister pined: 'I miss him terribly' – and took him angel cake.

In 1911 her brother 'Alec' died of an unexplained illness. It was believed to have been the result of being hit by a cricket ball. Sensing her daughter's loneliness, Lady Strathmore sent Elizabeth to a 'select' academy for girls in Kensington run by Miss Irene and Miss Dorothy Birtwhistle. Here she spent eight months and won a prize for literature.

Then she was sent to Tuscany, where she stayed with her grandmother, Mrs Caroline Scott, at her Medici villa near Florence. This sophisticated woman had remarried Harry Warren Scott of Ancrum after the death of her clergyman husband, Charles Cavendish-Bentinck, and had been widowed again so was spending much more time in Italy. She tutored well-bred young English girls in the history of Italian art.

There could have been no one more receptive than her granddaughter, who loved the pink stoned Villa Capponi with its tiger lily-scented, calm, private chapel, cool damask red interior, and ornate Italian furniture. The Queen Mother would be drawn back again and again to this part of Italy where she first sipped dry vermouth at Doneys' celebrated café, a refresher after long days in the museums and galleries of Florence where her grandmother believed in enjoying one picture at a time.

She loved to walk at dusk along the terracotta footpath leading to the lemon garden, which was surrounded by roses, azaleas and oleanders. She listened to the goat bells, scenting whiffs of rosemary and thyme on the air as she looked across over the Tuscan hills dotted with formal cypress trees.

Here she would meet a colourful relative, Lady Ottoline Morrell, niece of Mrs Scott and the Duke of Portland's sister. This Bloomsbury Group *grande dame* may have sneeringly been called 'horse faced' by Lytton Strachey, but he, like the rest of the set, enjoyed her hospitality at Garsington Manor, her home near Oxford. Quentin Bell put it succinctly in his biography of his aunt, Virginia Woolf: 'Ottoline brought petticoats, frivolity and champagne to the buns, the buttery and the high thinking of Fitzroy Square.' Memories of the Villa Capponi inspired Lady Ottoline to create the graceful Italianite gardens enjoyed by opera-goers at Garsington today.

Elizabeth was receiving the 'best' sort of education, moving in cultivated circles, speaking French, reading poetry, learning colloquial Italian and acquiring a passing knowledge of art. Her grandmother took her to the Uffizi and all the best art galleries in Florence. Even at that early age, Elizabeth developed a passion for religious paintings.

At eight she acquired a Raffaelino del Garbo painting of a Madonna and Child. Now in an ornate round gold frame, it has a cherished place in her bedroom in Clarence House, which has a distinctly Italian flavour. However, looking slightly incongruous on the chimneypiece below are a couple of porcelain corgis and white geese amongst the tiny Florentine Revival Medici paintings. In Bordighera, where Mrs Scott had another villa, Elizabeth used her wiles to persuade the owner of an antique shop to let her have two golden carved angels for just three lira. The angels in their brocade robes stand sentinel by her bed; sometimes they are dressed in starched white linen.

By now a precocious collector, back in England Elizabeth sent a letter to a governess inviting her to come and see 'my objays (sic) d'art'. Any charge of philistinism in the royal family could not be levelled at the Queen Mother.

CHAPTER 2

Anyone Seen Those Rascals?

As the tingling notes of The Last Post echoed over the blue-grey Grampians, a bearer party of gamekeepers carried the body of the 13th Earl of Strathmore and Kinghorne from the castle. Young men of the Scots Guards lifted their trumpets towards the battlements to sound the Reveille.

This was 1904 and Sir Claude Glamis had succeeded his father to become 14th Earl of Strathmore. He inherited Glamis, St Paul's Walden Bury and Streatlam Castle in Durham, which had to be demolished in 1915. David Bowes-Lyon told a family friend that the children saw 'Glamis as a holiday place, Streatlam as a visit, and St Paul's as Home'.

The family would now spend much more time at Glamis, their fourteenth-century ancestral castle, with its ghosts, romance and secret stone staircases. The imposing structure, with quirky French turrets and 25,000 acres, had been a gift to a Bowes-Lyon ancestor, Sir John Lyon of Forteviot, when he married Princess Jean, daughter of Robert II of Scotland.

According to popular legend it was here Macbeth murdered King Duncan in 1040, and King Malcolm died of battle wounds in 1034. Allegedly the blood on the stones could never be washed away. Mary Stuart and her Four Maries were welcomed to the castle in 1562, as was the Old Pretender after the battle of Sheriffmuir in 1715, where the Earl of Strathmore was killed.

The family crest included the gold lion of Lyons, a rose motif and the green thistle. There were gilded lions all about: as nutcrackers, on either side of the fireplace, on letter boxes and as doorscrapers. Glamis was the stuff of a child's fairy story, with friendly ghosts, Earl Beardie, The Grey Lady and a Monster.

The Bowes-Lyon family had long borne with the Monster, less of a legend than guidebooks suppose. Mentally and physically handicapped with minikin arms and legs and a black hairy body, the Monster was Thomas, eldest son of the 11th Earl of Strathmore. He roamed round a dark room in a lonely far-flung wing of the sandstone castle. Each Glamis heir was told about the Monster when he was twenty-one; some never quite recovered from the shock.

The 11th Earl assumed that because of his disabilities, his heir's life would be short. Thomas was kept out of sight, but reputedly lived to be a hundred. Debrett recorded Thomas' death as having been on the day he was born; his younger brother, also conveniently called Thomas, became the 12th Earl.

But the spectre of the Monster was relentlessly present. A workman thought he saw him shambling about his cell and foolishly told other estate workers about his discovery. For this indiscretion, he was sent to the Antipodes with a pension for life.

Every summer nursemaids, valets, cooks and 'tweenies' would set out from London for the 400-mile journey on the 'Flying Scotsman' to Dundee, twelve miles from Glamis. When a great-niece complained once to the Queen Mother about the hardship of a trip from London on a train without a buffet, she was sweetly told, 'Why, I once made a banana last the whole journey.'

The Queen Mother's friends always insisted that marrying into the royal family held few terrors for her, as 'things had been done on such a grand scale at Glamis.' The Strathmores were one of the last aristocratic families to employ a private jester. So Elizabeth Bowes-Lyon, a Scottish princess, was not easily awed.

Elizabeth galloped side-saddle on her pony, a picture of Edwardian comeliness in her pink riding habit and soft hat, or joined picnics, riding her elderly donkey through the heather. Days were spent on the grouse moors, waiting for the boys home from Oxford and Eton, or watching them play cricket in their 'ducks', the Glamis team against the Dundee Drapers.

The Castle had its own bakery and distillery, and two to three hundred people worked for Lord Strathmore. In this feudal village Bent Tosh, the tailor, and the carpenter, Frank McNicol, would smile as they watched the girl they called 'our

Lady Elizabeth' race pinkly out of breath with brother David to buy bullseyes. Loyally they looked blank when Lady Strathmore, in full pursuit, charged in demanding, 'Anyone Seen Those Rascals?'

The emphasis was on self-reliance, and that happiness should be self-made. The Queen Mother had lyrical memories of delving into a 'wonderful chest full of period costumes … a great collection of the wigs that went with their gorgeousness'. Charades or Clumps remained favourite drawing room romps and in later years many a bishop or cabinet minister was persuaded to jump over cushions at The Royal Lodge in an imaginary Grand National.

In the candlelit fifteenth-century drawing room at Glamis, with its eight-foot thick walls and tree trunk logs glowing like amber in the Tudor fireplace, Lady Strathmore would sit comfortably at the piano to play 'Scotch Maiden's Dream', accompanied on the violin by the castle chaplain the Reverend James Stirton. His white pointed beard made him a family favourite. 'The Benjamins' joined in: Elizabeth in rose pink and silver brocade, a James I period dress from the chest. Poised and solemn, she would dance for half an hour with her brother, who was dressed in candy-striped jester's costume with cap and bells.

They were not always such a decorous pair and enjoyed pouring cold water on the heads of visitors arriving at the castle. This jape, called 'repelling raiders', discomfited guests who were preening themselves as they waited for the door with its 1659 iron knocker to be opened, especially as the water in the ewers was often ice cold.

In London on 4th August 1914, there was a family party to celebrate Elizabeth's birthday and her good results in her Oxford 'local', an exam equivalent to O-levels. The Strathmores took her to the Coliseum, that 'Palace of Entertainment', to see Charles Hawtrey and Fedorovna, a celebrated Russian ballet dancer. By the end of the birthday celebrations, lamps were 'going out all over Europe' and Britain had declared war with Germany.

CHAPTER 3

The Lassie

Adolescence is rarely a time of enchantment and now Elizabeth, this sheltered girl who would mature quickly, was catapulted into World War I and the start of what she later described as 'those awful four years'.

Suddenly the dreamy days of tennis parties, make-believe and fey innocence were over. The London house was shut down. Glamis became a military hospital for 1500 wounded and shell-shocked soldiers. Elizabeth, with her sister Rose who had trained as a nurse in London, helped out under the supervision of their mother. As the wounded arrived at the Castle, Lady Strathmore met them at the door, welcoming them as if they were her own family.

Four of her sons were of military age. Patrick joined the Scots Guards; Michael, who had been up at Magdalen College, Oxford, volunteered for the Royal Scots; Jock and Fergus chose the Black Watch. Years later the Queen Mother was invited to be their Colonel-in-Chief, a duty which gave her undisguised pleasure. A favourite pair of earrings were her Black Watch 'Jimmies', the St Andrew's Cross badge normally worn on Glengarry and sporran.

When the Regiment was leaving for Korea in 1951, the 'Jocks' were astonished to see the familiar face of their Colonel-in-Chief in the dawn mist, peering through a gap in a hedge. There had been formal farewells the night before, so she was the last person they expected to see at five the following morning, smiling and waving goodbye. But that was typical and meant a great deal to the men.

Too young to nurse, Elizabeth was best at cheering people up. At this early age she learnt the knack of hospital visiting, stopping at every bed with solicitous inquiries: 'Are you in pain?' 'Would you like me to write a letter home for you?' and the most popular inquiry was always, 'Have you enough tobacco?' She would have their Gold Flake and Navy Cut cigarettes fetched from Forfar.

The soldiers marvelled at the maturity of this 'womanly' fifteen year old, so kind-hearted and sympathetic. They were struck by her grace and appreciated how nothing was ever too much trouble, how when she wrote letters for them she often had to mask her own tears.

She could make them laugh on days when she sensed the pain was almost unbearable, by skidding about the lawn on her bicycle, taking her hands off the handlebars and tumbling into the flower beds. She played patience with them, and beat them at billiards and dominoes.

Her own memories were of '... knitting, knitting ... The billiard room was piled high with handknitted mufflers and homemade shirts. Sheepskin coats to be cut out and treated with some kind of varnish ... My chief occupation was crumpling up tissue paper until it was so soft that it no longer crackled, to put in the lining of sleeping bags ...' The only good thing, she cheerfully admitted later, was that, 'Lessons were neglected.'

Christmas was spent in the castle crypt. The wounded gathered round the great dark fir tree and the suits of armour looked friendly in the candlelight. Brightly, Elizabeth encouraged sing-songs, loving as she did the old vaudeville standards. Her distinctive voice joined in 'Goodbye Dolly I must leave you' and 'It's a long way to Tipperary.' As part of one entertainment, she introduced a knowing, exotic beauty under a provocative sprigged veil. The men were disappointed to find the saucebox in disguise was twelve-year old David Bowes-Lyon.

Seeing her wandering round Glamis 'in a spring dress and swinging a sunbonnet' with Peter her black satin cocker spaniel, the soldiers thought of Elizabeth simply as 'the lassie'. One reflected, 'She had a very taking habit of knitting her forehead just a little when she was speaking and her smile was a refreshment.' Yet under this disarming Bo-Peepery there was a surprisingly decisive young woman.

When she was sixteen, she showed a presence of mind which helped save Glamis and its treasures from destruction by fire as adults stood around horrified and immobilised. The fire began in the Castle Keep in Leigh Tower. The staff relied on water from the river Dean but had not anticipated the need for a ninety-foot hose to reach the Keep, where a high wind fanned the blaze and spread the flames wildly along the turrets.

As the fire roared to a crescendo, the local Forfar Fire Brigade admitted defeat. Some of the family and servants huddled together in disbelief on the lawn, thankful that most of the convalescent soldiers billeted at Glamis for the war had been well enough to go out to the cinema that day.

Seeing their dismay, Elizabeth quickly took control. Reassuring those standing around aghast, she said coolly, 'Don't worry – the Dundee fire brigade will be here soon, for I telephoned them when I called the local brigade.'

Then there was a second drama, potentially as destructive as the fire, when a huge lead tank used for water storage burst in the heat and bubbling water came cascading down the stone staircase, about to swamp the carpets and castle treasures. Quickly Elizabeth galvanised the onlookers, calmly giving orders. Those formerly paralysed with dismay were now told to get busy with sweeping brushes to divert the oncoming water into the basement.

The thirty volunteers lined up between the front door and the rooms containing family treasures. Elizabeth and her brothers created a human chain as paintings and antiques were passed from hand to hand and put in a safe place. While this was going on, the fire brigade arrived from Dundee. It took them some time before the flames were extinguished. Considerable damage was done to the castle but Elizabeth became known by the villagers as the 'braw lassie', praise indeed in those parts, where people are not given to extravagant compliments.

She touched many hearts that summer. Before leaving Glamis, a soldier, W H Harrup of the Eighth Seaforths, wrote prophetically in her autograph book, '... May the owner of this book be hung, drawn and quartered. Yes, hung in diamonds, drawn in a coach and four and quartered in the best house in the land.' That was on 12th September 1917.

In common with nearly every family in the country, the Bowes-Lyons would experience loss during the 1914-18 years. It accelerated the growing-up process and brought hard-earned maturity. Brother Fergus died in Flanders in 1915. He had been married a year earlier to Lady Christian Dawson-Damer, a daughter of the Earl of Portarlington. Sharing his youngest sister's canny intuition, he insisted on leave. He came home in September 1915 to celebrate his first wedding anniversary and to see his two-month old baby daughter for the first and only time. He was killed the day after his return at the taking of the Hohenzollern Redoubt.

When Michael Bowes-Lyon was reported missing, believed dead, neither 'Benjamin' could accept his death. David dreamt he saw his brother alive surrounded by trees. This 'second sight' or 'giftie' triumphed with the discovery of the adored older brother, found alive in a German forest. He had been taken prisoner of war and had severe head wounds. He was to have been invalided home, but with Strathmore thoughtfulness had sacrificed his own chance to give the opportunity to another wounded soldier. When he did get back to England he married Elizabeth Cator, a friend of Elizabeth from their Sloane Street schooldays. Their son Fergus would become 17th Earl of Strathmore and Kinghorne.

At the start of the war another brother, 'Jock' Bowes-Lyon, had married the Honourable Fenella Hepburn-Stuart-Forbes-Trefusis. They had five daughters. One, Anne, was particularly close to the Queen Mother. She married Viscount Anson and their two children are Lady Elizabeth Anson, who runs Party Planners, and her brother, photographer Lord Patrick Litchfield.

There was tragedy however for Jock and his wife: two of their children, 'Nicky' Nerissa (born in 1919) and 'Tinky' Katharine (1926), were mentally impaired.

The sisters' hereditary mental illness was linked with a disorder known as the 'fragile gene', passed through the mother's line. In large Victorian families it was not unusual to have at least one child less well able to cope. But Jock Bowes-Lyon doted on his children and could never come to terms with their heartbreaking vulnerability.

'They were incredibly beautiful little things and very sweet ... you couldn't help liking them,' their Leveson-Gower cousin Lady Mary Clayton recalled. 'They were,' she said, 'like some little wild creatures in the woods ... They couldn't speak, but they were very sensitive and responsive to you.'

When Jock died in 1930, caring for the girls at home was too stressful for his widow so the family decided they should be sent to a private school. This was Arniston, near Hemel Hempstead, where one of the nurses, Isabel Waghorn, remembered them as 'two dear little souls ... known as the "Ga-Ga Girls".' It was, she explained, 'our affectionate nickname for them.'

The mentally disabled daughters of Fenella Bowes-Lyon's sister Harriet, who had married Coldstream Guards officer Henry Fane, were further tragic proof of the genetic theorists' view.

These daughters, Ethelreda, Idonea and Rosemary, joined their cousins Nerissa and Katharine, who had been moved to the Royal Earlswood Hospital in Redhill, Surrey.

When first admitted the sisters were incarcerated for much of the day. Earlswood was the first purpose-built 'asylum for idiots', a flagship. A vast rambling pile of bricks, it epitomised classic wrong-headed Victorian insensitivity towards mental incapacity: unawareness rather than a deliberate callousness prevailed. Under the National Health Service, the institution was revamped, the patients were given light sunny rooms and cared for by a compassionate staff.

Understandably ostrich-like, members of the Strathmore family, some genuinely believing the girls to be dead, were shocked when in 1987 it emerged that three survivors of the five cousins had been locked in institution for forty-six years. These revelations unleashed a torrent of outrage and sensational newspaper headlines – such as 'Queen's Cousins Locked in Madhouse'. These three gentle creatures, Ethelreda aged sixty-four, her sister Idonea aged seventy-two, and Katharine, were sharing a seven-bed ward. All remained unaware of their illustrious kinship.

Suggestions of duplicity were hurled against Mrs Fenella Bowes-Lyon and she has been seen as heartless and unloving. This outcry was handled with dignity by her granddaughter Lady Elizabeth Anson, who explained that visits to the sisters became too distressing as there was no recognition. But she and her brother Patrick changed the minimal marking on her aunt Nerissa's grave in Redhill with its plastic tag, serial number M11125, and added the name Bowes-Lyon.

The secrecy had partly been to protect the Queen Mother, patron of Mencap, a society for the mentally handicapped. Relationship to royalty creates an intangible barrier, and the threat of any scandal can silence the relatives of those elevated by marriage.

Even in an enlightened climate, mental disability has been royalty's unspoken fear. Prince John, the last of King George V and Queen Mary's family of six, survived to the age of fourteen, epileptic and mentally 'defective', his existence at Sandringham known only to a few trusted servants. When he died in 1919, Queen Mary grieved about the 'poor little troubled spirit'.

Meanwhile in the winter of 1917, in a climate of austerity and mourning, Elizabeth, exhausted by her war effort, went to Suffolk to keep her newly-married sister Rose Leveson-Gower company while the latter's husband, a naval officer, was away at sea. Here the sisters would help catch a German spy.

A dentist living near Rose's house in Felixstowe held a lot of late-night drinking sessions with his patients, who always seemed to be in uniform. Elizabeth and Rose became suspicious. They hid in the bushes outside his house, eavesdropping, and discovered that the dentist was spying for the Germans. In return for over-generous drinks, so hard to come by in wartime, the young servicemen, tongues loosened by the welcome hospitality, were innocently giving away secret details of future manoeuvres.

The next day, the sisters reported their findings to Sir John Fisher, an elderly Admiral and also a family friend. The dentist was taken away by the police and Rose and Elizabeth became heroines. When George V was told, 'He was all for giving them medals,' said Lady Clayton, but they said, 'No, oh no'.

After this excitement, and in the euphoria at the end of the Great War, Elizabeth was ready to take London by storm.

CHAPTER 4

Ma, He's Making Eyes at Me

A five year old girl captured a future king's heart by offering a glacé cherry from a piece of iced sponge cake, though he was only ten at the time. The Queen Mother met her husband, Prince Albert, the King's second son, at a children's party. 'Bertie' and Lady Elizabeth were guests of Lady Leicester.

When all that 'creamy English charm', as Evelyn Waugh described it, had blossomed, Lady Elizabeth and the Duke of York were to meet again at a Derby Day dance in Mayfair in June 1920 given by Lord and Lady Farquhar.

Prince Albert, along with many others, thought Elizabeth 'absolutely ravishing'. He was an accomplished ballroom dancer and so was Elizabeth, whose tiny feet had fairly twinkled across some of the best ballrooms in London. They shimmied to the Missouri Walk, Jog Trot and Twinkle, and smiled at each other when Jack Hylton and his band struck up 'Ma, He's Making Eyes at Me'.

Elizabeth's appeal was neither flip nor sophisticated. It was more ingenuous and homespun. Her Twenties long-waisted tea-frocks, embroidered jumpers and baggy tweed coats gave her an altogether 'picturesquely unfashionable' look in comparison with Flapper contemporaries. But she would conquer the sprigs of the aristocracy.

It was said that she was 'irresistible to men' but she was neither arch nor coy. However, one look from those Mediterranean blue eyes under a feathery fringe could make admirers feel like Sir Galahad. As Dorothy Parker astutely suggested: 'Protectiveness and passmaking are not far apart.' Lady Elizabeth could be very funny but she was also discreet and, head on one side, a good and sensitive listener.

A 'noticeable debutante', wrote the American diarist Chips Channon, who was captivated by Elizabeth's 'curious sideways lilting walk'. Part of her charm was perhaps the very fact that she had not been presented at Court. The war had intervened and her parents were spared the £750 cost of 'bringing out' a debutante.

Instead, as bridesmaid to 'Rosie' her favourite sister, Elizabeth was launched quietly in May 1916, 'coming out' unofficially at her sister's wedding to William Spencer 'Wisp' Leveson-Gower at St James' Piccadilly. She wore a jacket of pink chiffon over a filmy white frock, a Dutch bonnet with silver ears, wide pink ribbons and carried roses. Her grecian bun had disappeared and instead her curly hair was cut in a more fashionable bob. She would quickly take London by storm and Lady Buxton wondered 'how many hearts Elizabeth will break'.

Her values were old-fashioned. She did not smoke, or care for the new American craze for cocktails, unlike Robert Benchley, who said on getting out of a swimming pool: 'My, I must step out of these wet things and into a dry Martini.' Later in life, the Queen Mother would not be averse to a cocktail or three.

Lady Strathmore had groomed her daughter expertly, giving her a natural poise and grace, teaching her never to make a superfluous gesture or even glance at her feet. After the grimness of wartime, there was a release of social energy and a return to a fashionable hedonism.

At tennis parties, girls arriving for tea on the lawn for raspberries and cream and Dundee cake sheltered under parasols to keep their skin pale. 'Debs' wore opaque stockings; Queen Mary hated seeing bare legs. After tea, they wound up the His Master's Voice gramophone and danced, carpets brought home from India rolled to one side; she saw shows like 'Fol-de-Rols' and 'White Coons', with cleanshaven young men who flattened their hair with pomade. They lit up De Reske cigarettes; it was 'bad form' to offer cigarettes from a packet – one always had a slim gold or silver case, Turkish on one side, Virginia on the other. If no Turkish, then profuse apologies, 'Sorry old thing, only got gaspers.'

Lounge lizards aped Rudolf Valentino and lured 'sporting' girls into their 'cuddle bucks' – Morris two seaters and Austin Sevens, which could cost anything between £100 and £200. They roared away, putting extra passengers in the dickey and sometimes breaking the twenty mile-an-hour speed limit. Hurrah.

Lady Elizabeth's admirers were many. Her innocent sensuality intrigued Prince Paul of Serbia; Sir Arthur Penn, later her Private Secretary, was also smitten; so were the Airlie boys, especially the younger, ukelele-playing Hon.Bruce Ogilvie and the amusing Lord Gage, who inherited Firle Place in Sussex at the age of seventeen. But he was not in the running because, as Chips Channon observed, 'Alas, he is far too heavy, too Tudor and squirearchical for so rare and patrician a creature as Elizabeth.'

Quite a different suitor altogether was Jamie Stuart, the 17th Earl of Moray's handsome son, who was in the Royal Scots. Posted to Belgium in 1915, his insouciance earned him a Military Cross on the Somme. Dismissive of the honour, he liked to pretend that as a sporting squire he missed his hunting, and to compensate had merely gone out and 'potted a few Huns before breakfast'. His bravery earned him a second MC at Arras. After the war, he became the Duke of York's first equerry.

He was less successful in his siege of the Strathmore girl, although she thought him amusing when they met at a music hall when he was home on leave. Stuart, an incorrigible philanderer, was enchanted. Ironically Prince Albert asked him, 'Will you introduce me?' when he saw Stuart partnering Elizabeth at the Farquhar ball. The Prince had been watching her, in her simple white dress ... 'the instinctive mistress of the arts and crafts that please ... small, wistful, yielding'. What distinguished her from so many of her contemporaries was her maturity.

Now two months after that first meeting, Jamie Stuart was so in love with Elizabeth that he broke off his engagement to 'Elfie' Evelyn Louise Finlayson, the appealing daughter of a Glasgow millionaire. But Lady Strathmore, who had chaperoned her daughter on many occasions, did not approve of Stuart and made a point of inviting his new rival to Glamis.

So young Prince Albert came over the mountains from Balmoral for the Forfar Ball. Elizabeth appeared on the great stone staircase at Glamis wearing a rose brocade Vandyck dress and small roses and pearls in her hair. He liked what he saw.

Queen Mary also drove across to Glamis. Lady Strathmore had been ailing for some time, devastated by the death of two of her sons. She was frail after surgery in 1921, so the running of the castle was handed over to Elizabeth, who became an accomplished *châtelaine*. The Queen was impressed. In the absence of her mother, Elizabeth was an assured hostess. The Queen quickly formed the opinion that this young Strathmore girl would be an eminently suitable wife for 'Bertie'.

As a mother-in-law, Queen Mary was hardly cosy. Painfully stiff and shy, she stalked about in forbidding pre-1914 toques and long grey coats with high fur collars. Privately however she could be quite skittish, occasionally sticking a matchbox on the end of her nose and passing it to whoever was sitting next to her – sometimes a bishop – and she might burst into song: 'Yes, we have no bananas'.

As Princess Mary of Teck, coming from a relatively impoverished German royal background, she had lived in Florence until the age of eighteen where she developed an acquisitive regard for *objets d'art*.

Engaged at first to the Duke of Clarence, Edward VII's eldest son, Princess 'May' was considered so eminently suitable that when the heir to the throne died unexpectedly in 1892 the royal family simply switched her to the next brother. There was no question of love. They married on 6th July 1893 in the Chapel Royal, St James' Palace, London.

Mary grew to love grumpy George V, with his stern 'We sailors never smile on duty', and uncompromising attitudes: 'I won't knight buggers ... thought fellows like that shot themselves.' The King had changed the family name from the inflammatory Germanic 'Guelph' to Windsor during the First World War, but none the less the royal family often spoke German privately and the King retained a high regard for Teutonic formality. Evenings ended at eleven o'clock sharp. He deplored any decline in Victorian standards of etiquette.

Queen Mary dressed to please him and never showed her legs because he did not approve of short skirts. She never spoke in public or used the telephone. He thought of her simply as 'his darling May'.

Always correct, the Queen Consort never lost self-control, even when her husband seemed to have disappeared underwater in a submarine at Portsmouth for an unconscionable time. Turning to Admiral Sir John Fisher she remarked, 'I shall be very disappointed if George doesn't come up again.'

As parents, George and Mary were remote figures not aware of the anxieties of their six children. Sir Owen Morshead, the royal librarian, held a critical view of the royal family's cold, authoritarian attitude. 'The house of Hanover, like ducks, produced bad parents. They trample on their young.'

If ever a child needed careful nurturing it was Bertie, who was completely overshadowed by his older brother Prince Edward, heir to the throne. Edward was born 23rd June 1894, and was known in the family as David. He was a golden boy with a sunny personality, quite unlike his younger brother who was born on 14th December 1895 at York Cottage.

'Bertie' was withdrawn, prone to tears and stuttered from the age of seven, later calling it 'God's curse on me'. He had a particularly sadistic nanny, Miss Green, who terrorised this gentle boy.

Even when he was happily married he could still fly into 'gnashes', the family name for sudden irritability and believed to date back to this bullying in the nursery. In later years, the Queen would just take his pulse and count 'one, two, three, tck tck Bertie,' until he smiled and cooled down.

Unlike his older brother, who shone, he irritated great 'Gangan' Queen Victoria by howling whenever he saw the black bombazined figure approach. In her eyes he had already committed an unpardonable offence. He had arrived in this world on the anniversary of the death of her beloved Albert, the Prince Consort. The Queen had had to be revived with a drop of Scotch mixed with her claret.

When Lord Derby gently suggested to the King that his sons should not be so frightened of him, George V replied: 'My father was frightened of his mother; I was frightened of my father, and I am damned well going to see to it that my children are frightened of me.'

'We were so terribly shy and self-conscious as children', the Duke of York admitted later, but his grandfather King Edward frightened Prince Albert less than his own father did. The King affectionately referred to him as 'my dearest little Bertie' and the two had a jokey relationship. At lunch, when nobody ever talked about anything except generalities, the weather or possibly the French, Prince Albert was told off for trying to attract his grandfather's attention: 'Don't talk my boy until we have finished luncheon.' Politely the young prince waited until the King, by now in avuncular mood, leant across and asked benevolently, 'Now, what is it you wanted to say to me?' Bertie replied with humour which was to endear him to his future wife: 'It doesn't matter grandpa. I was only going to tell you that there was a caterpillar in your salad, but you have eaten it now.'

In the schoolroom it was Princess Mary, born 25th April 1897, who was capricious and spoilt. Harry, the Duke of Gloucester, 'Glossipops', born 31st March 1900, was nervous, highly strung and given to sudden swings of mood, either tantrums or uncontrollable giggles. Prince George, later the most charismatic of them all, born 20th December 1902, was considered the brightest and most artistic. Prince John, born on 12th July 1905, was not brought up with the other children.

All his young life, Prince Albert struggled. He was susceptible to every bug and got whooping cough, measles and stomach upsets. Left-handed and nervy, he was forced to change his writing to the more accepted right-handed style, and this may have contributed to his difficulties with mathematics. His tutor Henry Peter Hansell, an Oxford man, complained irritably to the King: 'Division by two seems to be quite beyond Prince Albert.'

More important perhaps than academic laurels was a report describing him as a 'nice ... unspoiled, honest, well-mannered boy'. He passed out of the Naval College, Dartmouth, sixty-first out of sixty-two.

Later he served as a midshipman, cheerfully slinging his own hammock and eating cheese and onions, which may not have helped a volatile digestion. Three weeks after the declaration of World War I, while serving on HMS *Collingwood,* he developed appendicitis. He had to be whisked ashore through fog and past eight battleships and twelve destroyers to Scapa Flow. Even after a successful appendectomy, he was dogged by stomach upsets, prompting the King's Private Secretary Lord

Stamfordham to wonder if this young man would be 'able to continue in the Navy with the recurrence of these mysterious and unsatisfactory abdominal pains'. He did not take into account Prince Albert's doggedness and will to overcome all obstacles.

After the appendectomy Albert fretted at his desk job in the War Room at the Admiralty and then went back to sea. In those days a Prince did not abandon a chosen course – a far cry from the freedom which permitted Prince Edward to quit the Marines in 1987, not for health reasons but because he was attracted to a life on the boards.

At the Battle of Jutland in May 1916, Prince Albert impressed fellow officers with his seven-hour stint in the gun turret. He had been exhilarated by the challenge, telling his brother, David: 'D ... it seems curious but all sense of danger and everything goes except the longing to deal death in every possible way to the enemy.' He made cocoa for his gun crew.

None of this fitted him for Twenties' drawing room chatter, but it moulded his character; he was notably different from flippant contemporaries, Etonian friends of the Bowes-Lyon brothers. Outwardly he was more urbane and at ease with girls.

The King appreciated the struggles, physical and psychological, of this introverted second son and made him Duke of York in 1920, two weeks after his meeting with Lady Elizabeth. Honoured by his father with the oldest royal Dukedom and the King's belief that 'this splendid old title will be safe in your hands', the Duke's self-confidence soared.

He was lithe, a superb tennis player, and won the the RAF doubles finals at Wimbledon with his mentor, Dr Louis Greig. Greig had been instructed to toughen him up, but found a young man already of character and courage. He always beat the Prince of Wales at golf.

His persistence would win Elizabeth's hand, though half the men in London were in love with her. It is said she was slightly attracted to the Prince of Wales, the 'Little Man' as he was affectionately known. Her niece, Lady Mary Clayton, later recalled seeing the brothers together at Glamis and thought, 'Uncle Bertie was more of a dish ... actually more dashing.' She said later, 'The Duke of York may have had a stutter, but he was decisive, he had initiative and he wasn't shy in private company at all.' Besides, her aunt Elizabeth would never have married a weakling.

The Duke was pursued by racy hostesses, who plied him with whisky and found him shy but charming. He was never physically strong, but any impression of frailty was misleading.

In the end serendipity and Princess Mary would help secure Bertie's happiness. Elizabeth and the Princess Royal were good friends and enthusiastic Girl Guides.

A sympathetic listener, Elizabeth knew that Mary's real love had been the Duke of Dalkeith, but after Queen Mary caught them in each other's arms the romance was speedily concluded on the grounds that the Buccleuchs were not rich enough for the King's only daughter.

When Princess Mary became engaged she invited Elizabeth to be her bridesmaid. The new, approved suitor was Lord Lascelles, 6th Earl of Harewood, a millionaire three times over. On the eve of the wedding on 28th February 1922, the bride-to-be wept bitterly, yet this solid union would produce two sons – one artistic and musical, the 7th Earl of Harewood whose first marriage was to pianist Marion Stein, later the wife of Jeremy Thorpe the former Liberal leader.

Tatler, reporting on the wedding of the King's daughter, noted that three of the bridesmaids, 'the exquisite Lady Mary Thynne, Lady Rachel Cavendish and Lady Elizabeth Bowes-Lyon', were persistently tipped as possible brides for the royal princes. It was true that Elizabeth in her silver and white dress was unknowingly being admired by the Duke of York, and was also subjected to his mother's special 'intent, questioning gaze'.

Queen Mary had long suspected that 'Bertie' was in love with this 'charming girl' but wondered if anything would come of it. She knew how tongue-tied he was in her presence and 'unable to utter'.

CHAPTER 5

A Perfect Little Duck

Whenever the Duke of York joined a shoot at Glamis with the Bowes-Lyons brothers he was struck by the happy and relaxed atmosphere, so unlike Balmoral which he found tedious and dull. He would complain about 'a lack of originality' in conversation with his own family, surrounded by 'nothing but a dreary acquiescence'; the royal family despise obsequiousness.

The Duke naturally hesitated to put this abrasive point of view to the King. James Thomas, a royal favourite, tried. This outspoken engine driver and Bolshevik sympathist, who had masterminded several railway strikes, explained to the King why the young princes did not like Balmoral. 'Sir,' he said in his blunt way. 'It's a bloody dull 'ouse.'

Meanwhile the Duke of York had royal duties to fulfil. He represented the King at a royal wedding in Belgrade, when Marie of Roumania married Alexander, King of the Slovenes, Serbs and Croats, in 1922. Instead of travelling by limousine or carriage he was given a highly-strung Irish horse which cantered through the streets of the city. Fortunately the Duke was an assured horseman.

Back in London, he enjoyed a few desultory dalliances. He had lost his virginity in Paris in 1919, and had been attracted to eighteen year old Helen 'Poppy' Baring, who was flirtatious, fun and wealthy, and from the well-established banking family.

The pair became inseparable, dancing exclusively with each other at Cowes Regatta. Her brother Charles Baring, who had a home in the Isle of Wight, recalled, 'Those were magnificent days; the royal princes would sail down in their yachts and take over a country house.'

The Duke proposed. But the royal network quickly flashed this intelligence to the Palace where there were instant rumblings of disapproval. Queen Mary acted promptly and put a stop at once to the engagement between her inexperienced, diffident son and the flighty Poppy.

A telegram was sent to Prince Albert immediately. 'On no account will we permit your marriage, (signed) Mama.' He could be in no doubt about her wishes. There were a few other flirtations; one with bossy but beautiful Lady Maureen Vane-Tempest-Stewart who later married Oliver Stanley, the 17th Earl of Derby's son.

So there was nothing serious except for a brief affair with Viscount Loughborough's attractive Australian wife. Albert was also attracted by a dancer, Phyllis Monkman, who had great legs and was an immediate hit with the Duke when she appeared in a West End show called 'Tails Up' in 1919. He invited her to dinner but not to meet his mother.

Queen Mary intimated to Lady Strathmore that the royal family considered Lady Elizabeth a possibility as a future bride for Bertie. Elizabeth, according to Admiral Beattie, was a 'perfect little duck', appearing at dances and parties in soft pastels and ivory lace, with a blush of roses pinned on the hip, full of social skills and comeliness. Yet even she could not help her stuttering royal suitor to say what was really in his heart. It was not a romance which leapt forward with fiery momentum.

In the end, it was the Duke of York's character and doggedness which won Lady Elizabeth's plump little hand. It helped too that his only real rival had been seen off. Jamie Stuart suddenly resigned as his equerry in 1921, deciding to go and work in the oilfields of Oklahoma. It has been suggested that North America was not his idea of heaven, but he was warned off.

'There is no doubt Stuart had pursued her rather,' an old friend recalled, or that twenty-one year old Lady Elizabeth had been attracted to him. 'Jamie never stopped loving her', but gallantly left the way clear for the King's son. The Queen Mother's niece Lady Mary Clayton said years later, 'She was very lucky she didn't marry him. He was very attractive, but there were many more attractive people who loved her.'

Proposing to Lady Elizabeth Bowes-Lyon was agonising for the Duke. The difficulty, he confided in 'JCC', John Cohn

Campbell, a thirty-three year old Scottish MP, the Prime Minister's Parliamentary Private Secretary and later Viscount Davidson, was that although 'desperately in love', he 'could not risk refusal because he was a king's son.' He had sent an emissary and this, understandably, had not been successful. Davidson comforted the Duke, saying his own wife had indeed refused him several times and suggested the very best thing was to propose personally.

So, on 16th January 1923, just when everyone had begun to despair of this romance, the Duke of York's engagement to Lady Elizabeth Bowes-Lyon appeared in the Court Circular. After three proposals, the Duke had finally been accepted by 'this enchanting girl'. The wedding would be on Thursday, 26th August 1923.

Lady Elizabeth's hesitation, according to Lady Airlie who was a friend of Queen Mary's, had been a 'longing to make Bertie happy' but 'a reluctance to take on the big responsibilities which this marriage must bring ... But she finally accepted.'

'Oh Bertie, yes,' she had replied when he asked her to marry him. 'Because,' she explained in the end, 'I couldn't live without him.'

The Duke proposed in the rose garden at St Paul's Walden Bury on Sunday, 13th January, when the Strathmores were at church. Chips Channon mournfully observed that there was not a man in England who did not envy him. 'He is the luckiest of men ... the clubs are in gloom.'

Queen Mary reported 'Bertie looks beaming.' Her heart had leapt at his economically worded telegram when it arrived at Sandringham with the news she had been praying for: 'All right, Bertie.' It was to be more than all right. Albert knew he was marrying one of the most popular girls in London. 'I know I am very lucky to have won her over at last,' he admitted to his mother, and in all the years of their marriage he was never complacent about his good fortune.

As for Elizabeth, her misgivings soon evaporated. Elated, she admitted, 'I feel very happy but quite dazed, the cat is completely out of the bag nor does there seem any possibility of stuffing him back again.'

A few months later on 26th April 1923, Jamie Stuart, now Viscount Stuart of Findhorn, married a friend of Elizabeth's, Lady Rachel Cavendish, daughter of the Duke of Devonshire.

It is said that for years afterwards, there was a photograph of Elizabeth by his bed signed 'All my love, Betty.'

The Strathmores had moved to 17 Bruton Street from St James' Square in 1920 and here Elizabeth would give her first and last newspaper interview. A reporter from the *Daily Sketch* called and was invited into the morning room. He described 'Lady Elizabeth's merry laugh' and was delighted at the open way in which she seemed to be handling the interview.

When asked if it was true that the Duke had proposed three times, she said that this was news to her, but confided, 'I am so happy, as you can see for yourself'. In the beginning the Duke was referred to as 'Bertie' then, correcting herself, she explained how everyone knew him as 'Prince Bertie'. This anodyne interview when it appeared in the newspaper enraged the King. Elizabeth learnt her first lesson about the need for royal reticence, so much so that she never gave an interview again; indeed her voice was rarely heard again in public.

Amongst the first to see her Kashmir diamond engagement ring was Janet Fox, a chambermaid at Glamis, who would always remember how Elizabeth skipped over a gate by the cricket pavilion, not bothering to open it, in her excitement to talk about the wedding.

As a couple, the Duke and Elizabeth looked well together. There was a touch of Dornford Yates about his well-cut suits and Homburg hats. Group Captain Peter Townsend, who was to become one of his equerries, thought the Duke 'a marvellous looking man ... not a spare bit of flesh to be seen when he was in swimming trunks'.

Seven days after the engagement, Elizabeth was taken to Sandringham to stay with the King and Queen. For many young women, this could have been daunting. Her royal in-laws were sticklers for protocol. Those early years of training by Lady Strathmore however stood her in good stead and Elizabeth acquitted herself well. The King thought her charming from the moment she arrived in a fetching flapper cloche hat and coat with fur collar. They got on famously.

She would be his first and favourite daughter-in-law. And she was clever enough to be nice to Charlotte, his parrot. Of her father-in-law, Elizabeth said, 'I was never afraid of him.' He called her 'Lilibet,' the affectionate family nickname for the present Queen.

It would be just an ordinary royal wedding: 3,000 invitations and a dinner party for 600. The King gave to Elizabeth an ermine, a full-length sable squirrel fur, and an evening wrap of white lapin, and to Bertie an antique pedestal table. Other gifts included a sports car from the Prince of Wales who thought Elizabeth 'delightful', hundreds of gold needles and a Cartier clock in Russian enamel. Elizabeth always loved clocks.

For her wedding the bride chose music by Purcell and the hymn 'Lead us, Heavenly Father'. Her creamy camellia silk crepe wedding dress studded with crystal beads and real pearls, and with sleeves of Nottingham lace, is preserved at Clarence House. Her shoes were embroidered with silver roses. Over her veil of Flanders lace dotted with the white rose of York, the bride wore a simple wreath of orange blossom.

Two of her nieces, Elizabeth Elphinstone and Cecilia Bowes-Lyon, were trainbearers. Six of her friends were bridesmaids: Betty Cator, the girl who would one day become Lady Strathmore; Lady Mary Thynne; Diamond Hardinge; Lady Katharine Hamilton, the Duke of Abercorn's daughter, who would later become Lady of the Bedchamber, and Lady Mary Cambridge, once tipped as a possible bride for Prince Albert. They all wore white roses and heather in their hair.

The Earl of Strathmore, in his uniform as Lord-Lieutenant of Forfar, looked suitably proud of his daughter as they left Bruton Street for Westminster Abbey. All misgivings about one of his children becoming part of court life had evaporated as they travelled by state landau with four mounted policemen.

They arrived at the West door at half past eleven in the morning and began the long walk up the aisle, following a golden cross held high. A beadle in scarlet handed Elizabeth her handkerchief bag, which she had dropped. In remembrance of her brother Fergus, killed in France, she placed her bouquet of white roses at the tomb of the Unknown Warrior. A bridesmaid managed to smuggle in the bride's gloves, left behind on the hall table.

Not since 1269 when Henry II's son was married had there been a wedding of a reigning King's son in Westminster Abbey, yet the service could not be broadcast. The Archbishop of Canterbury, Dr Cosmo Lang, forbade this sharing with the people, fearing that men might listen to the wireless in public houses and forget to remove their hats.

The wedding breakfast at Buckingham Palace for 138 guests included *Supremes de saumon Reine* Mary, *Cotelletes d'agneau Prince* Albert, *Fraises Duchesse* Elizabeth and baskets of spun sugar. Pieces of the nine-foot-high wedding cake, baked in Edinburgh by Mcvitie, were sent to 100,000 underprivileged children and some found a lucky gold charm in their slice.

The newlywed Duke and Duchess appeared on the balcony at Buckingham Palace. The bride, now Her Royal Highness and the fourth lady in the land, mouthed a smiley 'thank you' to the crowd. Chips Channon thought her more 'lovely and exquisite than any woman alive'.

In those days, royal couples did not kiss and hug in public, unlike Prince Charles and his bride whose wedding kiss was flashed around the world in 1981. The only tactile gesture the crowd would see was Queen Mary wrapping a shawl about her daughter-in-law's shoulders and trying not to appear too pleased with the bride's grace on this, her first appearance on the Palace balcony.

As their carriage, trimmed with gold brocade and sprinkled with lilies of the valley and the inevitable lucky white heather, pulled out of the Palace courtyard, Queen Mary scattered 'favours', or knots of pink, yellow and blue ribbons and rose petals. In a brown, feathered hat, the Duchess of York looked jubilant as they drove away. She had gone to her wedding as a commoner in an ordinary state landau, but had left it as a Princess in a Glass Coach.

The royal brothers threw sugar plums in gilded baskets at the newlyweds, yet there was a hollowness about the Prince of Wales in spite of his urbanity and showy self-confidence. The King watched the Yorks leave for Waterloo. He was later to say prophetically, 'I pray to God that my eldest son will never marry and that nothing will come between Bertie and Lilibet and the throne.'

CHAPTER 6

Carefully Orchestrated Appearances

The train pulled into Bookham Station at ten past five after a thirty-five minute journey from Waterloo, for a honeymoon slightly different from today when royal newlyweds fly off to a tropical island and the paparazzi compete for the most intimate shot.

The Duke and Duchess of York chose to go to Polesden Lacey, Mrs Ronnie Greville's Edwardian house in Surrey. They had been frequent quests at her 'riotous evenings' in London and the country. The Duchess always had a penchant for luxury, and even her husband found 'Maggie's' ostentatious hospitality agreeable after his spartan upbringing.

Rich enough to indulge royal whims, including appetites for 'baby tongues' and 1810 Grande Champagne brandy, Mrs Greville had no difficulty securing crowned heads at her table. She once complained, 'One uses up so many red carpets in a season.' Her attitude to the Duke and Duchess was maternal and she would lament the day they became King and Queen, sensing she might no longer be so acceptable in court circles. 'I was so happy,' she liked to say, 'when they used to run in and out of my house as if they were my own children.'

One of the great hostesses of the Twenties, her link with the royal family had been through her husband's friendship with Edward VII – and his mistress Mrs Alice Keppel and her husband. The Keppels had two daughters. The eldest, Violet, proved a trial. Conventionally married, there was a huge scandal when she ran off with writer Vita Sackville-West. Their husbands, Denys Trefusis and Harold Nicolson, chased all over Europe in hopeless pursuit of the sapphic lovebirds.

Mrs Greville was godmother to Sonia, the Keppels' younger daughter. When her goddaughter wanted to marry Ronald Cubitt, heir to the Ashcombe title, she tried to stop the marriage. The trouble was that he was in 'trade', his family having built most of Belgravia. There is no one more snobbish than a nouveau riche and Mrs Greville, as the illegitimate daughter of a self-made Scottish brewer, William McEwan, was no exception. Lady Ashcombe was not enthralled either by the prospect of her son marrying the daughter of the King's mistress. She was quite unwelcoming at first and she could hardly bring herself to address Sonia directly. She would inquire sniffily, 'Will the young lady have a scone?' staring coldly into the middle distance of the drawing room.

Eventually Sonia did marry her 'builder'. One of their daughters, Rosalind, married Major Bruce Shand and their first child was born in July 1947. That baby, who was to have so much in common with her great-grandmother, was Camilla Parker-Bowles. Mrs Keppel never saw her replacement in royal affections, but her granddaughter Rosalind Shand was later devastated by the unsavoury publicity by her daughter Camilla and Prince Charles. Mrs Shand held firmly to the view that one's name should appear in the paper only three times, birth, marriage and death.

The Duke and Duchess of York liked the somewhat manipulative Mrs Greville and always remembered her with affection. She had gone to a great deal of trouble to ensure that the first part of their honeymoon should be idyllic.

They relished the seclusion of Polesden Lacey. 'The silence and the spaciousness that comes from long established wealth', was Chips Channon's view of 'old Maggie's country house' with its hall of dark oak, taken from an abandoned church, and gilded Italian palazzo drawing room.

The house, perched on a wooded hillside overlooking today's mock-Tudor Surrey, had elaborate gardens where the couple wrote thank you letters for their presents, which included a bow-fronted Sheraton chest of drawers, Chippendale mirrors and an ormolu bureau. They thanked their parents for the wedding, played golf and tennis, and reminded each other of some of the highlights of the wedding.

Part of the trousseau included an unsporty apple green crepon tennis frock trimmed with periwinkle silk. The Duchess wore this for a little putting in the afternoons and then would collapse gracefully into a wicker-work Lloyd Loom chair, to do nothing more strenuous than admire the camellias and tulips.

They were meticulously cared for by Mrs Greville's legendary butlers Boles and Bacon. The pair had a disconcerting talent for encountering the unexpected. The celebrated hostess never spoke to her servants directly but wrote them messages. This remoteness would cost her dearly. Once, when Bacon, who had been on a Bacchanalian binge, was tottering round the dining table with hot gravy he was handed a note from his mistress which read 'You're disgracefully drunk. Please leave the room at once.' Unperturbed and ignoring these instructions, the tipsy butler carried the note on a silver salver to the teetotal Nancy Lady Astor.

However, when Mrs Greville died on 18th September 1942, it was a sad Boles who was amongst those who saw her buried near the dog's cemetery in the garden at Polesden Lacey. The Queen said, 'She was so shrewd, so kind and so amusingly unkind, so sharp, such fun, so naughty ...'

The Yorks spent the second part of the honeymoon at Glamis. The industrious Lady Strathmore had re-embroidered the apricot satin hangings of the four-poster where Bonnie Prince Charlie's father had slept, and left a watch under the pillow. The names of her nine children were stitched with bubbles in delicate shades of blue, yellow and pink. Here the bride would spend most of her honeymoon with whooping cough. 'Not very romantic,' the Duke told his parents.

For him Glamis no longer seemed to have quite the same appeal. To his wife it was home and she was being cosseted by the two people dearest to her in the world, her husband and her mother. The Duke began to find the castle gloomy and oppressive, especially after the sybaritic comfort of Polesden Lacey.

The Strathmores had gone to a lot of trouble carrying out improvements for the honeymooners, putting a new bathroom in their wing. The Duke was often lonely. Not a great reader, although he liked *The Empty Tomb*, a book about the Resurrection, and sometimes a Conan Doyle novel, he would do *petit-point* on his own, sitting in the pretty sitting room with its blue Delft-tile fireplace.

His parents-in-law were kind and solicitous but he missed his young wife's cheerful company; over ten days of honeymoon the Duke had grown pleasantly accustomed to her vivacity and humour. Now he was forced to rely on himself while she was ill, without even the support of attentive courtiers. In common with other royal princes, he got bored if left to his own devices. He needed to be active, stalking, hunting, shooting rather than listening to a string quartet.

The Duchess, on the other hand, had inner reserves; she happily read Jane Austen and Rudyard Kipling, a taste she shared with the Prince of Wales. The second part of the honeymoon in this vast Scottish fortress was not perfection. Her recovery had been slow.

The King was showing a new respect for the Duke of York which had nothing to do with his bravery at the Battle of Jutland. He had been impressed by the Duke's ability to win such a 'charming and delightful wife'. 'Dearest Bertie,' he wrote, 'you are indeed a lucky man,' seemingly surprised at such a perfect choice made by his unassuming son.

First home for the newlyweds was a Georgian hunting lodge in Richmond Park with tennis courts, a lily pond, a park full of deer and five bosky acres. This was White Lodge. Today it is the Royal Ballet school. Full of history, it was here Nelson traced his tactics for Trafalgar on the dining room table with a finger dipped in wine. Later the house belonged to Queen Mary's mother, the Duchess of Teck, who lived there for nearly thirty years. The darkly formal rooms and corridors reeked of Germanic solemnity.

The Yorks moved in on 7th June 1923 and found the house lacking any 'airy lightness'. Besides, it was 'altogether too far from London'. The Duke and Duchess liked to go hand in hand to the cinema at Marble Arch or dancing at Ciro's. Once, spotting them at the theatre, Lady Diana Cooper thought they were 'such a sweet little couple and so fond of one another' as they enjoyed 'private jokes'.

In those early years of marriage, the Duchess was happier than she could have imagined possible. Formal demands made on her by the royal family were surprisingly few. They loved her. Her mother-in-law, invited to lunch, was warned by the Duke in advance: 'Our cook is not very good but she can do plain dishes well and I know you like that sort'. He aimed to protect his new wife from potential criticism from Queen Mary, but the two women got on well.

In the 1920s there was no intrusive, beady scrutiny of a young royal wife. Women in the royal family performed a string of bland, unperturbing engagements; these were recorded in the Court Circular with a respectful caption. They made carefully orchestrated appearances and their voices were rarely heard in public. They were protected from grisly sights, in sharp contrast to the Princess Royal today or Diana the late Princess of Wales, who visited leper colonies, AIDS victims and saw the desolation of camps of starving refugees.

For the Duchess of York, each morning began with nothing more arduous after breakfast than sifting through invitations. Lady-in-waiting, Anne Ring, would help with the formal correspondence. The Duchess wrote beautiful letters by hand, thanking people for the smallest kindness. Letters to friends signed 'Ever yours' were treasured.

The choosing of the right societies for patronage was a delicate task. Charity work had to be undertaken; hampers of biscuits sent to crippled children at Christmas; an appearance made at a charity fête at Balmoral and a visit to the British Empire Exhibition at Wembley made in 1925. An ability to handle a shovel was helpful for tree-planting ceremonies.

These engagements were few, at first, until the Duchess with her sense of fun became increasingly popular. There was her charm of course, but she was also was refreshingly natural. Whenever she appeared in public, she received nothing but praise and became known as The Smiling Duchess. The King was delighted with her.

The Duke and Duchess of York's first public appearance abroad was in Belgrade on 21st October 1923 for the christening of the son of King Alexander of Serbia. Still in honeymoon mood, they went reluctantly. The Duke was an embarrassed godfather, or *Koom* which is the Serbian word, but moved swiftly when the butter-fingered, elderly Patriarch dropped the six week old heir, Crown Prince Peter, into the font.

Elizabeth relished the sight of her husband scooping up the howling baby and carrying it, naked on a cushion, three times round the altar in a sea of incense. In the streets of Belgrade, the Duke was later surrounded by begging children shouting, 'Oh Koom your purse is burning' as they scrabbled hopefully for coins from the chief sponsor of the future King Peter II of Yugoslavia.

The English King thought the Duke and Duchess had acquitted themselves well. He was concerned about his eldest son, the Prince of Wales, his flippancy, and the women to whom he was attracted. Queen Mary had never been kind about the Prince of Wales' girlfriends, nicknaming Freda Dudley Ward 'Miss Loom'. Her father was a Northern textile magnate and though sophisticated and worldly, Freda's 'trade' background could never be overlooked. Had the King and Queen realised what lay ahead, they might have been less demanding and not rejected Lady Rosemary Leveson-Gower as insufficiently well bred for marriage to the future Edward VIII.

The Duke and Duchess of York went on safari in December 1924, and spent Christmas in Mombasa. They loved Kenya; 'the colony,' the Duke wrote to Queen Mary, 'was utterly different from other parts of the Empire … the settlers … a very nice lot and for the most part real gentlemen.'

They went off into the foothills of Kilimanjaro and slept in 'bandas' or small bamboo huts, wore bush hats, safari shirts and trousers, and were stunned by the romance of seeing ostriches picking their way delicately round the camp. Butterflies and birds were the colour of jewels. There were swollen silty rivers to be crossed, treacherous tracks to be negotiated, and sometimes the royal party picnicked under a tree with a leopard stretched indolently on a branch overhead.

The Duke of York always found big game hunting exciting and his wife made him proud. Smiling sweetly, she received the compliments of the rangers when she coolly bagged a Grant gazelle, a water buck, a buffalo, a rhinoceros, a dik-dik, a wart-hog, a Kenya hartebeest, an antelope and an oryx with her .275 Rigby rifle.

They went on to Uganda but liked it less, then travelled down the White Nile until they reached Khartoum. It had been a grand Imperial adventure and Elizabeth would never lose her affection for Africa. Even in her nineties, the Queen Mother remained nostalgic for the old colonial order and could never understand why those 'dear African states' wanted to break away and be independent.

Back in London, the Duke and Duchess felt refreshed by this escape from the rigidities of Court life.

CHAPTER 7

A Drop of Dill Water

When Princess Alice, Countess of Athlone, heard that the Duchess was expecting her first baby, she remarked: 'Kenya is famous for having that effect on people I hear.' Her theory, though charming, was not quite convincing as the baby was not due until April 1926. The pregnancy was kept fairly quiet.

With a baby on the way and no word about a town house from the King or Queen Mary, it was Lady Strathmore who, practical as always, came up with the offer of the family home in 17 Bruton Street. Relieved, the Yorks moved to Mayfair where they would spend an enjoyable waiting time during the pregnancy with quiet dinner parties. They entertained friends like Lady Doris, sister of the 9th Duke of Richmond, and her husband Commander Ronald Vyner, who were also married at the same time. The Spender-Clays, Lord and Lady Plunket and the Marquess of Salisbury were further visitors.

Princess Elizabeth, the future Queen, was born at 2.40 am on Wednesday, 21st April 1926 'feet first' as the happy mother later told friends. It had not been an easy birth. The King and Queen, woken at four o'clock in the morning, knew their 'dear daughter-in-law' had been in labour all day and that eventually the baby was born by Caesarean section, delivered by Sir Henry Simpson and obstetrician Walter Jagger, a consultant at the Samaritan Hospital for Women.

The Duke, highly strung and naturally anxious, was irked by the ancient custom of the Home Secretary, then Sir William Joynson Hicks, being present at a royal birth.

Queen Mary, who had been so worried about 'our darling Elizabeth', now felt only 'such relief and joy'. Bertie, who had been the first of her sons to marry, told her when she called with bouquets of pinks and lilac from Windsor: 'We always wanted a child to make our happiness complete ...' He confided, 'I am so proud of Elizabeth at this moment ... after all that she had gone through during the last few days.' There were so many visitors the bell broke.

The baby, blue eyed and blonde, was called Elizabeth and christened on 29th May 1926 with Jordan water at the gold lily font at Buckingham Palace. A drop of dill water soothed her as a few tears dropped on the Brussels lace robe used for all royal babies. At the age of six months, Princess Elizabeth, rather like her mother, was 'sitting up by herself in the middle of a huge Chesterfield'. Anne Ring thought 'her fair hair beginning to curl charmingly ... was like white fluff', a piece 'of thistledown'.

Four years later, on 21st August 1920, Princess Margaret was born at Glamis, on a wild windy night. Thunder claps and sheets of lightning heralded her arrival at half past nine in the evening. Lady Strathmore had given up her own bedroom for the birth rather than have a royal baby born in the Duchess of York's old apartment in the nursery wing. The Duchess felt happier this time about the compulsory presence of Mr Harry Boyd, the Ceremonial Secretary of the Home Office, because he was a distant relative. Making light of it, she remarked that if there had to be gentlemen waiting outside her bedroom door for the birth then 'I hope it's someone we know.'

The Duke never forgot the uncomfortable feeling of being forced to entertain a senior civil servant during one of the most intimate times in any couple's life. When he became king, he banned the archaic custom so the Queen's four children were born at Buckingham Palace without a single bureaucrat being present.

The new baby was called 'Bud' by her sister, and 'a darling' by Queen Mary. The King refused to allow them to call the baby Ann, though the Duchess had pleaded 'Ann of York sounds pretty ... and Elizabeth and Ann go well together.' George V was adamant. The baby was christened Margaret Rose on 30th October 1930 at Buckingham Palace.

In charge of the nursery in Bruton Street was 'Alla', Clara Knight, a motherly body glad to be caring for her 'Benjamin's' second baby. Pinching this trusty nanny from one of her married sisters, the Duchess slyly reminded her: 'She was mine first.' When Mrs Knight died, at Sandringham in 1946, there was a posy of violets on her coffin and a message, 'In loving and thankful memory' signed Elizabeth R.

Helping out in the nursery was Margaret MacDonald, 'Bobo' to the Princesses, because they thought her unsurpassed at playing 'Peek-a-bo.' She would later become indispensable as the present Queen's dresser, a model of discretion, refusing to retire even when crippled by rheumatism and in her eighties. The neat little hunched figure was usually to be found on the Queen's side of the interconnecting bedroom doors at the Palace, busying herself by putting away her 'little Lady's' jewels as Prince Philip tried to talk to his wife about his day.

When Princess Margaret was three months old, the Duchess took her home to stay with her parents and 'Bud' was wheeled through the Italian gardens which were the creation of a green fingered Lady Strathmore.

The Duke and Duchess' happiest home in London was undoubtedly the old town house at 145 Piccadilly, demolished now. Ideal for their young family, they moved into this 25-bedroomed house in 1926, not long after Princess Elizabeth's birth. Lady Agatha Perowne, who lived next door at 144 as a child, thought it 'wonderful for a dance' and remembers a grand staircase leading to three drawing rooms, one in red satin, one in yellow and one in blue. Outside, liveried chauffeurs waited by Rolls Royces and Daimlers. You could smell the polish on the upholstery. The staff – butlers, footmen, cooks, laundry maids, kitchen maids, dressers and the steward's room boy – all travelled by horse-drawn buses. Years later, when driving with the Queen Mother round Hyde Park Corner, she would become wistful and be reminded of how 'Poor Piccadilly got a direct hit in the war, you know', and sigh.

The Duchess immediately set about making 145 Piccadilly 'cheerful and homely', with shades of apricot, comfortable squashy armchairs and newly acquired paintings, many stacked against a wall in what she called 'a state of consideration'. Window boxes, a new craze in Mayfair, were a riot of blue hydrangeas.

Two boy scouts stood sentinel in the green pillared hall, coopted as part of the Duke's Youth Welfare Scheme. One answered the telephone and the other would dart across the moleskin carpet to open the heavy black double doors.

The Prince of Wales was a regular visitor. It was sometimes hinted that the Duchess had been attracted to him as the more dazzling of the two brothers. Happily married, the Duchess still liked to flirt. As her brother-in-law prepared to go on another royal tour, she would tease him: 'Ah, you old Empire builder', and then laughingly they would quote Gungha Din together. At this time the Prince of Wales was a fan of his sister-in-law and thought her 'the one bright spot' in the royal family.

Long after his death, a jokey photograph of the Duchess of York with a pipe was found in an old chest at the Duke of Windsor's home in Paris. Enmity came later, fuelled by what the Duke saw as the royal family's disdainful attitude to his American wife.

In those carefree days in the 1930s though, the Prince of Wales liked nothing better than visiting 145 Piccadilly at the end of the day. As he arrived he was greeted by 'Jimmie', a white parrot who would squawk 'Have a drink.' If it was bath time, he would run upstairs following the sound of laughter in the nursery to find the Duke and Duchess of York wrapping the Princesses in big bath towels. They would chorus, 'Uncle David please read *Winnie the Pooh* to us'.

Nobody ever thought of the glamorous Prince of Wales being lonely, but he confessed he thought 'Bertie had one matchless blessing' and that was 'a happy home with a wife and children'.

The King would lean on them more and begin to groom the young couple for what he suspected would be inevitable. His instincts told him that the Prince of Wales never would be King.

CHAPTER 8

The House Was Filled with Laughter

The King was dotty about his daughter-in-law. 'Everyone falls in love with her,' he told the Archbishop of Canterbury, and added, 'were it not for a little unpunctual streak, she would be perfect.' It was extraordinary to his own family how indulgent he was towards the Duchess, who once arrived two minutes late for dinner and apologised. 'My dear,' said the King comfortingly, 'you are not late. I think we are early.' Such gallantry, not even the mildest rebuke.

George V had rather dreaded his sons' wives, imagining they would be Bright Young Things, part of the nightclubbing cocktail set, wearing short skirts and flame red lipstick, so unlike his 'darling May'. The elegant Marina, wife of the Duke of Kent, earned royal disapproval almost immediately when she wore scarlet nail polish at Buckingham Palace before her wedding in 1934.

'I'm afraid the King doesn't like painted nails. Can you do something about it?' Queen Mary suggested stiffly, but Princess Marina of Greece and Denmark, with that Almanach de Gotha confidence and secretly feeling superior to the short-waisted Windsors, replied in broken English: 'Your George may not, but mine does' – shades of Prince Michael of Kent's imperious wife Marie Christine today, bearing out the old adage that men sometimes marry women who remind them of their mothers.

The Duke of Gloucester's wife was an altogether more pliable addition to the stable of royal wives. A daughter of the 7th Duke of Buccleuch, Princess Alice had shared with Elizabeth Bowes-Lyon the same misgivings about marriage to a king's son. Dreading it would mean the end of 'a truly private life', she was thirty-four when eventually she agreed to marry Prince Henry in November 1935.

He steadily became more blimpish with the years, bellowing at the opera when the diva disappeared behind a tree, 'Has she gone now, can we all go home?' and on another occasion, almost a caricature, asking a belly dancer in Cairo, 'D'yer know Tidworth?' The widowed Princess Alice, Dowager Duchess of Gloucester, always trod a careful path. Although sixteen months younger than the Queen Mother, in her later years she was not often seen on public engagements and certainly not on race-courses or picnicking by the River Dee.

The Duchess of York was the first of the King's daughters-in-law. Attractive but not showy, she could make him laugh out loud. Outgoing by nature, she struck a subtle balance between warmth and accessibility, and a gentle separateness; she quickly acquired that indefinable royal aura.

'She knows exactly what to do and say to all the people we meet,' the Duke of York told his father after a visit to Northern Ireland. The King did not need any convincing. He was delighted with her and like a puppet-master gave his daughter-in-law every encouragement in her public life. The Duchess blossomed under this benign approval; although not ambitious for herself she wanted the best for her husband, and their appearances together on engagements began to bolster his fragile ego. A 'simpleton' Hitler had called him when he saw him amiably miming 'Under the Spreading Chestnut Tree' at a Boys' Club Jamboree.

George V had astutely recognised that underneath all the winsome charm, Elizabeth had a strength and almost steely determination to give moral support to the anxious 'Bertie'. Here perhaps was even a little parental guilt. George V had beaten his sons and now could see how the Duke of York had been personally damaged by such an apprehensive childhood, not in itself uncommon in aristocratic circles at the beginning of the twentieth century when children were sometimes the victims of sadistic nannies and bullying fathers.

Now happily married, the Duke became more at ease with himself and relaxed enough to begin to enjoy an easier relationship with his father. 'I can make him listen and I don't have to repeat everything over again.' The King decided that they were ready for the relentless public gaze of a world tour. The purpose of the visit was the opening in Australia on 9th May 1927 of the new Parliament building in Canberra.

They protested, hating the idea of leaving their eight month old baby Elizabeth and, with reason, asked: 'Why us, why not the Prince of Wales?' The King dissembled, making an excuse about how only recently 'David' had been Down Under. He insisted the Duke and Duchess of York should go instead. It was their duty.

Famous for his outspokenness even by Australian standards, Stanley Bruce, the Prime Minister, had misgivings. He was not sure the visit was a good idea, voicing honest fears about the Duke's stammer. Would his countrymen and those busy sheep-shearers pause long enough to wait for the next word?

Since these tours are often planned years ahead, there was time to go and see a speech therapist about the Duke's inability to communicate in public, let alone make a speech. Lionel Logue, an Australian himself, was a gifted therapist who had enjoyed almost uncanny success healing speech defects during the First World War. His first impression of the future King was of a 'slim, quiet man with tired eyes' who had been persuaded to visit his consulting rooms, then in Harley Street, only at his wife's insistence.

After several disheartening visits to specialists, she had pleaded, 'Have just one more try'. It was a success. The Duke would visit Logue almost every day for two months. There was a lot of laughter when the Duchess helped him struggle with speech exercises as her husband studiously recited, 'She sifted thick stalked thistles through a strong thick sieve' and stood by an open window intoning vowels.

The Duke persevered but told his father, 'I am sure I am going to get quite all right in time, but twenty-four years of talking in the wrong way cannot be cured in a month.' It would take longer to heal his bouts of anger, a symptom of years of pent-up frustration at his agonising inability to speak without stuttering. It was no wonder he occasionally got through a decanter of whisky at one sitting.

It was the age of the wireless and the improvement in his speech meant that during the war, George VI's rich voice would go out directly to the people. Even the slowness was an advantage, reassuring those listening to their brave King and appreciating his personal courage. His sincerity shone through while the Prince of Wales' speeches, though altogether more assured, could sound glib.

Before the six-month tour of Australia and New Zealand, the Duke and Duchess were given their instructions by the King. They must remember Queen Victoria's edict that the royal face could never be 'too earnest' in public. The Duchess of York would break this rule at once, being first Princess to smile in public, bringing freshness to royal tours and a quality nobody else in the royal family could ever quite capture.

They left England on 6th January 1927. Heartbroken, they hugged their baby, the parting almost unbearable. The Duchess had to be driven round the block at Grosvenor Gardens three times before she felt composed enough to face the crowds. 'The baby' she said, 'was so sweet playing with the buttons on Bertie's uniform ... it quite broke me up.'

The present Queen has always cherished the coral and pearl necklet seen in photographs of her as a baby which was made specially from 'Mummie's necklaces' to wear while her parents were abroad. The Duchess' heart was often with her baby, but none of the people she met could have guessed how much she was pining; she seemed so convincingly happy to be in their country. In her absence, the royal grandparents would care for the 'bambina', as Queen Mary called the infant Elizabeth, and she was allowed the honour of an occasional tug at the King Emperor's beard.

On board HMS *Renown* the royal couple entered the Pacific on 28th January 1927. Crossing the Line four days later, the Duke was greeted by a recital of 'Now is the winter of our discontent, made glorious summer by this sun of York' by sun-tanned matelots who had been brushing up their Shakespeare.

In Canberra, in naval uniform and watched by a crowd of 20,000, the Duke took a gold key, unlocked the doors to the new Parliament building and then standing on the steps made a major speech. The Duchess, in grey chiffon trimmed with fur, looked serene. They had rehearsed the night before and now she sat calmly on the platform while the Duke spoke slowly but with hardly any hesitation.

After terrific applause Dame Nellie Melba, still in soaring voice at the age of sixty-six, sang 'God Save the King'. The Duke was everything the Australians liked, a diffident, modest man, neither arrogant nor standoffish but serious, a keen fisherman, champion class tennis player and a good horseman.

His speeches struck the right 'down to earth' note, not distant but with emphasis on family values. 'Take care of the children and the country will take care of itself.' One of his more moving speeches was at an Anzac Day ceremony celebrating the Gallipoli landing when he spoke to army veterans: 'They gave their all for the King and Empire.' The warmth towards him generated in the Duke a novel feeling of self-worth. His confidence soared.

It was a triumph for them both, a turning point. Afterwards, whenever he was complimented on a speech the Duke would look towards his wife and say simply, 'She helps me.' His success was hers.

A member of the Household who travelled with them, on this first major tour abroad, thought Elizabeth 'a marvellous helpmeet' to her husband but added, 'he was perfectly his own man. She provided him with just the sort of ambience that he liked. But he was never over-dependent on her.' The Queen Mother always disliked the image of herself as manipulative and the stronger of the two, and the misleading impression of weakness created by her husband's speech impediment.

The Duchess on this, her first world tour, 'achieved the responsibility of having a continent in love with her'. According to the Governor of South Australia, Sir Tom Bridges, she had become the 'Empire's Darling'. A young Scotsman noted, 'The Duchess shines and warms like sunlight.'

On the morning of 21st April 1927 at eight o'clock in the morning there was a birthday salute on board *Renown* for one year old Princess Elizabeth. Apart from three tons of presents, the baby was given possums, kangaroos and wallabies, two singing canaries and twenty parrots. The bigger and furrier live gifts were not installed in the nursery at 145 Piccadilly.

Hundreds of letters and requests came from children all over Australia and New Zealand, 'I am four and a half months old, and I should like a photograph of Princess Betty.' The Duchess did confess she was worried about the attention the Princess was attracting. 'It almost frightens me that people love her so much … poor little darling.'

The children all had personal replies and that was one of the things which made the Duchess special. Not for her the standard, formal 'royal' letter.

The trip, clearly successful, was still being monitored by the King who sometimes, like an angry old hawk, would send grumpy missives. On spotting a member of the Household stood in the wrong place, he sent a message to the Duke: 'I send you a picture of you inspecting the Gd. of Honour ... Yr Equerry should be outside & behind it, it certainly doesn't look well.' This would once have been deeply upsetting for the Duke, but now he was more assured and could even smile at some of his father's rebukes: 'an unfortunate moment for the photograph to be taken', he replied emolliently.

If George V was scolding one minute, the next he was a devoted 'Gramps', loving the presence of the baby Elizabeth. 'I am glad to be able to give you the most excellent accounts of your sweet little daughter, who ... has four teeth now ... she is very happy and drives a carriage every afternoon.' The King and Queen enjoyed their granddaughter more than their own nervy children.

In triumph, the Yorks sailed home, coping sanguinely when fire broke out on board ship. A long way from land, with four of the boiler room staff gassed and badly burnt, the Captain was worried they might have to abandon ship, 'Ma'am, did you realise how bad it was?' he later asked the Duchess. 'Yes indeed,' she smiled. The Captain looked puzzled; he had hoped she had not been aware of the danger. 'I knew there was real trouble ... because every hour someone said there was nothing to worry about.' Ships' captains were impressed, children soothed, the elderly cheered as the image of a desiccated, detached monarchy began to recede.

The tour's success meant that the Duke and Duchess had a new identity in the eyes of the British public. As a mark of his approval, the King sent the three Princes, royal brothers David, Harry and George, to Portsmouth to meet them on Monday 27th June 1927. But he could not resist a few more crusty commands: the Duke would arrive 'without medals and ribands, only stars'. The King and Queen Mary would be at Victoria Station to welcome them home after their arduous six months, but on no account would father and son embrace before so many people; and most important, Bertie must remember, 'When you kiss Mama take yr. hat off.'

The Duchess' natural inclination was to race instantly to Buckingham Palace to see her baby. Instead, she had to do her duty, bear with ceremonial greetings at the station, those polite restrained exchanges, and then thank the host of dignitaries.

It seemed an eternity but at last they reached the Palace. When Princess Elizabeth was brought in by a nanny the Duchess ran forward crying, 'Oh you darling, you', and held her child close to her for several minutes.

The Yorks would now be carrying out more engagements which they found rewarding. Public life had become much less of an ordeal. Behind the King's grouchiness there was a sensitivity and a kindness. To show his appreciation of their recent achievements, in 1931 he gave them a present of The Royal Lodge in Windsor Great Park. George IV described this hunting lodge, designed by Nash, as 'that stately pleasure dome'. Yet even this gift carried a stern proviso. The King got exceptionally cross if its distinctive 'The' prefix was ever omitted in speech or writing.

In love with this dilapidated house and tangled gardens, the Duke and Duchess cheerfully set about renovating the grace and favour 'cottage' which to them would always be 'home'. It was given a rose pink wash, naturally the Duchess of York's choice.

The Wyattville saloon was restored and here, in their green-panelled drawing room, the contented couple would sit side by side at their desks. After her husband died, the Queen Mother never allowed his desk to be removed from alongside her own and always tried to spend the anniversary of his death at this beloved home.

The Duke was an exceptional gardener and an expert on shrubs and rhododendrons. This passion for gardening would compensate for having to abandon hunting and other expensive pastimes. Due to the Depression, and not for the first time, members of the royal family felt a chill financial wind. 'I must sell my horses too,' he sadly told his friend Ronald Tree, adding, 'This is the worst part of it all and the parting with them will be terrible.'

Revelling in home life however, the Duke created an admired garden at The Royal Lodge with its camomile lawn, shrubby azalea walks, flowering cherries, magnolias, sky blue hydrangeas and for his wife, favourite yellow rhododendrons and pink camellias. The Queen Mother later was always proud to remind guests, 'The King made all the garden himself ... it had been a sort of jungle,' as she strolled along some of the paths where she had known the greatest happiness with him.

The Duke liked to communicate in botanical Latin. Humorously explaining to the Countess of Stair at Lochinach Castle how the Duchess had been ill, he wrote: 'I am glad to tell you that she is much better though I found her looking *microleucrum* (small and white) ...' He would complain of a *recurvum* (bent back) and that he was somewhat *lasiopodum* (woolly footed).

The Princesses had their own tiny gardens. As a child at Frogmore, little 'Bertie' had grown Brussels sprouts, radishes and peas. Now he encouraged his children to plant montbretias and baby azaleas. They liked to impress him with their diligence with their own sets of hoes, rakes and brushes. They were given a fifteen foot high model of Welsh cottage Y Bwthyn Bach – 'Little House'. 'All the generations loved this little house,' the Queen Mother would say, watching great-grandchildren exploring this gift from the people of Wales.

Lunch, or 'luncheon' as the Queen Mother insisted was the correct word, was at half past one. If ever the weather was warm enough for a swim, there was a pool surrounded by cherubs on pedestals, fountains and a sundial and, in the hothouse, peaches, melons and apricots.

Dinner on fine summer evenings was on the paved terrace, scented by lavender and rosemary. Leading from the restful terrace there was a sunken garden outside the Duke and Duchess' bedroom planted with damask roses and white tobacco plants for exotic scent at dusk. In the greenhouse, there were richly scented African Moonflowers. And a favourite with the couple was the myrtle tree which they had grown from a sprig of the Duchess' wedding bouquet.

They were enchanted by this weekend home and so were the corgis, Dookie and Jane. Also, chauffeur driven from London, was a fashionable Tibetan lion dog called Choo-Choo accompanied by three yellow Labradors, Mimsy, Stiffy and Scrummy.

Each August the Duke and Duchess would go to Scotland for the grouse shooting, and in early autumn, pheasant and partridge. Birkhall had a heather-thatched summerhouse and Wendy house and was perfect for summer holidays. Here the Princesses picnicked and a rose called Honeymoon was planted near a yew tree shaped like a cottage loaf. Holidays abroad were never considered, anymore than the Queen would go anywhere but Balmoral for the late summer.

The Duchess of York loved children and, from a large family herself, had hoped for a third child though neither birth had been easy. Several gynaecologists were consulted and the children's pram was kept hopefully in evidence for rather a long time before it was put reluctantly away. Even when the Duke of York became King, Princess Elizabeth was not immediately named official Heir Apparent. The Princesses were being groomed only as daughters of a royal duke.

The house was filled with laughter. The Princesses amused the Duke whenever he caught glimpses of them being given early lessons in deportment and grace by their mother. 'Now I am the Archbishop of Canterbury,' the Duchess would say, or 'Now I am Grannie,' meaning Queen Mary. They had swimming lessons and played with toy horses, They nibbled their parents' coffee sugar crystals at dinner, always at half past nine in the evening. Princess Margaret, sitting on her father's knee, would demand 'windy water' – soda water. It was often suggested that 'Margo' was Papa's favourite.

In London they had dancing lessons with the celebrated Madame Vacani. For parties and visits to the King and Queen at Buckingham Palace, they wore dresses with flouncy, frilled organdie skirts or ruched pink tulle over rose satin. Otherwise, for outings to Hyde Park or Battersea, sitting in a carriage drawn by a pair of bays, they wore pale rose or primrose hand-smocked silk frocks with matching knickers, white ankle socks, straw bonnets trimmed with forget-me-nots and blue coats with velvet collars.

Queen Mary disapproved of their late hours, wondering why the Princesses did not spend more time behind the green baize door as royal children had done for centuries, hardly ever seeing their parents. Princess Elizabeth was always orderly, and loved playing at housework – a craze only for those who never lift a duster. Lady Airlie had given her a scarlet housemaid's outfit for Christmas with a dustpan and brush. Queen Mary thought now that she was four, it was more appropriate that she should learn about the Empire and sent her building blocks to make it easy.

The Duchess, so well grounded herself in 'the arts that please', was not going to insist that her daughters studied Latin or Greek. Instead she wanted them to be able to play the piano, read nicely and acquit themselves at parlour games, to have good handwriting and perfect poise rather than the ability to discuss the theory of relativity.

In 1932 a presentable twenty-two year old from Scotland, Miss Marion Crawford, was appointed governess to the Princesses. Embraced by the family, she became known as 'Crawfie'.

'Crawfie', who stayed for seventeen years, worried about the Princesses' excessive love of horses but the Duke reassured her. 'Think nothing of it, it is a family idiosyncrasy. My sister Mary was a horse.' The Duchess, who was reading *Black Beauty* to her daughters, jokingly admitted, 'Yes … anything we can find about horses and dogs.'

Their governess would take them incognito to Woolworths for Christmas shopping – 'so exciting'. On the rare occasions when she was cross with them they called her 'Gruffenough'.

Crawfie put off her marriage to Major George Buthlay until 1947 when she was thirty-eight because of her commitment to the Princesses. She would never be forgiven, though, for writing a harmless enough book called *The Little Princesses* in which she made a few anodyne revelations: how she had to keep the peace between Elizabeth and Margaret; how they squabbled, hated wearing hats, 'you brute, you beast' they would cry, snapping the elastic under each other's chins. Princess Margaret was a biter and, as for Princess Elizabeth, 'she never cared a fig about clothes.' When Crawfie died in 1987 almost a recluse, there was not a flower or a word of condolence from any of the royal family.

Afterwards, an old shoe box was found amongst Crawfie's possessions crammed with loving mementoes from the Princesses and letters daubed with charcoal kisses.

The Duke and Duchess of York enjoyed their children; their family warmth gave a reassuring picture of conventional domesticity and people could identify comfortably with this neat, traditional, happy family. There was the Duchess, the pretty mother, with her earnest, devoted husband and two well brought up children. Motherliness was in fashion again after years of being stifled in the post-war era of the flat-chested Twenties. Royal women used never to hug a gloomy little prince or princess in public, but the Duchess broke with this convention, always holding the Princesses warmly by the hand.

'What fun she is ... How easy to talk to,' Sir Fitzroy Maclean's wife Veronica recalled of entertaining the Duke and Duchess of York. The impression they created was that 'they were not at all like other royalty ... whose formality usually created a kind of frozen space around them, paralysing all normal and, certainly, youthful conversation.'

Profoundly depressed about the heir to the throne's lack of seriousness, the popularity of the Yorks was giving the King even more proof of their eminent suitablity to succeed him. He was already grimly aware that 'David', bored by his own charm, flashing 'his dentist's smile' (Chips Channon's description), was preoccupied with his social life rather than his duties as heir to the throne.

'You dress like a cad, you act like a cad,' the King barked when his eldest son had the temerity to arrive at the Palace with turn-ups on his trousers. 'Is it raining in here?' his father raged, unaware of this latest fashionable trend. Almost as upsetting to the King as the Prince's style of 'chic fatigue' was the fact that, in his opinion, 'David did not have a single friend who is a gentleman.' Intolerable.

Charmed by the warm security of his family and the love of his sweet wife, enjoying a carefree life and emotionally stable, the nightmare possibility never occurred to the Duke of York that he might one day become King. But the notion preoccupied his father.

CHAPTER 9

Wallis Blew in from Baltimore

'I want to introduce a great friend of mine,' the Prince of Wales remarked, sauntering across to Queen Mary at a wedding reception. His voice always sounded confident whether making a kingly speech, a dramatic 'something must be done' promise to hard pressed miners, or giving up a throne.

It was the Duke of Kent's wedding day, 29th December 1934, and in that festive atmosphere the Queen was obliged to meet Mrs Wallis Simpson. She hoped that the American with the harsh laugh was just another of David's infatuations and, in her experience, 'they never lasted.' However, by the following May, the Queen shared her daughter-in-law's view about Wallis Simpson as a predator. The Duchess of York was fond of her brother-in-law, but she developed a deep-seated intuitive dislike of the glossy American, and would disparagingly refer to the day 'when Wallis blew in from Baltimore', making her sound like a damaged autumn leaf.

Queen Mary could never be reconciled to her American daughter-in-law, declaring bitterly that Wallis had come between her eldest son and herself like a 'coiled malevolence'.

The Prince of Wales, eighteen months older than the Duke of York, had been showing no inclination to marry until meeting this latest girlfriend at Melton Mowbray in 1931, where he had gone to stay with his brother Prince George and to enjoy some hunting. Born in June 1896 in Virginia, Wallis Warfield was a witty, sophisticated woman who came from old established American stock and who would never be intimidated by royalty.

First married in 1916 to Earl Winfield Spencer Jr, a lieutenant in the US Navy, Wallis, for a time, thought he was the world's most fascinating aviator. But then he took to drink and would fly less through the skies and more into sadistic rages. They separated in 1921, divorcing soon afterwards on grounds of desertion.

Somehow the divorce had not prevented her from being presented at Court in 1931. Her headdress of aquamarines complimented her ivory complexion and black hair, which always had a severe middle parting. Ironically she was presented at the same time as fashionable Thelma, Lady Furness, whom Cecil Beaton thought had the pale beauty of a magnolia. Even this hot-house appeal was not enough however to prevent Wallis replacing her, after four years, in the affections of the Little Man, one of her pet names for the heir to the throne.

Ernest Simpson, her second husband and a stockbroker, was a naturalised Englishman whom she had married at Chelsea Register Office six months after her divorce. A civilised man with a taste for the classics, opera and *objets d'art*, he bore with the Prince of Wales' attentions to his wife but warned her that she was probably only 'the froth on his champagne'.

Soignée in her 'messenger boy suits', as Cecil Beaton called them, Mrs Simpson wore strong colours well, especially scarlet. Slim to extinction, she rejoiced in being a modern day X-Ray. Obsessional about her looks and self-absorbed, for thirty years her hair was done at least once a day by Alexandre, the celebrated French hairdresser from Paris. She was never without multiple pairs of gossamer silk stockings at any one time, whether in New York, Paris or London.

Opinionated and with a raucous laugh, she was, however, often the most striking woman in any smart gathering and closely watched by 'cold jealous English eyes', which was her own vivid impression after that first meeting with Queen Mary.

The Prince became a regular visitor at Bryanston Court, the Simpsons' minimalist, fashionable flat with white leather furniture near Marble Arch. White arum lilies and orchids complemented the black and white decor by interior designer Lady Colefax (who had briefly been the wife of Somerset Maugham). 'It was the only Household where the water in the vases was always crystal clear,' recalled the Baroness de Cabrol, a close friend from Paris, savouring this aesthetic detail.

Mrs Simpson, perfectionist and model of self-improvement, paid minute attention to aesthetic detail and not just her own metallic elegance. When Duchess of Windsor, her kitchen staff were instructed to make sure that when a salad was served in the dining room, every single lettuce leaf should match; her sheets had to be freshly ironed every day; a maid later complained: 'Her Royal Highness would never think of having a wrinkle on her bed.'

Even the pugs, Trooper, Disraeli, Imp and Davy Crocket, had to be sleekly groomed. 'We did have one called Peter Townsend,' the Duchess later recalled, 'but we gave the Group Captain away.' The Queen Mother may have pampered her corgis, with baskets made up like proper beds with pillows and sheets, but in her Household they made do with ordinary bowls, not solid silver.

'The babies send you eanum flowers,' the King wrote to his love in 1936. Eanum was their intimate word for 'tiny' or 'little'. In a demonstration of affection, Mrs Simpson would send 'a pat to Slippy Poo' the dog but the hapless Slipper was killed by a snake bite at the Château de Cande in France just before they married. 'Now the principal guest at the wedding is no more,' lamented the bride.

About this time Lord Dunsany, an Irish peer who died in 1998, met the Prince of Wales by a swimming pool in Marbella. Both men were in shorts but Dunsany, soldierly and correct, came to attention, snapping his bare ankles together. He explained, 'Everybody knew about her. Mrs Simpson was fun, articulate, safely married, ideal.' No threat to the monarchy then. In the north of England, children sang a cheeky ditty which echoed public disapproval.

'Who's this coming down the street?
Mrs Simpson with her smelly old feet,
She's been married twice before,
Now she's knocking at Edward's door.'

George V celebrated his Silver Jubilee on 6th May 1935. His 'dear people' shouted their approval as he drove to St Paul's and sang 'For he's a jolly good fellow'. Rather surprised, he chuckled 'They must really like me for myself,' and turning to Archbishop Lang said: 'But I cannot understand. I am quite an ordinary sort of fellow.' 'That is just it,' the Archbishop replied.

By November, the King was gravely ill with acute septicaemia in the right lung and the Duke of York, who was hunting at Naseby, had to return to London. After an operation, the King seemed to recover. At Sandringham, he touchingly insisted on going out on his white pony with Queen Mary walking beside him. But the following day, 16th January, he was too ill to leave his room and the Queen sent for all her sons.

The Prince of Wales, returning from East Africa, was later teased by his younger brother Bertie: 'There is a lovely story going about ... that the reason you are rushing home is that in the event of anything happening to Papa, I am going to bag the throne in your absence. Just like the Middle Ages.' What irony.

Queen Mary, not usually extravagant in her praise of her family, would say gratefully 'my children were angelic. I sent for Bertie to help me with the party.' The usual royal house party went on even if the host was dying. The Duchess of York had pneumonia and remained at The Royal Lodge while the Duke sped to Sandringham. Mrs Simpson confided to an indiscreet friend, 'Soon I shall be Queen of England.'

Queen Mary – as always – bottled up her emotions. When her husband lay dying, even then, the Duke of York told the Prince of Wales, 'Through all the anxiety she has never revealed her feelings to any of us ... she is really far too reserved ... I fear a breakdown if anything awful happens.' It was typical. As the Duke of Windsor would remark later and a shade remorsefully, in the royal family 'Whatever was gnawing at their souls, nobody talked about it.' They believed that whatever the heartache public life should go on, their insistence on ritual a grim salvation in itself.

On the 20th January 1935, Privy Counsellors gathered round the King as he sat in an armchair wrapped in his beloved Tibetan green, blue and yellow dressing gown. They heard him finally admit 'Gentlemen, I am unable to concentrate.' Close to tears, they filed out. Even when he was dying, he would concede no more than 'I am very tired', but finally wrote in his diary, 'I feel rotten', and died that same evening at five minutes to midnight.

The Royal Physician, Lord Dawson, revealed that three hours earlier, when it was evident that George V's life was 'moving peacefully towards its close', he had been injected with a shot of morphine and cocaine 'into a distended jugular vein'.

The decision had been sanctioned by the Prince of Wales, so his father should have 'dignity and serenity' in his last few hours. It has since been suggested that the fatal shot was timed to enable *The Times* to carry the news of the monarch's death the following morning.

Now a widow of only a few hours, Queen Mary wrote a poetic note in her diary and confided that she was 'heartbroken'. It had not been a spontaneous love match but over forty-two years it had developed into a tender, loving marriage. She was stirred by memories of their courtship and how 'Georgie' had asked her to bear with him though outwardly he might appear 'shy and cold'. For her 'the sunset of his death has tinged the whole world's sky.'

Men in the royal family may have been frightened of the King, but the women loved him, knowing that his bearishness disguised a gentle man. The Duchess of York would miss him 'dreadfully ... Unlike his own children,' she said, 'I was never afraid of him ... he never spoke one unkind or abrupt word to me ... He was so kind ...'

On the night of George V's death Queen Mary inclined a curtsey and kissed the hand of the new King – Edward VIII. The King is dead, long live the King.

Mrs Simpson heard the announcement that evening in a cinema in Piccadilly and, in the accommodating darkness, reflected on her relationship with the new King: 'My head was spinning ... Was I going to revert to being plain Mrs Simpson, a discarded woman?' Hardly. On the evening of his Accession, royal advisers were horrified when the new King flamboyantly met her at the Ritz.

This hotel reeks of royal associations. It was here that Prince Charles would first show off Lady Diana Spencer at Princess Margaret's birthday party, and in 1998 was to present his mistress Mrs Camilla Parker-Bowles to the world when they both attended her sister's birthday party.

The relationship with Wallis Simpson had been drawing room gossip, but was not taken seriously until this defiant gesture. Surely the flashy Mrs Simpson – 'common and vulgar' – had been just a dalliance and her husband Ernest a 'man complaisant'? It seemed not. The observant Chips Channon recorded the unpalatable 'The King worships her'.

During George V's funeral there were one or two strange portents: in the middle of the solemn procession, a sudden flash of light was seen dancing along the pavement. This was the Maltese Cross, a jewel set with a giant sapphire and hundreds of diamonds on top of the Imperial Crown, which had toppled off the coffin and fallen into the street, watched by a stricken royal family. The superstitious in the silent crowd were made more fearful by this 'most terrible omen', Harold Nicholson wrote in his 1936 diary.

The new King's reaction to his father's death had been almost hysterical and an equerry, Major Verney, had been one of those genuinely puzzled as father and son had not been particularly close. At the same time Edward VIII was shaking off some of his father's idiosyncrasies which he found irksome, immediately correcting all the clocks at the Palace. George V liked to keep thirty minutes ahead of Greenwich time. This was hardly a harsh gesture but the speed at which it was done was insensitive and deeply upsetting to his mother, who had always indulged her husband's lovable eccentricities.

For the royal family, the worst thing was being received at Balmoral by Mrs Simpson, who rested her well-groomed head on the feathered royal pillows. The hospitality was now excellent. On one occasion, a witty all rose-coloured dinner was served instead of the more usual robust meat and white sauced vegetables. Although an experienced and assured hostess, Mrs Simpson was humiliated by the Duchess of York, who walked straight past her saying, 'I came to dine with the King' and seated herself on his right. Acting as principal guest and then as hostess, icily sweet, she invited the women guests to follow her out of the dining room.

The King enjoyed Balmoral as never before, humming strains from Gershwin's 'Rhapsody in Blue'. Only a month after his father's death he played the piano and marched round the table in Highland dress and tam o'shanter playing the bagpipes. There is no doubt that as hosts, he and Mrs Simpson were great fun.

Previously he had managed to escape the traditional royal family summer holiday in Balmoral. He hated the Victorian baronial gloom and unsubtle tartan. Never a keen hunter, he was happier in August playing golf at Biarritz or swimming at Eden Roc. Instead of the hardship of shooting parties in Scotland and those stodgy royal picnics, he preferred 'la chasse Européene'; he would rather velvet knickerbockers than rough tweed in which to stalk chamois in the Tyrol or shoot partridge in Hungary.

The King and Mrs Simpson went on a cruise on Lady Yule's yacht the *Nahlin* to Yugoslavia. Attired in couture beach clothes, bermuda shorts and striped tops, they were spotted shrimping, lounging on deck and generally having great fun. The King felt liberated: 'It was my impulse whenever I found myself alone to remove my coat, rip off my tie, loosen my collar and roll up my sleeves. Wallis calls this my striptease act.'

He engineered a teatime visit with Mrs Simpson to The Royal Lodge, ostensibly to show off his new American station wagon to his brother and sister. If the visit was resented, it was masked by the Duchess' 'justly famous charm'. It had been clever of the King to make the call so apparently informal. Gallant and well mannered with a true affection for his starry brother, the Duke of York warmly welcomed the couple. But as the two brothers went spinning off in the new toy, they were blithely unaware of undercurrents of feminine antipathy between the women they loved.

While the two could not have been outwardly more different, both were made of tensile steel. The Duchess of York, in delicate pastels, with Gainsborough prettiness, looked as safe as a Jane Austen heroine. A model wife and mother, she was known for her modesty and impeccably high moral standards and her reputation was pristine. Now she switched the full beam of 'her startlingly blue eyes' on Mrs Simpson, the racy American who would make her Queen.

Mrs Simpson, not easily outfaced, complained later about the Duchess' eyes, 'Why, they went right through you.' She got her own back by nicknaming Elizabeth the 'Dowdy Duchess'.

Pandering to Mrs Simpson, the King could always make her smile if he called the Duchess of York 'Cookie'. This was not an affectionate nickname, but stemmed from the malicious view that her bonny features and rosy cheeks made her look like their Scottish cook.

Mrs Simpson later scathingly referred to 'Elizabeth' as the 'Monster of Glamis'. In the language she knew best – that of precious gems – she relegated her appearance to a mere 'fourteen carat beauty'.

The royal governess, Marion Crawford, ever watchful, on bringing the Princesses in to meet the King thought Mrs Simpson 'a smart attractive woman with that immediate friendliness American women have'. Princess Elizabeth innocently asked the million dollar question, 'Who is she?' and was swiftly taken out of the drawing room. They learnt they were not to mention Uncle David's vivacious new American friend who laughed at her own jokes and made frequent references to 'K Ts', cocktails. How this slang grated on their parents.

Telling the Duke, who prided himself on his gardening expertise, that he ought to cut down some trees for a better view, was not the most tactful thing for the American visitor to suggest. Yet he did think her amusing, which could hardly have helped her relationship with the Duchess.

The Duke and Duchess loathed Wallis' flippancy and thought her humour cruel. When it was suggested that she go out for a walk with a man she did not care for at a weekend house party, Mrs Simpson, declined saying, 'I can't, I'm fresh out of leashes.' She was a gambler, and she made them wince when someone remarked at a game of gin rummy, 'Why Wallis, you've thrown away three kings.' 'But I kept the best one didn't I?' she answered smartly.

Her accent and loudness were bad enough but what really incensed the Duke and Duchess was the way in which she appeared altogether 'too proprietorial' with the King. They might have been even more appalled had they heard her snap impatiently at him at a Fort Belvedere dinner party, when he was pouring wine, 'You can't serve Graves, it is the commonest wine in the world.'

Winston Churchill, who liked Wallis Simpson, shocked a dinner party by emphasising the King's need for her. 'Make no mistake,' he observed, 'he cannot live without her.' This passion would shake to their foundations those old aristocratic, establishment families who orbited royalty. Not particularly glamorous or entertaining, their particular strength was conforming, as their ancestors had done for centuries: public school, army, colonial service; predictable, dynastic marriages, then running the family acres, steady as the turning of the agricultural seasons. Loyal to the Crown, these stolid god-fearing people were now hearing that their King, the Supreme Head of the Church and Defender of the Faith, was 'insane' about an American divorcee. The *mot juste,* they sniffed.

The second divorce, from Ernest Simpson, came through quietly on the 27th October 1936 in Ipswich, Suffolk, on the grounds of his adultery at the Hotel de Paris in Bray, Berkshire, with a woman called Buttercup Kennedy. The forty-two year old King and his love hoped that her divorce would free them to be acceptable to the nation as a couple. Like Prince Charles and Camilla Parker-Bowles, some sixty years later, they were blithely unaware of the deep well of pain inflicted by their relationship. The Abdication crisis was now inexorably gaining momentum.

1. Lady Strathmore called her youngest children her 'two Benjamins' because they were so close in age
David, born in 1902, is here with his sister Elizabeth, aged four. Unable to pronounce his sister's name
David called her 'Buffy'. The bond between them was to last all their lives.

2. An early soft focus shot of Elizabeth's womanly curves, showing a sensuous hint of self-awareness and a touch of a budding actress.

3. The newly married Duke and Duchess of York with both sets of parents after their wedding on 26th April 1923. The bride looks suitably solemn, flanked by her mighty in-laws, King George V and Queen Mary. Her parents, the Earl and Countess of Strathmore, appear to be taking the honour of their daughter marrying into the royal family in their stride. The Queen Mother inherited her original, free-flowing style of dressing from her mother.

4. The Duke of York was keen on the Boy Scout movement and his wife shared his enthusiasm, spreading the word to 'new chums' on a visit to Australia in 1927. The Duchess was always involved with the Girl Guide movement and was District Commissioner of the Glamis troop before she got married.

5. This photograph from a private collection has a charming informality and has never been seen before in public. It captures the Duchess of York's pleasure in her children on one of her frequent visits to the chintzy nursery. A bouncing Princess Margaret is the centre of attention, Princess Elizabeth showing no jealousy of the attention attracted by 'the Bud' - her name for her baby sister.

6. Before she married into the royal family, the Duchess dreaded public engagements. But her easy charm carried her through. An ability to handle a shovel was a prerequisite in those days for the royal family for tree planting ceremonies. Here, the Duchess acquitted herself well on a visit to Sheffield in July 1934 digging potatoes in the Deep Pit allotments provided for the unemployed. A country girl at heart, her deftness with a shovel did not go unnoticed by some of the out-of-work onlookers.

7. King George V was a stickler for sartorial correctness, so that even for romping family get-togethers, everyone should be formally dressed. The Duke of York was a devoted family man. Here, Princess Elizabeth is five and Princess Margaret is ten months. The Yorks were disappointed that they were unable to have any more children.

8. The prettiness of the Queen is shared by her daughter Princess Elizabeth who is wearing the coral necklace given to her by her mother, both sharing enviable English rose complexions.

9. An early taste of France. Not long married, the Duke and Duchess of York were given a dutiful civic reception at the Paris Hotel de Ville. But when they visited in 1937 as King and Queen, the Parisians were absolutely bowled over. 'We have taken the Queen to our hearts,' was the cry wherever the Queen appeared in long white Winterhalter dresses under her white parasol. 'She rules over two nations,' the French cried, 'France is a monarchy again.'

10. Girls in pearls in April 1940. The Queen with her daughters Princess Elizabeth and Princess Margaret, who had specially rag-rolled her hair for the photograph. Determined to make life fun for her children and to protect them from the horrors of war, there was an indestructible bond between mother and daughters which has lasted to this day.

11. George VI shortly after the Abdication in December 1936. A reluctant new King, he looks gaunt and strained but the Queen has that gift of being able to perform well and gives a gracious wave. Through their marriage, she could disguise any anxiety in public and this helped the King. The two Princesses are too young to be aware of the momentous changes about to overtake them, particularly Princess Elizabeth - now directly in line to the throne.

12. It was the King and Queen's war effort which won them the enduring affection of the British people. They never shirked visits to bomb-damaged cities and the Queen, seen here in South London in September 1940, had a knack of touching the right note with her quick, sympathetic smile and readiness to listen. She felt the suffering endured by the people during the war 'almost too much to bear.'

13. This first photograph of the King since his operation for lung cancer in September 1951 was at a children's party celebrating Prince Charles's third birthday on 14th November 1951. The King has dressed up for the occasion in his new suede shoes. The Queen is amused by her husband's uncertainty about the bundle of granddaughter, Princess Anne, just plonked in his lap. Meanwhile the Queen's fur is slipping and likely to provoke a sleeping corgi. Prince Charles treasures this photograph.

14. Prince Charles was the son she never had. During the Queen's coronation in 1952, it was the Queen Mother who comforted him and kept a supply of sweets for her favourite grandchild in her handbag during the long service at Westminster Abbey. The bond between them has been indestructible.

15. A trying time in the company of the Windsors, at the 1967 unveiling of the memorial tablet to Queen Mary; the Queen had amicably invited 'Uncle David' to bring his wife. The Queen Mother remains 'utterly oyster' on matters close to her heart, but the Duchess appears only too aware of some evident antipathy. Prince Philip, the Duke and Duchess of Gloucester with Lord Harewood standing behind the Queen Mother all look as if anything might happen.

CHAPTER 10

An Airy Telegram

In November 1936, the Prime Minister Stanley Baldwin left Buckingham Palace in a state of shock after a meeting with the King. Edward VIII had briskly announced that he would marry Mrs Simpson as soon as possible, preferably as King but if that was not possible he would abdicate.

'I have heard such things from my King tonight that I never thought to hear'. Baldwin's words still echo an eloquent dismay.

The Duchess wrote to the Prince of Wales appealing to his better nature. She told him of her anxiety over her husband, how the Duke of York's social phobia made public life a nightmare. He was now in a 'constant agony of foreboding'. 'Darling David,' she wrote. 'I am terrified for him so do help him ...'

Meanwhile the Duke went about his engagements dreading the call that would mean being led to the slaughter 'like the proverbial sheep'. He would 'have to take over ... and do his best;' otherwise the fear was that 'the whole fabric might crumble under the shock and strain of it all.'

The Yorks were in Edinburgh on 29th November 1936, where the Duke succeeded the Prince of Wales as Grand Master of the Freemasons. He and the Duchess would receive the freedom of the Scottish capital. With her uncanny Bowes-Lyon sixth sense the Duchess feared all was not well and was increasingly depressed. A timely virus always seemed to attack and lay her low at emotional times in her life.

As they returned to London by train on the night of 2nd December, newspaper billboards at Euston blazed the worst: 'King gives up throne for "The Woman I Love."'

Mrs Simpson was in France. She had always known of the hostility towards her, but now the agonising was over. The King had made his decision; there would be no more wondering if he thought of her as 'a woman only to be enjoyed and not to be taken seriously'. He would marry her.

With the Abdication crisis at its height, the King would have been horrified had he known about Mrs Simpson's written declaration that she was 'giving up any interest in marrying His Majesty'. In hiding at a villa in Cannes, this bombshell came on typically tasteful grey writing paper and was probably the result of pressure on Mrs Simpson from royal advisers. Another theory is that Mrs Simpson, exhausted and appalled by the depth of feeling against her and seeing the gilded fun evaporating from the relationship, wanted to break with the King and scuttle back to America where they knew how to make a decent cocktail. It is doubtful if anything could have deflected the King at this late stage from his obsessional love.

In the car between Euston and Piccadilly, the Duchess struggled to control her emotions. 'Her heart,' she admitted later, 'dropped' when she saw the newspapers. When she turned to her husband and saw how drawn and tense he looked, a nerve working in his cheek, she was overwhelmed. Her love for him from that moment would be encased in a deeply embedded anger against Mrs Simpson. Later she would say, 'I just felt sorry for her by the end,' her pity perhaps even more devastating than her anger. She never forgave Mrs Simpson because she believed that from the time of the Abdication, her husband's lifespan was brutally curtailed.

That bizarre evening, close friends who were entertaining the Duke and Duchess of York to an intimate supper party at their mews house in Mayfair remembered how they were an hour late, and how unusual that was for the punctilious Duke. When they finally arrived all their resentment and anger against this 'scheming woman' poured out. The Duke felt horribly let down but the Duchess was 'undoubtedly furious'. 'Mrs Simpson,' they said, had 'wrecked their lives.'

The Duke was now only eight days away from becoming King and was reeling from the sequence of events. He confided in his cousin Lord Mountbatten: 'This is terrible, Dicky. I never wanted this to happen. I am quite unprepared for it. David has been trained for it all his life whereas I have never seen a state paper ... I am only a naval officer. It is the only thing I know about.'

'Gay as a lark', lighthearted about his decision, the King entertained the Prime Minister and members of his family to a convivial dinner at Fort Belvedere on 8th December 1936. His sister-in-law Elizabeth was thankful she could miss the dinner at the Fort. She had gone to bed soon after they returned from Scotland, 'so glad she had 'flu'.

Almost the hardest thing to bear for the royal family was the way in which the King appeared to be in such irrepressibly high spirits at the prospect of leaving them. Lord Mountbatten thought unforgivably so.

The King embraced his brother 'Bertie', who had whispered to Sir Walter Monckton during dinner, 'this is the man we are going to lose,' of a brother who 'was the life and soul of the party.' The new King, bemused, still in a state of shock, would always recall how 'D and I said goodbye ... kissed, parted as Freemasons and he bowed to me as his King'.

On the night of 10th December, after 327 days on the throne, Edward VIII signed the Instrument of Abdication declaring, 'My irrevocable determination to renounce the Throne for Myself and My descendants'. The former king, now Prince Edward of Windsor, then had a pedicure for a troublesome corn, and embarked on the destroyer *Fury* at two o'clock in the morning on 11th December 1936 and sailed for Boulogne, leaving both country and throne.

The new King Emperor George VI would sob for an hour on his mother's shoulder at Marlborough House, and there was something magnificent about this old lady of unbending rectitude now coping superbly with 'this incredible tragedy'. It was a compliment to her that 'Bertie' should feel free to weep so easily in her presence.

The new Queen worried. 'Those last days of the Abdication crisis had been,' she said, 'like sitting on the edge of a volcano'. Now she prayed that her husband 'would be granted not a lighter load but a stronger back'. She knew he had 'great guts' and was determined to steady a 'rocking throne'.

Queen Mary had called on her and spent an hour and a half with her, helpless in the face of her paroxysms of grief: 'the tears were streaming down my dear daughter-in-law's face'.

Some of the tears were angry and fretful, an outpouring of resentment. The Queen was outraged, aware now of the speculation about which royal brother would make the best king: not the Duke of Gloucester, an uncomplicated soldier; nor would the Duke of Kent do, attractive but wayward and with his taste for exotic substances, hardly the solid phlegmatic character needed to stabilise a discredited monarchy.

For a year there had been a charismatic king on the throne. Now the country would have to do with the Duke of York, hardly ideal, a reluctant choice. Provoked by this apathy, the spirit of 'the lassie' was to help George VI become one of our most universally respected kings.

White and tense but of compelling dignity, the new King attended his Accession Council at St James' Palace. Privy Counsellors were struck by his presence and diarist Harold Nicolson noted his 'most beautiful speaking voice'.

'I meet you today in circumstances which are without parallel in the history of our country'. After his succession George VI spoke to the people: 'With my wife and helpmeet by my side I take up the heavy task which lies before me'. Earlier that day, he had been moved when, inspired by their mother, the two Princesses had gravely curtsied to him, their King, in the hall at 145 Piccadilly. Respect for the monarch within the royal family is such that Princess Anne will leap to her feet and remain standing if she receives a telephone call from the Queen.

An airy telegram arrived from 'D', the ex-King now in France: 'Had a good crossing. Hope Elizabeth better. Best love and best of luck to you both,' as if on the start of a motoring holiday on the continent. On New Year's Eve he had joined Mrs Simpson in France and gave her a pair of aquamarine flower clips from Cartier to add to her dramatic and sensual collection of jewellery.

As a love match it seemed to endure. Sir Walter Monckton, Edward VIII's lawyer and a stalwart friend through the Abdication crisis and long afterwards, wrote about the 'intensity and the depth of the King's devotion to Mrs Simpson, it was a great mistake to assume he was merely in love with her. There was an intellectual relationship and there's no doubt that his lonely nature found in her a spiritual comradeship'.

Lord Monckton's view of the Windsor marriage, revealed in papers released at the Bodleian Library, Oxford, in March 2000, hint at that solitary and individualist streak in the Duke's make-up which might explain his rejection of a conventional royal marriage to a suitable aristocratic virgin selected for him by the Palace.

The Duke always treated the Duchess with unquestioning devotion even when worn out by her unrelenting social appetite. In America once when she had danced till five o'clock in the morning, long after the Duke had gone to bed, he reappeared on the staircase in silk pyjamas and dressing gown. Putting his head on one side, he called gently, 'Yankee, come home.' In his eyes she was, quite simply, Lord Monckton said, 'the perfect woman'.

Working at the needlepoint taught him by Queen Mary and which he did so beautifully, gardening, paying attention to his wardrobe, entertaining and designing jewels for his Duchess, helped the Duke while away the unforgiving years of exile in Paris. He was immensely bitter that his wife was never given a title or accepted by the royal family.

About the only recognition she received in England was a waxwork figure at Madame Tussaud's in London in an unbecoming long red dress.

'Is there any way you can have that appalling wax figure of me removed,' she asked in a letter to the King's lawyers in 1936. 'It really is too indecent and so awful to be there anyway.' Obsessed by her appearance, her attempts to have the hateful dummy melted down were unsuccessful.

The Queen Mother, mellow in outlook on most things, tends to vagueness now at any mention of earlier antipathy to the Windsors. Imbued with her Edwardian background, when men leapt to the defence of their country in a time of war and wives stayed home supportively knitting socks, the Windsors' flirtation with Hitler had particularly incensed her. In July 1940 in an uncharacteristically angry letter to the Colonial Secretary, Lord Lloyd, the Queen objected strongly to the appointment of the Duke as Governor of the Bahamas.

'The people in our lands are used to looking up to their King's representative – the Duchess of Windsor is looked upon as the lowest of the low ...'

The Duke could not but be aware of the Queen's antipathy. His resentment spilt over in March 1953 when in England at Queen Mary's deathbed. Complaining about the tedium of waiting for his mother to die, he confided in the Duchess who had stayed in America: 'It's one of the most trying situations I've ever found myself in and hanging around someone who has been so mean and vile to you my sweetheart is getting me down.'

As he and the rest of the royal family waited in the sickroom at Marlborough House he observed: 'What a smug, stinking lot my relations are ... You have never seen such a seedy, worn out bunch of old hags; most of them have become ... ice-veined bitches;' these were petulant outpourings of a fragile justification of life in exile.

Only the Queen and Princess Margaret ever had a real inkling of their mother's true feelings about the Duke and Duchess of Windsor. A meeting with the Duke was engineered some years later at Clarence House with the not long widowed Queen Mother, which he found 'informal and friendly'. She told him how it 'was nice to be able to talk about "Bertie" with somebody who had known him so well.' Perhaps the Queen Mother was thinking back to when she was first married and the Duke was the glamorous heir to the throne. They had got on well with him then and she wrote comforting, teasing letters when George V was angry with him. 'Dear David, of course you are very very naughty, but delicious.'

When the Duke was dying of cancer of the throat in 1972, the Queen, Prince Philip and Prince Charles visited him in Paris. They assured him that the Duchess would be buried alongside him in the Royal Mausoleum at Frogmore.

Prince Charles tried hard to fix a friendly visit back to England for the man he called 'Uncle David' but the Queen Mother was implacably opposed to the idea. He died on 28th May 1972. 'I know how you feel,' the Queen Mother nevertheless said at the funeral. 'I have been through it myself,' taking the distraught Duchess by the arm.

They had met briefly in June 1967 when the Queen, in a conciliatory gesture, had invited the Duchess to accompany her husband to London for the unveiling of a memorial plaque to Queen Mary. Wallis would not curtsey. There were perfunctory kisses and it was left to the Duchess of Kent – the saintly 'Katie' who works for Age Concern and Hospices for the Dying – to look after the Windsors at lunch. The Queen Mother went to the Derby with the Queen.

For someone so fastidious the Duchess' last years of bedridden senility were a final indignity. No longer a threat, this once chic figure lay in a darkened room. Her plight moved the Queen Mother, who told Kenneth Rose, author of a best-selling biography of George V, how, contrary to public opinion, she had always made a point of inquiring about the Duchess' health whenever she was passing through Paris, and sent her flowers. So have rumours of the Queen's animosity towards the Duchess been greatly exaggerated?

As the Queen Mother blossomed with the years, the Duchess of Windsor declined, dying of arteriosclerosis in Paris in 1986. That year, the Duke and Duchess' Paris home in the Bois de Boulogne was leased to Mohamed Al Fayed, the Egyptian owner of Harrods, who considered it sufficiently elegant for his son Dodi and Diana, Princess of Wales.

In July 1997, in readiness, he ordered that the house be cleared of all Windsor clothes, furniture and artefacts. A month later his son and the Princess were killed in a car crash in Paris. The following February the Windsor possessions were auctioned in New York. The proceeds went to the young couple's favourite charities.

CHAPTER 11

Too Many Damned Parsons

The King and Queen were filled with foreboding. Even the deference shown them by the royal family was depressing, further proof of the 'intolerable honour' this unassuming couple now bore.

The year opened with a sense of unease. For the demoralised Royal Family, there was the slightly encouraging news that a proposal to abolish the monarchy had been defeated by 403 votes to 5 in the House of Commons.

Succession to the throne is challenging enough when you have been groomed for the role all your life; now this second best King struggled in the shadow of his assured older brother, with whom he was constantly and unfavourably compared. George VI, a nervous man anyway who hated heights and public speaking and was subject to fits of depression, was frank about his feelings of inadequacy. He told the Prime Minister's wife, Lucy Baldwin, that all his life he felt outshone by 'his brilliant brother'.

In the solitude of his study, he rehearsed for the Coronation on 12th May 1937 – his cruel date with destiny. Worried about the seven-pound St Edward's Crown he would have to wear for the ceremony, he spent hours practising, walking about or sitting at his desk with a weight on his head.

At Glamis, the Countess of Strathmore gathered her grandchildren round her and instructed them: 'Now that Uncle Bertie and Aunt 'Peter' are King and Queen you've got to show more respect ... You've got to call Uncle Bertie Sir and the Queen you must call Aunt Elizabeth.' The children, who always found 'Elizabeth' unpronounceable, would go on calling her 'Aunt Peter', the same name as her much-loved spaniel.

The Queen tried to be supportive but often was tearful. She would break down suddenly and cry: 'I can't go through with it. I can't be crowned.' Desolate moments were aggravated by rumours of her husband's apparent fragility: 'They say the King has epilepsy and might fall down during the service'; ill-founded gossip and well-aired doubts circulated about his ability to face the Coronation service. He would confound them all and managed to make a joke of the hurtful speculation. 'According to the papers, I am supposed to be unable to speak without stammering, to have fits and to die in two years. All in all I seem to be a crock.'

The gods, not kindly disposed to this reluctant King, had not allowed for his spirit. Having overcome severe hurdles in his life, now he faced one or two more, but of terrifying magnitude.

In addition to his speech impediment, the King was cursed with a quick temper and fits of rage, frightening especially to women at Court as he often seemed so explosive and out of control. This gave him what he least needed, a horror of public occasions which were a nightmare for him. Both handicaps would prove more difficult to conquer than the stutter.

The phobia, a form of agonising shyness, was exacerbated by the prospect of having to make his Coronation speech which for the first time ever would be broadcast by the BBC. It needed to be flawless. There were five months to prepare.

He rehearsed his responses and speech in his bedroom. It was not easy for a king to have to stumble and stutter in the presence of courtiers and officials. On hand, of course, was the Queen, by his side as he doggedly struggled with his c's and g's. During the many toe-curling pauses when he got stuck Lord Reith, Controller of the BBC, and Lionel Logue would tactfully look round the room perhaps focussing on some of the King's many jewelled cigarette cases. Smoking was his weakness and would ultimately be his killer.

The new King's forty-first birthday was on 14th December 1937. Immediately after his Accession, he had given the Queen the Order of the Garter. In a handwritten letter to Queen Mary, she gave a touching description of the ceremony, when the King had presented her with the highest and oldest order that he could bestow. There was her pleasure in receiving it. 'Bertie discovered that Papa gave it to you on Papa's birthday June 3rd, and found the coincidence so charming that he has followed suit and given it to me on his birthday.'

On the Sunday before the Coronation, the King and Queen spent a quiet time with the Archbishop of Canterbury, Dr Cosmo Lang, at Buckingham Palace and knelt down and prayed. The Archbishop noticed 'the tears when we rose up from our knees' but also a new sense of peace about the couple after they had been blessed. The King felt uplifted and seemed to gain an inner strength.

This was not the first time they had knelt and prayed together. They often read the Bible and had a strong spiritual commitment, especially the Queen; taking a moment to pray beside her husband had been one of her first reactions to the Abdication.

Now with a new courage and the tears mopped away, the first British Queen Consort since Tudor times was ready to prepare for her Coronation. Duff Cooper, then Secretary of State for War, was impressed by the transformation. He was invited to dinner at Windsor Castle which was always at half past eight. After soup, fish, fowl, meat, ice and a savoury eaten at boarding school speed, ladies left the dining room at half past nine. He was then summoned to the Queen's sitting room for tea, when everyone had retired at half past ten. She looked 'too ravishing in a gloss of satin – a lily and rose in one' with her feet up on a sofa. She talked calmly to him until midnight about the responsibility of monarchy.

Duff Cooper and his wife had been part of the 'smart set' surrounding Edward VIII. Now they attached themselves swiftly to the new King and Queen's inner circle. Lady Diana Cooper was confident enough to make a joke of this rapid shift of allegiance, telling the King, 'I'm afraid I'm a rat, Sir.'

Even though she dreaded the Coronation, Elizabeth found pleasure in being fitted for a new Queen Consort's crown. It was the first British crown in fashionable platinum, a great favourite of hers, with impressive arches and sixteen diamonds taken from the circlet which had once held the Koh-I-Noor Moghul diamond.

She may have been the last Queen Consort to wear the diamond as, in 1999, an elderly Punjabi man called Sikh Beant

Singh Sandhanwalia, living in Holland, claimed it back. He said it had been taken from his family 'by the British, by force or trickery'. It had belonged to ruler Maharaja Duleep until the British took possession of the Punjab in 1849. The jewel was presented then to Queen Victoria.

The crown had to be modelled fairly speedily as the expectation had been for a ceremony for a bachelor king. The celebrated 106-carat Koh-I-Noor itself was about the size of a modern fifty-pence piece. By tradition a woman's diamond, it was considered unlucky for men, who suffered all sorts of misfortune if they wore it. The new King felt his luck could hardly be worse.

Not even for the Coronation would the Queen abandon her usual high-heeled shoes. She wore a pair of embroidered white satin. Most women might have chosen a safer, lower shoe but the Queen liked the flattering extra few inches height even if she was carrying the 'Mountain of Light' diamond on her head.

Two days before the Coronation there was a subdued family lunch. Normally there would have been a feeling of elation with an unflappable King reassuring his relations. But this was a low-key occasion. Afterwards presents were exchanged. A tortoiseshell and diamond fan for Elizabeth which had belonged to 'Mama Alix', Queen Alexandra, and from the royal family, 'For Bertie and E', a gold tea set which had belonged to the Duke of Cumberland. The King particularly cherished his own gift from the Queen and the rest of the royal family, a dark blue enamel snuff box with miniatures of his parents on the lid.

In the week of the Coronation, the Palace kitchens prepared over eighteen thousand meals.

On Coronation Day, a wet and mournful Wednesday, the King woke at three o'clock in the morning as loudspeakers were being tested in the Mall. 'One might have been in our room,' he grumbled. He could eat nothing and 'had a sinking feeling inside … I knew that I was to spend the most trying day'.

Princess Elizabeth, twelve years old, was up almost as early at five o'clock. Curled up on a windowsill, she intently watched the Royal Marines in the Mall. Crawfie put an eiderdown round her charge's shoulders. Hanging on the door of her wardrobe, she could see her dress for the Coronation – a confection of white lace and silver with gold bows.

Like her sister Princess Margaret, who was seven, she would wear a light silver-gilt coronet made up by a theatrical costumier. Real ones in gold were too heavy for young heads easily distracted by a yearning for a sweet or hunt for a lace handkerchief.

Just before ten the King and Queen appeared in their Coronation robes. The normally imperturbable Palace staff held their breath, struck by the serenity of the thirty-seven year old Queen in her Coronation robes. Her Princess-style dress made by Court dressmaker Madame Handley Seymour had a square neck and slashed sleeves flounced with lace. Becoming bosomy, the dress made the most of the Queen's extra bit of weight and complimented her presentable waist. It was dotted with the symbols of a then flourishing Empire and the Welsh leek, the English rose, the Irish shamrock and Scottish thistle, all embroidered in gold and diamanté. Her eighteen-foot long train in royal purple velvet was lined with ermine and trimmed with three rows of gold galloon lace.

Pale and tense, the King was too distracted to notice how uncomfortable the journey was to Westminster Abbey. It was a spectacularly bumpy ride as the eighteenth-century gold State Coach clattered along on iron wheels. The Queen felt helpless, seeing the tell-tale muscle in the King's cheek now working overtime again, and vowed that the ornate coach with its gold cherubs and ample goddesses supporting a laurel crown should be overhauled smartly.

Lady Strathmore, already in the Abbey and impressive in biscuit rhinestones and studded lamé, watched her daughter without anxiety, even when her procession was halted by a chaplain fainting in a heap in the aisle. In a not very ecumenical spirit George VI later noted with amusement that the collapsed cleric was Presbyterian.

The hope was that the Queen felt some of the 'positive wave of widespread affection and admiration for her', as described by Lord Mersey when she took her place in the Abbey, watched by some 7700 guests: maharajahs, peers, European crowned heads and the Sultan of Zanzibar.

A 'spellbinding Queen' said Lady Diana Cooper, and Winston Churchill, suddenly feeling humbled, whispered to his wife, 'You were right. I see now that the "other one" would not have done.' Clementine Churchill had never been a supporter of Mrs Simpson. Now people were no longer feeling palmed off with second best, a replacement King and Queen.

Princess Elizabeth's impressions of the Coronation were vivid: 'When Mummy was crowned and all the peeresses put on their coronets it looked wonderful to see arms and coronets hovering in the air and the arms disappear as if by magic. Also the music was lovely and the band, the orchestra and the new organ all played beautifully.' A fair account by a young royal reporter with a ringside view.

As the Queen moved to her throne she gave a bow to the King who sat still and intense in his robes and golden tunic. They both seemed to be in a trance as the massed choirs sang Parry's 'I Was Glad'. Fortunately the King remained alert since as he stood up to walk to his throne with the Crown of England on his head, he was brought up short by one of the Bishops standing on his robe. 'I had to tell him to get off it pretty sharply as I nearly fell down.' He shared his father's view that there were altogether 'too many damned parsons'.

There were other gremlins about. The King complained that when the great moment came for him to declaim the Oath, the Archbishop 'held the book down for me to read, but horror of horrors, his thumbs covered the words ...'

In the Recognition prologue the Archbishop asked the congregation if they would accept this man as King as he turned north, east, west and south. To Handel's powerful coronation anthem 'Zadok the Priest' George VI was anointed from a gold ampulla on brow, breast and palms with a concoction of holy oil dating back to Charles I. Then he moved to his seat in the Edward I Coronation Chair which had special meaning for the Queen. It had been created to hold the Stone of Scone on which the ancient kings of Scotland were crowned. It also has a spiritual symbolism as it is believed that on this stone Joseph of Arimathaea had a vision and that he brought it to Britain from the Holy Land.

Now exchanging his King Edward crown for a lighter Imperial Crown of State made for Queen Victoria, the new

King looked across at the Queen, his wife, 'my helpmeet and my joy', and she smiled lightly back, the sceptre and rod of ivory in her small hands. From the moment the crown was placed on her head, the Queen said she never felt the same again. She had a new strength which she attributed to the mystical quality of the Coronation; it empowered them both. Now everyone rose to their feet as the Abbey resounded with 'God Save the King'.

Queen Victoria's granddaughter Princess Alice, Countess of Athlone, who had been to four Coronations, thought 'Bertie's was the most moving,' he looked so fine.

Queen Mary watched through her jewelled lorgnette and pronounced the King and Queen 'quite perfect'. That night the newly-crowned King Emperor spoke movingly to his people.

'It is with a very full heart I speak to you tonight,' he said, and few heard him without a sting of tears. 'The Queen and I will always keep in our hearts this day of inspiration.' His gallantry was affecting.

That evening he made a gift of a badge and star of diamonds, sapphires and emeralds for his Scottish Queen, investing her as the only Lady of the Thistle. The Queen could not speak because she had lost her voice with the strain of the day, but laughed when she heard him say of the jewelled Order which he had designed himself: 'We have only one Thistle. I wear it one night, the Queen the next.' His quiet humour saved her; she might otherwise have wept for the love she bore this decent man. He had triumphed and that was her joy.

Harold Nicolson was another who had perhaps been a little patronising about the new reign, but he too was astonished at the King and Queen's new confidence. 'He was so gay, and she so calm. He is now like his brother.' Elizabeth may not have seen this as much of a compliment.

He said of the new Queen of England, 'Nothing could exceed the charm and dignity which she displays, and I cannot help feeling what a mess poor Mrs Simpson would have made of such a situation ...'

There had been persistent telephone calls from the South of France from the former Edward VIII, who spent the Coronation Day knitting a sweater for Wallis. Now he was preparing for what had become the biggest event in his life, a wedding rather than a Coronation.

It was not until after the Coronation that Edward's future title, Duke of Windsor, was given legal formality and he would be known as 'Royal Highness'. What irked him was not the fairly frugal allowance George VI had settled on him, £60,000 a year and a capital sum of £1 million for his life tenancy of Balmoral and Sandringham. What he wanted most but still did not receive was a title for Wallis.

'What a damnable wedding present'. The Duke was furious when the King told him the news. This title would have meant far more to his American wife than his presents, which included a sapphire and diamond bracelet and a pug dog. Insulated by their infatuation, the Duke and Duchess had never doubted that they would continue to enjoy royal privileges.

On their wedding day, 3rd June 1937, at the Château de Cande, Tours, the Duke was careful to compliment his bride on her blue crepe wedding dress, clinging to her boyishly narrow hips: 'It's lovely, very pretty,' but the bride snapped 'Shut up'. Perhaps the reason for her bad temper was that she now knew she would never be named Her Royal Highness.

Across the Channel, the King and Queen were closer than ever. 'We are so particularly together, leaning so much on each other,' the Queen had written to the Archbishop of Canterbury. 'I can hardly believe that we have been called to this tremendous task and (I am writing to you quite intimately) the curious thing is that we are not afraid. I feel that God has enabled us to face the situation calmly.'

Sustained by each other, their happiness would lighten the gloom of the Palace. The monarchy was about to be reinvented. Exciting times lay ahead.

CHAPTER 12

A Born Homemaker

Far from disintegrating, as had been the fear only months earlier, the monarchy was growing as a symbol of unity. The King and Queen, with their two daughters a close and happy family, were beginning to inspire confidence in a nation no longer depressed by the Abdication.

George VI and his family moved into Buckingham Palace on 15th February 1937. Surprisingly sanguine about this upheaval, the King disliked the Palace less than Edward VIII. He still found it coldly formal, like 'an icebox with its six hundred and ninety rooms, vast ballroom, musicians' gallery and three miles of corridors' where, as a child, he had never been allowed to run or play.

Displaying the practical good sense of his great-grandfather, Prince Albert, he had been asked to streamline Sandringham when 'Little D', as he called his older brother, was King. Now he would do the same for Buckingham Palace and added a heated swimming pool.

The Queen, a born homemaker anyway, busily set about cheering up the unrelieved gloom of the Palace, which was just the sort of challenge she enjoyed. When first they had moved in, she was amused to find a different bottle of whisky put out each night by her bed. The custom dated back to Queen Victoria. The great Empress enjoyed a little cocaine but was also partial to a dram ever since she had tasted a hot toddy as a cure for a sore throat.

Now it was as if heavy Victorian drapes were being pulled back – letting 'daylight in on the monarchy'. Depressing corridors were being brightened with billowy mixed flowers from Windsor. Hydrangeas, roses, sweet peas, carnations and luxuriant greenery now filled the Palace urns, symbolic of freshness. And on the Queen's desk, in spring, a sprig of her favourite lily of the valley.

Money had been short when as Duchess of York she tried to furnish 145 Piccadilly and The Royal Lodge. One of the perks of being Queen was the amount which could now be spent on furniture and paintings. Although there were already 10,000 pieces of furniture in the Palace, much of it was redolent of repressive reigns. Her preference was for the gilded Italianate style. But she was receptive to guidance. Sir Arthur Penn, a devoted friend who later become her Treasurer, helped hunt out antiques including the distinguished eighteenth-century drawing room furniture bought at Preston Hall, Midlothian, and found craftsmen who restored other country house bargains.

Although not sporty or outdoorish, the Queen had many interests. She was a discerning collector of porcelain, Sèvres and especially Chelsea Red Anchor with its leaves and flowers, anything with a hint of chinoiserie, silver tea caddies and Fabergé. Her aesthete's eye for beautiful things was a bond shared with Queen Mary and together they would explore antique shops in Mayfair and Chelsea and search for bargains in the East End.

The Queen had the knack of getting what she wanted, once placing the bait nicely before the unsuspecting Queen Mary. Telling her about a piece of Fabergé, oats in a crystal pot with a cornflower, so 'beautifully unwarlike – charming in these grim days', she cannily suggested that if her mother-in-law was still searching for a birthday present for her, a donation towards this piece would 'be most acceptable'.

The Fabergé was hers. 'I send you most loving thanks for a lovely present.' This would launch her fabulous collection of Russian enamelled miniatures, picture frames and flower sprays, which included the enamel and rose diamond gold box with the last Tsar's crowned cypher and some of the charming Easter presents he commissioned for his wife and the tsarinas.

Another of the Queen's passions was for musical clocks, especially the nineteenth-century John Smith of Pitween now in the Outer Hall at Clarence House, where it plays 'My Nanie O' or 'God Save the King', causing the visitor to straighten his shoulders. In Buckingham Palace there were one thousand clocks.

The Queen had been knowledgeable about art since childhood. Those happy afternoons at the Uffizi and Pitti Palace in Florence with her knowledgeable grandmother had nurtured a sophisticated, catholic taste. She appreciated the royal Lelys and Angelicos at the Palace, but the Queen now bought paintings not just for the Royal Collection but because she loved them.

Confident enough to choose what she really liked, her taste indicated a romantic sensibility, a love of portraits, of still life: *Jugs and Apples* by Matthew Smith; seascapes like *Newhaven Pier* by Bloomsbury artist Duncan Grant and calm, pastoral watercolours. Lucky enough to own at least one French Impressionist, her great favourite was Monet's *Study of Rocks*; another was Walter Sickert's *Ennui* though the owner herself never seemed to experience a moment's boredom. Later she would be more adventurous.

When she first started collecting seriously, two of the people who influenced her were Sir Jasper Ridley and Sir Kenneth Clark. Sir Jasper was an old family friend and collector of modern art, but more credit perhaps for her mouth-watering art collection should go to Sir Kenneth Clark, Surveyor of the King's Pictures and Director of the National Gallery, who was enthralled by her. In the course of seeing young artists and going to galleries, these two mentors reported back to her about any new exciting work. The Queen would then visit the gallery, or the budding young artist would be only too pleased to bring his portfolio to the Palace.

Once she liked a painting and wanted it, no amount of persuasion could make her part with it. One of her favourites was of Field-Marshal Montgomery in his HO Mess Tent in Belgium in 1944, by Sir James Gunn. It had been sent to the Royal Academy and the Queen was assured that the Field-Marshal did not want the painting himself so bought it. Then he changed his mind, but none of his brilliant wartime strategy could get it back from its royal owner. Gunn had to paint another for Montgomery.

The Queen used her artistic acumen to commission the artist John Piper to do a series on Windsor Castle, fearing it might be bombed to extinction. She was excited by the work of this spare ascetic. A friend John Russell declared he had the features of 'an accessible Montezuma'.

The King, who found the paintings grey and depressing, teased the artist, suggesting that the weather must have been so unrelentingly dreadful at Windsor it influenced his palate. The Queen appreciated Piper, who would become a great friend, and they would explore old churches and ruined abbeys together until his death at eighty-eight. 'Gone upstairs,' the Queen Mother would say as she stood in front of these gloomily eloquent watercolours. The same instinct to preserve in the face of imminent destruction may have inspired her choice of Henry Moore's figures from the Blitz.

She was the first member of the royal family to buy modern paintings. She had a restrained passion for contemporary art, and her choice was not exactly Francis Bacon, more L S Lowry's *A Fylde Farm* and some Australian work. Sidney Nolan's *Green Swamp*, Russell Drysdale's *Home Leave* and Kenneth Jack's *Storm Approaching Marree* were not in keeping with her perceived cosy image. Later these parched Down-Under landscapes were relegated to a corridor in Clarence House. A friend explained, 'Her interest in modern art stopped with Sutherland.' She continued to attend exhibitions and enjoyed buying the odd landscape or 'charming watercolour' throughout her nineties.

Not only had the Palace been neglected by Edward VIII during his brief reign, but the 230 staff had become disheartened and apathetic; there had been no female presence around to encourage them. Now they emerged from a cavernous below-stairs existence like troglodytic creatures blinking in warm sunshine. The Palace tingled with a new energy.

If a banquet, party or reception had gone particularly well, they would be especially thanked by the Queen. So as the atmosphere changed, they began to smile and warm to the sight of her tripping down to the kitchens to make scrambled eggs or scones for the Princesses, who were finding it difficult to adjust to their new home.

'The little girls' lives are all upset,' the Princesses' governess complained, stating the obvious. They were missing the pleasant homeliness of 145 Piccadilly: the gaiety, the sound of their mother singing, the piano music and games of Snap or Sardines with their parents, now so so busy and preoccupied. The King pretended that he would build them a secret passage back to the 'dear old house' but still they pined. To try and cheer up ten year old Princess Elizabeth, her parents would tell her she looked like Shirley Temple, the cute Hollywood child. Not surprisingly, this did little to encourage her; she was the most affected by the sudden change in their lives.

In private, the King and Queen were still indulgent, almost boisterous parents and not afraid to show affection – an old-fashioned, loving upbringing not reflected in the next royal generation. The King talked openly about his fear of his own father and always said, 'I don't want my children to be frightened.'

Weekends were spent at Windsor Castle with their dogs and ponies, Scotland was for summer holidays, the King had a shooting lodge at Naseby in Northamptonshire, 'very ordinary and very homely' – an escape. There was a conscious return to family values.

CHAPTER 13

No More High-Hat Business

Hitler thought the Queen 'the most dangerous woman in Europe' and watched with dismay as she won over first the French and then the Americans.

It was the Spring of 1938 and the King and Queen were beginning to feel more assured, so it was now important to solicit more friends overseas in view of the threat of war with Germany. First, a major State Visit was arranged to France to secure the *Entente Cordiale*. Just as they were about to set off there was a blow for the Queen as her mother, the Countess of Strathmore, collapsed with a heart attack.

Now, in her last hours, all thoughts were with this indomitable matriarch to whom they both owed so much. She died aged seventy-six on 23rd June 1938 at her London home in Portman Square.

The Queen was heartbroken. 'I have been dreading this moment ever since I was a little child and now that it has come one can hardly believe it,' she said in a letter to Prime Minister Neville Chamberlain. Her mother, she said, was 'a true Rock of Defence for us ... a young spirit, of great courage and unending sympathy' and with 'a heavenly sense of humour', qualities her youngest daughter had inherited.

Immediately there was a sympathetic call from President Albert Lebrun of France who commiserated and looked forward to their visit, now postponed until 19th July 1938. He had happy memories of being entertained by the King and Queen, and of seeing a young Peggy Ashcroft and John Gielgud doing the balcony scene from Romeo and Juliet in the Durbar Court at the Foreign Office.

One of the problems now was arranging the Queen's wardrobe for France. Bright colours would no longer be appropriate but black would not do either.

Norman Hartnell was a young designer working in Mayfair whose clothes were seen mainly on actresses such as Gertrude Lawrence and other svelte shapes. The Queen had first been made aware of his style at the Duke of Gloucester's smart wedding to Lady Alice Montagu-Douglas-Scott on 6th November 1935.

When he was called to the Palace, Hartnell brilliantly suggested that white was also a colour of mourning, 'second mourning' as it was called in royal circles when pearls and white jewellery were worn. The Queen's collection for France would be remade, thirty voluminous frocks in pristine white in under a month. This quick-wittedness would make Hartnell indispensable as a royal dressmaker for many happy and lucrative years to come. The Queen was relieved she could fulfil family and royal duties and took fifty trunks with her to France.

The King, who had been stung by criticism of his wife's early homespun style, invited Hartnell to walk with him along the Palace corridors. When they came to the State Apartments they paused by the luscious Franz Xavier Winterhalter portraits and the King, without any hesitation in his voice, told the waiting needle-meister, 'This is what the Queen should wear.' He spoke with authority, no hint of a stammer, so convinced had he been that the romantic look of this nineteenth-century German artist would be right for his wife.

Hartnell immediately caught the imagery of those spangled crinolines in silk, taffeta, tulle, chiffon and lace; of Viennese waltzes on polished parquet, dancers behind gilded Corinthian columns toying with sugar-nymph ices, before joining their partners for another polka under crystal chandeliers.

Sensual yet demure, the Queen, with the aid of 'dear Mr Hartnell', would fulfil the King's dream. Both men helped create her uniquely fragrant image, a style she would favour for the rest of her life. And women were not wearing crinolines in the thirties; it had been the King's strong influence which was responsible for the Queen's perfect operetta-heroine style. Husbands may not understand the nuances of high fashion, but they can usually tell what looks best on the woman in their life.

Always dedicated to the spangled fairy-queen look, the Queen Mother would say years later when embroidered sequins had become prohibitively expensive, 'Oh but I do adore those little paillettes.' It was old-fashioned and not easy to wear but it suited her roundness.

All Paris fell at her feet. Instead of appearing in the pleasant but hardly spectacular jackets and nicely cut frocks planned originally, the Queen now wore sensational long white lacy crinolines and in the afternoon, too. Not since Tum-Tum, the Prince of Wales, paid a visit to Paris in 1852 and appeared on stage starring as a dead body opposite the great actress Sarah Bernhardt, had the British Royal Family been such an uproarious success.

'We saw the King and Queen ... coming down the Champs Élysées with roofs, windows and pavements roaring exultantly, the Queen a radiant Winterhalter.' Lady Diana Cooper was in a crowd which went wild and she was besieged by 'crying old ladies' begging her for a spot on the royal path to catch a glimpse of the Queen. 'You see her all the time,' one said, nudging the legendary beauty aside.

Chic Parisians lost their *sangfroid*, pushing and elbowing each other to see the Queen in the middle of a springy velvet-green lawn at Versailles opening up a matching white lace parasol; or watching a ballet on the aptly named Ile Enchantée, or at a garden party in a hat trimmed with osprey feathers; at a banquet at the Élysée Palace in a dress of Valenciennes lace. They stood for hours but their patience was rewarded at the Opera where the Queen appeared in a white crinoline, dotted with white camellias and magnificent diamonds.

The Queen brought £7 million worth of royal jewels to Paris. Some of them were now twinkling in the waxy luminous light of the tall white candles in twenty-branched candelabra which was held high by *les chandeliers*, an escort of valets who went ahead to light the marble stairs for the royal visitors. Lady Stanley, from a balcony view, thought 'The King slim and handsome in evening dress and decorations, and the Queen radiant in diamonds'.

'*Et La Duchesse est délicieuse*,' a distinguished old French soldier Marshall Lyautey had remarked when he met the Queen once when she was Duchess of York. It still applied.

The chocolate box creations had been a gamble, especially in a city like Paris with its reputation for *haute couture*. But they were a triumph.

Appreciative and, as usual, thoughtful, the Queen invited Hartnell to the royal suite at the Élysée Palace. He was impressed by the two mosaic bathrooms, one in silver, one in gold, both decorated with what Hartnell puckishly recalled as 'crystal fiddle-de-dees rampant'. He was welcomed warmly and urged, 'Please have a glass of champagne before you leave'. The King, also delighted with the success of his Winterhalter idea, added: 'It's very good champagne, I assure you.' The three celebrated.

Elated by the success of the royal visit, Republican France cried, 'We are a monarchy again,' and hoped the threat of war would recede. But it was Herr Goering's enormous uniforms which would hang before long in the cupboards of the King's dressing room in the Élysée Palace, when the Germans occupied Paris in 1940.

As militaristic rumblings from Germany grew louder, it became important to secure friends on the other side of the Atlantic, too. The situation in Europe was becoming increasingly volatile. The King was embarrassed by the Duke and Duchess of Windsor's visit to Hitler, which further inflamed the Führer's wildly acquisitive dreams of world power. When Hitler declared that Wallis would make a good Queen, the Duke had decided the Austrian dictator was 'not such a bad chap after all'.

Embarrassing the King and Queen still further, the Duke was photographed with Hitler and saluted him twice in public. He had always spoken German well and gave teutonic orders to his gardeners at The Mill, the Windsors' country house in France where he marched about in brogues with silver acorn tassels, his idea of stout gardening shoes.

So there was increasing pressure on the King to visit Canada and America. He hated leaving Britain at such a time of uncertainty but agreed, amidst fears that their countries would soon be engaged in a life or death struggle against Hitler.

President Roosevelt charmingly suggested, 'If you bring either or both children they will also be very welcome and I shall try to have one or two Roosevelts of approximately the same age to play with them.' There was no question of the Princesses going on this seven-week trip. Theirs was a sheltered existence and the Queen was anxious that they should enjoy a simple, unspoilt childhood and 'spend as long as possible in the open air'.

The Princesses saw their parents off at Portsmouth on 5th May 1939. 'Handkerchiefs are for waving,' Princess Elizabeth told her eight year old sibling, who was having a little sniffle as 'Mummie and Papa' embarked on the *Empress of Australia* to sail off to the New World.

A week later the ship was stranded for days in thick fog and perilously near icebergs. Writing to Queen Mary, the Queen described 'the melancholy blasts of the foghorn' which were echoed back by the icebergs 'like the twang of a piece of wire … incredibly eerie'. The captain, she said, was 'nearly demented' because 'some kind cheerful people kept reminding him that it was about here that the *Titanic* was struck, and just about the same date'. But she had not been frightened: it had been 'a most interesting experience' to push through a quarter of a mile of near solid floes. The King actually enjoyed the enforced leisure. He said, 'An ice field is not ideal for a holiday but it does seem the only place for me to rest in nowadays!'

There was uncertainty about how the royal couple might be received in Canada; after all there had been talk of Canada leaving the Commonwealth and remaining neutral should there be a war. Mackenzie King, the Canadian Prime Minister, was confident however that, once the King and Queen arrived, anti-royal sentiments would vanish 'like clouds before a Biscay gale'.

'Are there any letters from the children?' was the Queen's first question when they arrived at the Château Frontenac in Ottawa. Duty came first and, before letters could be opened, she had to show a carefree, smiling face to meet politicians and their wives. She changed into a gold lamé, white slipper satin and lace dress. The Queen Mother and the Queen often laugh about the need to be quick-change artists. The world fondly imagines them enjoying all the time in the world in their dressing rooms but if you have to change your clothes at least four times a day, only speed counts.

In Canada the couple travelled 4,281 miles. After the unveiling of the War Memorial in Ottawa the Queen asked the

Governor-General, Lord Tweedsmuir, better known as novelist John Buchan, if it was possible 'to get a little closer' to the veterans. Within minutes, she and the King, with their 'capacity for getting in touch with the people', waded in amongst the old soldiers.

'It was extraordinarily moving because some of the old fellows were weeping and crying, "Aye man, if Hitler could just see this."' Tweedsmuir thought the Queen had a 'perfect genius' for the 'impulsive gesture'. When she heard that some stone masons who had worked on the new Judicature in Ottawa were from Scotland her face lit up. Breaking away from the worthy officials, surveyors, architects and government ministers, she reminisced with them about 'home'. The Queen was making history with this first ever royal walkabout.

Tweesdmuir thought, 'Our monarchs are the most remarkable young people'; it was 'the small unscheduled things that count most, and for these they have a genius.'

The King's sincerity and the Queen's effervescence made a successful combination, whether travelling through Kicking Horse Pass, overnighting in a log cabin in the Rockies, sailing through wooded creeks to Victoria (that bastion of imperial values), or meeting Indian chiefs Chief Jacob Too-Young-Man, and Chief Turned-Up-Nose who, wearing their best elk teeth and bear claws, presented the King with a coloured photograph of Queen Victoria in buffalo robes.

George VI was the first reigning monarch to visit the United States, and many Americans expected a stultifyingly, lacklustre royal couple. They had a certain empathy with the unstuffy, carefree Duke of Windsor who had undeniable glamour and an American wife. A five-page list was sent ahead of the visit including such gems as, 'The King does not like suet puddings or capers' and whenever their Majesties returned after midnight, 'ham sandwiches should be available.' Informal Americans were instructed, 'The King should be served his food thirty seconds before the Queen.' This protocol hardly mattered at barbecues where the Royal couple, 'Betty and Bert', enjoyed hot dogs and hamburgers and cooled off with water melon and icecream.

There had been a tip-off that Irish extremists and a pro-Hitler group of Californian Nazis planned to assassinate the royal couple, so some 50,000 armed men and an escort of naval planes guarded them when they arrived in New York on board the destroyer USS *Warrington*.

The King and Queen were given such an enthusiastic ticker-tape welcome they were hours late reaching the President's up-state home Hyde Park, ninety miles away in Duchess County on the banks of the Hudson River. Hot and and sticky, the royal couple were exhausted when they arrived. As their motorcade drew up, a smiling President was waiting at the door. 'My mother thinks you should have a cup of tea,' he said to the King, 'she doesn't approve of cocktails.' Mrs Sara Roosevelt had ordered English tea though it was eight o'clock in the evening. The King replied, 'Neither does mine,' gratefully reaching for a frosted martini glass from the silver tray held by a black butler who would refer to Elizabeth as 'honeychile Mrs Queen'. At once the royal couple felt at ease staying in this pretty, unpretentious house amongst its rosewood tables and Landseer engravings.

The house today, with its somewhat shabby chintz, is a place of pilgrimage for Americans. In the slightly overgrown grounds, there are warning signs not to touch the branches of trees or the shrubs for fear of Lymes disease, an infection spread by deer. The royal sitting room, still displaying black and white photographs of the King and Queen, is untouched and the royal visit is spoken of warmly. Their bedrooms were on the first floor with balconies and views across the Hudson. The President's formidable mother always insisted that she should sleep in the room next to her son, while his wife Eleanor was relegated to the end of the corridor.

From the moment they met, the King and President Roosevelt liked each other, the latter a fatherly figure in the wheelchair thirteen years older than the diffident English King. It was to be the start of a long friendship. The President, wise and charismatic, respected the King's common sense views and knowledge of world politics; he was always one of the best informed people in the country. They enjoyed several serious late night private talks in which Britain had the assurance of support from America, the reason for the King's visit in the first place. This was a welcome turning point for the King.

The visit was more of a success than the White House had anticipated and the only real security threat had been when the royal couple were driven around by the President in his Special Ford car, which only had manual brakes. 'Such fun,' the Queen said. The King shed his tie.

In Washington security was intense and temperatures a humid ninety-seven degrees, yet the Queen stayed cool when all around her were fainting. 'Never a hair out of place,' marvelled the President's wife. Crinolines and parasols were ideal for the traditionally enervating summer in the capital. After the royal visit an umbrella company was asked to make five thousand just like the Queen's in white silk to meet demand.

When asked by Mrs Roosevelt about her apparent ability to smile at hundreds of people at once, the Queen replied, 'The secret is to pick out an individual in a knot and smile pointedly, and to concentrate on faces in several rows.'

The Americans loved her. A senator from the Deep South slapped the King on the back, 'My, you're a great Queen picker,' and they both grinned like two good ol' boys.

For the King this visit to America was liberating. He came back feeling renewed and confident. Touched by the democracy of the States, his attitude became a trifle impatient with elderly courtiers who baulked at change. 'Sir, this is how things were done in Queen Victoria's time.' Although the King had a wholesome respect for continuity, he told an adviser on the tour, 'There must be no more high-hat business.' The tour to North America 'has made us,' the Queen said happily.

They arrived home on the 22nd June 1939 on board the *Empress of Britain*. The Princesses sailed out to meet them in the destroyer HMS *Kempenfelt* in a state of great excitement. The crew had clubbed together and given them nightdress cases shaped like pandas and at a hilariously happy reunion lunch, the King threw balloons out of portholes.

As the King and Queen drove into Buckingham Palace the roar of the jubilant crowd could be heard in the Strand. Even in the House of Commons, Bills were abandoned and MPs rushed into Parliament Square. 'We lost all dignity and yelled and yelled' to cheer home the King and Queen. Harold Nicolson reported, 'We returned to the House with lumps in our throats.'

Some 50,000 people gathered round the gates of Buckingham Palace. The normally cautious British public now cheered them and sang 'The Lambeth Walk' and 'Under the Spreading Chestnut Tree' until well past midnight.

The King, smiling like a boy in his Admiral's uniform, appeared on the balcony with the Queen alongside him and as they waved they had a look which asked, 'Can these cheers really be for us?' Nicolson thought the Queen was superb, 'managing to convey to each individual in the crowd a personal greeting'.

There was a surge of goodwill and national pride. The *Daily Mirror* fulsomely welcomed back the King and Queen 'To Our Love And Gratitude ... You Enter Once Again Your Home In The Empire's Heart.' The newly appreciative tone was quite different from that of the months before. Now there was a slightly mortified feeling in the country that once again the King and Queen had only received the recognition they deserved by going abroad.

Not long after the successful visit to North America in July 1939, the Royal photographer Cecil Beaton took official portraits of the Queen. These were classic, enduring photographs of her in the garden of Buckingham Palace holding a parasol to match the long lace crinoline which had been such a triumph at the Bagatelle garden party in France. Beaton thought her 'dazzlingly pink and white' as she posed on the steps of the Palace, by the Waterloo Urn and on the lawn in beaded embroidered creations, pale grey crepe day dresses, cobweb lace extravaganzas.

Formal photographs were taken and duty done, now it was time for the nation's model family to go to Balmoral where they would walk, fish and sing too. The King loved grouse shooting; the Queen would learn to land a salmon.

However on 1st September Hitler invaded Poland and ignored an ultimatum to withdraw his troops. War with Germany was declared at eleven o'clock in the morning of the golden Sunday on 3rd September 1939. An entry in the King's diary that day noted, 'Hitler would not and could not draw back from the edge of Abyss to which he has led us.'

That evening the King broadcast about 'dark days ahead' and at Christmas, prompted by the Queen, George VI ended his message to the Empire with a poem by Marie Louise Haskins. In his deep slow voice he spoke the words which are now so familiar: 'I said to the man who stood at the Gate of the Year'. Listening to the wireless in the sitting room next door, the Queen thought that the little hesitancy in his voice had added a special quality to what was to become known as the King's Prayer.

CHAPTER 14

Almost Too Much to Bear

At the beginning of the war, the Queen wrote two secret sealed letters to the Princesses, to be opened only if she was killed. She sent a copy of Hitler's book *Mein Kampf* to the Foreign Secretary, Lord Halifax, but advised him not to read it right through – 'or you might go mad and that would be a great pity. Even a skip through gives one an idea of his mentality.'

It had been assumed that the Queen and the Princesses would go abroad for the duration of the war. Canada was longing to offer them a haven, but the very idea was inconceivable to the Queen. She replied immediately that, much as the invitation was appreciated, 'The children could not go without me, I could not possibly leave the King and the King would never go,' and confided, 'I should die if I had to leave.'

The King and Queen were closer than ever, their glances and quick smiles their mutual telegram. The Queen's life revolved around her husband's. Whenever a lady-in-waiting tried to draw up the Queen's schedule, she would gently be reminded: 'The King must first be consulted.'

'We stay with our people,' the Queen explained, but she also meant, 'I stay with my husband,' and confessed, 'If things turn out badly, I must be with the King.' She would support him in many ways, and sustain him before those dreaded straight-to-the-heart addresses to the nation: 'Let no one think that my confidence is dimmed when I tell you how perilous the ordeal is which we are facing. On the contrary, it shines in my heart as brightly as it shines in yours.' Brave words on Empire Day 1940. Only those closest to him knew how difficult these morale-boosting broadcasts were for the King with his congenital stutter. His equerry, Group Captain Peter Townsend, noticed how George VI always tried to say 'monarch' or 'sovereign' instead of 'king' because of difficulty with the letter K.

The British people began to feel fortunate. In Europe other royal families were crumbling and fleeing as the Germans advanced, while the British King and Queen were becoming a symbol of strength.

A clutch of harassed European royals, including a suddenly homeless King Haakon of Norway, descended on Buckingham Palace. A distraught Queen Wilhelmina of the Netherlands, once considered the prettiest princess in Europe, had telephoned the King at five in the morning on 13th May 1940. 'It is not often,' he joked, 'that one is rung up at that hour and especially by a Queen'. As Holland was helpless against the German invaders, Queen Wilhemina reluctantly jumped aboard a British destroyer sailing from Rotterdam. Her son-in-law, Prince Bernhard, would later recall the family's escape with his daughters Beatrix and Irene, who was so small that 'We carried her in a little box with air holes.' Beatrix was to succeed her mother, Juliana, as Queen of the Netherlands in 1980.

The indignity of invasion, and the sight of Queen Wilhemina arriving without so much as a small suitcase or toothbrush, so shocked the Queen that she assiduously practiced with a .303 rifle and .38 revolver. This conjured up an unlikely if faintly comic picture of her, in high heels and powder blue duster coat intimidating a Nazi, but the Queen could handle a gun confidently.

Winston Churchill's regard for Edward VIII had been well known but the new Prime Minister, a devout upholder of constitutional monarchy, now supported the King wholeheartedly. A bond developed quickly between the two men. Soon the King was treating his Prime Minister as a friend – 'My dear Winston'. There had been no example, Churchill proudly suggested, of such 'intimacy' since the days of Queen Anne and Marlborough.

The Prime Minister now saw with his own eyes how George VI, with none of his golden brother's assurance, was meeting the challenge. He had feared that the new King, whose psychological and physical problems were so evident, would not be up to the task. But now, in the limelight which he hated, an impressive goodness and integrity shone through. Yet the King still had that reticence, disguising vulnerability, which the nation loved; it made Churchill admire him even more.

Antipathetic at first, for the Queen knew Churchill had doubted her husband's ability ever to be majestic, she secretly lamented Chamberlain's resignation. In time however she, too, warmed to the Prime Minister and they were to enjoy an enduring friendship.

To cheer the King at Christmas 1940, Churchill give him a 'siren suit' to wear in air-raid shelters. These floppy dungarees had become the Prime Minister's wartime hallmark. The King, though, who was fussy about dress, even disapproving of Field Marshal Montgomery's Tank Corps beret, never appeared publicly in the coverall.

Churchill joined the King and Queen for lunch every Tuesday, usually for beer and sandwiches. The King would say, 'I don't know what's in these, sawdust I expect,' but once proudly produced a château bottled claret. The secret behind this luxury was Captain 'Mouse' Fielden, who daringly ferried agents across the Channel and once, while in France, managed to smuggle back some decent Bordeaux, reporting happily to the King, 'Mission accomplished, Your Majesty.'

For four and a half years, the King, Queen and Prime Minister enjoyed these spartan but informal get-togethers. When the sirens went, they carried their glasses and plates down to the air-raid shelter in the Palace basement, formerly a maid's sitting room. The Queen used her ability to make things 'cosy' so even this functional Palace shelter was furnished with familiar comforts, gilt chairs, a large mahogany table and a Regency sofa.

Percy Benham, Yeoman of China and Glass, had put away most of the precious porcelain which had been in use since Queen Victoria's time. The royal jewels were wrapped in newspapers and stuffed into hatboxes in the Windsor Castle vault. In London when there was an air-raid warning the Queen carried her personal jewellery to the makeshift Palace shelter, the King carried a corgi. On one of their visits, while the air-raid warning sounded, the Queen saw a black cat crossing their path and refused to go down until she had given this good luck symbol a regal pat.

Balmoral and Sandringham were shut down. The golf courses and lawns were ploughed up for vegetable plots. The

King's nurtured flowerbeds and lawns, now tightly packed with sturdy cabbages and potatoes, helped to feed a staff of 200. A hamper of sixty rabbits was delivered to Windsor Castle each Saturday and the adaptable coney was on the menu at least twice a week. Staff Chef Peter Malan prided himself on his ability to skin a rabbit in a minute.

From the beginning of the war, the Queen refused to wear drab, statutory, utilitarian colours. Sidestepping wartime edicts with austere insistence on functionality, she wore pinks, blues and lilacs and felt these gentle pastels might do more for morale than a uniform she hated: those mannish jackets and skirts and worse, trousers, 'so unfeminine'.

Her theory worked, her appearance was cheered and often in unlikely places. Admiring cries of 'Ain't she luverly' and then a louder cry, 'Ain't she bloody luverly', echoed from a pile of debris as men and women, faces blackened by hours of delving in bomb damage, stopped shovelling to watch the Queen pick her way towards them. Even on bomb sites she wore pretty shoes and that tick-tock of royal heels made red-eyed rescue workers smile.

Warm, approachable, but practical too, the Queen struck 'just the right note' as she waded in with arms outstretched towards a badly injured mother trying to dress her frightened baby: 'Here, let me help.' Where there was despair, she could bring a feeling of hope; to a family who had lost everything, to a crying child, or to a wounded soldier; people felt she was their friend. For an older generation, some of whom have survived two World Wars, there will always be a feeling of indebtedness to the Queen Mother. As Mr Bill Bartley, a bomb blast survivor, said: 'The Queen went round putting her arm round people covered in blood and grime and consoled them.'

'The people are so wonderful, they deserve a better world'. The Queen felt that the suffering being endured was 'almost too much to bear'. Comforting an elderly woman whose daughter and grandson had been killed in south-east London, the Queen said softly, 'We are proud of you,' but the grieving woman quickly replied, 'And we are proud of you and the King.'

The war sealed her position as the most loved Queen Consort, and her husband's as a valued and respected King who never faltered. Queen Alexandra was popular and charming but had never touched people's hearts in the same way. The Queen thought it patronising to suggest that because of her influence during the war, the King had become a man of stature with a positive zest for courageous leadership. On one occasion a voice in the crowd shouted out 'Thank God for a good King.' Deeply moved, George VI replied: 'Thank God for a good people.' The regard was mutual.

And to think that at the beginning of the war there had been some discordant anti-royal voices, people who believed that the King and Queen, cushily protected in their Palace fortress, knew nothing about pain and hardship. No-one now doubted their courage. When the Blitz was at its most devastating, the King and Queen insisted on visiting the bombed cities, often arriving before the removal of unexploded bombs made it safe to inspect. The drivers of their train were told the destination only at the last moment and at night it was stopped near a tunnel for some form of protection against air-raids.

As part of her war effort, the Queen held sewing parties at the Palace twice a week. Helpers sat at trestle tables in the Blue Drawing room. The Queen sat in a straight-backed chair, repairing and altering things for the 'Tommys and Jacks'. However, 'She always seemed to have the same piece of knitting,' Mrs Winnie Weddle, whose husband Alec was a groom at the Palace, recalled. Social climbers soon found that only their expertise with the needle counted and not the ability to do a correct curtsey. Bomb damage victims suddenly found themselves owners of couture outfits and elegant pieces of furniture removed from the Palace vaults.

The Palace was too dangerous for the Princesses so they were moved to Windsor Castle. Two cumbersome armoured cars were converted for their use, with the machine guns removed. Linoleum was put on the floors, seats installed, and the gun turret reversed to keep out draughts.

They spent the next five years at Windsor. Typically, the Queen's gas mask had a black velvet cover. Valuable royal portraits were moved to the vaults for safekeeping. 'Do you like my ancestors?' the King asked guests as they faced pictures of Mother Goose and Humpty Dumpty, pinned up by the children to cover marks on the walls.

The King and Queen remained at the Palace during the week but on Fridays returned to Windsor, and this was the signal for the royal governesses to close the books for the weekend. An observant member of the royal Household said it was 'lovely to watch the great hullaballoo with the children. The King would lift them up in his arms – well the Princesses just threw themselves at him.'

On Mondays during the war, the King and Queen would say goodbye to the Princesses upstairs in the schoolroom in the Castle, where Henry Marten, the Vice-Provost of Eton, taught them constitutional history, vital for Princess Elizabeth who was still nonetheless praying for a brother. After a lifetime teaching boys, he could not help himself and addressed the Princesses as 'Gentlemen', amusing them when he produced a globe from inside his umbrella.

Lessons began after lunch at two o'clock. The King liked to pop into the classroom before leaving for London. He would look at their books. Once, when the Princesses were struggling with the German word 'hinterteil', he said, very seriously and slapping his behind, 'What is this?' Princess Elizabeth said – suddenly understanding – 'Oh Papa!' The King was fun, he could read German with a very good accent and did not stammer at all. But he always said 'I never really mastered this beastly language.' The Court stopped speaking German during the war.

Princess Margaret was the livelier, more demanding child. Her head had to be massaged daily by 'Alla' Knight because her hair had become so thin, possibly due to the stress of being parted from her parents. She would ask a governess, 'Why don't you teach us in the Little House?' And when told, 'It is too cramped', 'No, no,' the Princess would mockingly suggest: 'You teach outside and I'll go inside!' When she did not know the answers to questions she would artlessly reply: 'Oh I knew them this morning,' whereas Princess Elizabeth would apologise, or have a genuine excuse, 'I was having a fitting for a riding habit.'

'I had such a lovely time, 3 hrs riding with Papa,' said a happy note in her diary. Time with Papa was precious. The Princesses were Daddy's girls and pined because they saw less of him when he became King; now war took their father away from them all week.

At weekends, the Princesses provided amusement for their parents and would put on pantomimes helped by the royal Household. The King, perhaps an over-protective father, was once shocked by his eldest daughter's costume when she appeared in *Aladdin* showing off her legs: 'The tunic is too short, Lilibet can't possibly wear that.' Prince Elizabeth was seventeen at the time and Prince Philip was in the audience.

Concerned that the Princesses were not having a well-rounded education because of the war, the Queen was delighted when her friend Osbert Sitwell invited them to a public poetry reading in London's Aeolian Hall in April 1940. For all the wrong reasons, it turned into an hilarious evening. When Edith Sitwell, the 'prima donna assoluta' of modern poetry, started reciting her own 'Anne Boleyn's Song' in her own inimitable way, with those distinctive cadences, the Princesses found it hard to look serious, unable to keep straight faces.

Worse was to follow, as the Queen Mother told author A N Wilson years later. 'A rather lugubrious man in a suit read a poem; we didn't understand a word and first the girls got the giggles, then I did ...' With a mischievous vagueness, she insisted on referring to the poem as 'The Desert' when in fact it was 'The Waste Land', read by the greatest poet of his generation. The Queen Mother loved poetry but obviously T S Eliot was not a favourite; 'such a gloomy man,' she thought, 'looked as if he worked in a bank.' There was no tittering when the Queen and her daughters attended concerts given by pianist Myra Hess in the empty National Gallery.

The Queen hated the sound of her own voice in public, so she forced herself to become an expert with the microphone, (often speaking) on the wireless, with a tender note: 'The King and I know what it means to be parted from our children, our loved ones ...' She had intuitive messages for women, praising their 'fortitude' at being parted from 'the men at the front'.

She insisted on writing her own speeches, 'I fear not very polished', and refused to repeat, parrot fashion, something written by a courtier. The Princesses did their broadcasts too, in their distinctive, cutglass, piping, 'Hello children everywhere' voices.

The King and Queen were in constant danger, their personal security fragile. It was well known that the Germans had a plan to capture the royal family and hold them as hostages.

The War Office's worst fear was of a possible airborne assault on Windsor Castle. Fresh-faced young ensigns from the Guards Brigade were ordered to be alert for the sound of church bells, the warning of an airborne invasion understood in every corner of the land. They kept their eyes trained on the skies above Windsor, briefed by wartime intelligence that at any moment they could be filled with black figures, German parachutists disguised as nuns, who would whip out light machine guns from under voluminous black serge habits and pepper the Castle with bullets.

A shell-shocked deserter did get past the vigilant Brigade and slip into the Castle to hide in the Queen's bedroom. 'For a moment my heart stood absolutely still,' the Queen said later, describing how the intruder held her ankles in a vicelike grip as he prostrated himself at her feet. There was sympathy for him, 'Poor man … he had lost all his family in a raid,' but then a rebuke. Before he was removed by the Castle Guard he was given a ten-minute lecture. One of her few areas of intolerance was for those who contributed nothing to the war effort. So deserters were parasites: 'I advise you to serve your punishment like a man … and then serve your country like one' – strong words from demure lips.

A (longstanding) friend once said that, much as he doted on her, he would not like to be 'given a rocket' by the Queen Mother. Behind the floaty sugar-coated charm she could be withering if she thought someone had been disloyal, careless or unkind.

In September 1940 – Friday the thirteenth, and a grey rainy day – there was a direct hit on Buckingham Palace. The King and Queen narrowly escaped death. A German bomber zoomed out of the clouds near Admiralty Arch and down the Mall. The Luftwaffe pilot, intent on destruction of the Palace, hit it with six bombs.

The King and Queen heard the terrifying noise of a diving aircraft getting louder and louder, nearer and nearer. The King threw his wife to the ground and they watched the flashes as explosion after explosion shook the Palace, wrecking the Chapel. He wondered afterwards 'why we weren't dead'.

'A magnificent piece of bombing, Ma'am, if you'll pardon my saying so,' a police constable remarked. The Queen managed a smile as she and the King emerged from the bomb-damaged Palace. Typically, she was wearing impossible shoes which immediately became covered with black dust and grime, her legs too, as she stepped over the rubble, fallen timber and glass. Wearing pearls and gloves and another becoming off-the-face hat, head on one side, she listened as always to eye-witness accounts, only this time it was her own home which had been bombed.

Her immediate reaction was: 'I am glad we have been bombed. It makes me feel I can look the East End in the face,' while the King was annoyed, grumbling that it had probably been one of his relatives in the German air force. The King and Queen made little of this incident; they were outwardly brave, yet for a time it made them both nervy. The Queen became more prone to tears, the King found it hard to settle at his desk.

The depth of the Queen's feeling was expressed in a letter she wrote to Queen Mary. 'My Darling Mama ... it does affect me seeing this terrible and senseless destruction. I think I mind it much more than being bombed myself.' One of the results of the bomb was a swarm of rats at the Palace. 'Everyone had great fun pursuing them,' the Queen claimed, but she was terrified if she saw a mouse. There are all kinds of courage.

There was no time for self-pity. Moorfields Eye Hospital and St Mary's Paddington were taken under her wing. She would pray nightly that they be spared the bombing.

On a visit to the Docklands in 1958, where she gamely pretended to be enjoying a half pint of bitter in the Blacksmiths Arms, the Queen Mother told the landlord: 'We came here so often in the war, I am glad it has cheered up so much.'

Mrs Eleanor Roosevelt, who arrived in October 1942 to see how Britain was faring, was shocked by the frugality at the Palace. Rationing was taken so seriously that there was only turnip jam, frequent meatless days and fishcakes disguised as 'croquettes', but served on gold and silver plates. Another 'hardship' for the royal family was doing without fresh napkins.

When the Chancellor of the Exchequer, Sir Stafford Cripps, stayed with the royal family in Balmoral he was given an omelette which he much enjoyed. The Queen Mother revealed years later how this sacrifice was resented. 'My daughters were scowling at him with hatred; the Chancellor was devouring all our eggs for a week.'

The Queen went to the north of England where an ample lunch was laid on as a mark of appreciation. With that famous smile and a tilt of the head, the Queen turned to the Mayor: 'You know, at Buckingham Palace, we're very careful to observe the rationing regulations.' Her Lancastrian host replied: 'Oh, well then, Your Majesty, you'll be glad of a proper do.'

Standards were being maintained at the Palace, however, where the King and Queen still dressed for dinner even if it was only Woolton pie (a concoction of pastry crust and root vegetables).

Hartnell had designed a satin evening dress with hand-painted garlands of lilac which the Queen would wear again and again – not a habit she cultivated in peacetime, when she was rarely seen in the same outfit twice. Even if her evening clothes were restricted, unlike many British women she never had a dress made from a curtain. The King did, though, have her bath marked with a five-inch red water line to halt any extravagance in a time of wartime regulation.

After dinner, there were no brandy and cigars but rather Jingoistic films. The King particularly liked Noel Coward's *In Which We Serve*, about cousin 'Dickie' Mountbatten's loyal crew aboard the destroyer HMS *Kelly*, which was sunk off Crete. Coward was an implausible naval hero but a favourite of the Queen's since before the Abdication, when he fervently supported King George VI.

Both the King and Queen lost family members in the war. The Duke of Kent was killed on 25th August 1942 when his Sunderland flying boat crashed over Scotland. The King made a pilgrimage to the desolate spot where his youngest brother died. He thanked the farmers who led the search parties and the doctor who found the body, saying, 'We shall miss him all our lives.' After a service at St George's Chapel, Windsor, the King grievingly noted: 'I have attended very many family funerals in the Chapel but none has moved me in the same way.'

The Queen's nephew, Patrick, Master of Glamis, was killed in action in 1941 and another, Andrew Elphinstone, was taken prisoner of war.

The King became increasingly strained and was hardly eating. Someone remarked to the Queen how good an influence the Duchess of Windsor had been on the Duke, how the bags under his eyes had gone. 'Yes,' the Queen replied, 'but who has the lines under his eyes now?'

Some of the Duke's were caused by his inflammatory behaviour, his 'gilded lifestyle', his heavy drinking, and indiscreetly fraternising with wealthy supporters of the Nazis. Due to his position, he had access to privileged information and a real fear was that he was betraying Allied secrets. He was seen as a natural Fascist, because of his blatant love of all things German as well as his admiration for their efficiency. His continued flirtation with Hitler prompted a stern letter from Churchill warning the Duke that he could be liable for prosecution for treason to his own country.

It is said the Duke cherished a return to the English throne as promised by Hitler after a putative German victory. He was playing a dangerous political game, but was at the same time dealing in lucrative currency transactions which were strictly illegal under wartime exchange control regulations. The Queen Mother now despised him utterly, but was concerned that he had it in his power to undermine a still fragile monarchy.

His behaviour greatly distressed the King, who now admitted to feelings of utter exhaustion. 'I have,' he said, 'been suffering to an awful reaction from the strain of war.' Yet in spite of this, he made a 6,700 mile journey to boost the morale of British troops in North Africa in June 1943. He was never physically strong, and the tan could not disguise his weariness.

George VI arrived in North Africa without fuss. He was a slight, hesitant figure in khaki, and appeared on the verandah of a villa where, at first, the soldiers on the beach did not recognise him. Then a lone voice started to sing God Save the King until it reached a crescendo and 'swelled deep-throatedly from a mass of soldiers'. Then, as the last notes of the anthem died away, the King suddenly stepped down and 'as if called by one voice, thousands of men raced towards him like a human wave.' With his horror of parades, on one occasion needing to be strongly prompted to go out and inspect a line-up of troops, this was a quietly heroic moment. He stood chatting easily with the soldiers, who had no idea of the incalculable personal effort their King had just made for them.

When Princess Elizabeth was eighteen she joined the Auxiliary Territorial Service, wanting to do 'as other girls of my age do'. The other girls called her 'Ma'am'. The Princess, who was said to enjoy 'being ordinary', still always referred to 'the King, my father'. The Queen tried to be encouraging, but found the chatter at Windsor Castle about 'D and M' baffling as the King questioned Second Subaltern No. 230873, Elizabeth Windsor, about the day's driving and maintenance course.

At the ATS Training Centre in Surrey, the King and Queen saw their daughter working on the carburettor of a utility van. The smiling King leant over and asked, 'Do we know what we are doing?' Cheerfully trying to look interested the Queen nonetheless thought dungarees 'not becoming even on Lilibet,' who was by now a shapely young woman 'with blue grey eyes and crisp curly hair'. Three weeks after her course ended in 1945, the war in Europe was over.

The King thanked the War Cabinet: 'You have brought this country – may I say you have brought the whole world – out of deadly peril into complete victory. You have won the gratitude of millions and, may I add, of your Sovereign'.

A high price had been paid. Dowager Viscountess Hambledon, a lady-in-waiting to the Queen, said, 'We all felt whacked.' The royal family went to Windsor and the King told the Duke of Gloucester, 'I feel burned out.'

Churchill, eloquent as always, said in a letter to the King on 5th January 1941, 'This war has drawn the Throne and the people more closely together than ever before was recorded, and your Majesties are more beloved by all classes than any of the princes of the past'.

On VE night, 8th May 1945, exuberant crowds filled the Mall and surged towards Buckingham Palace with an insistent chant: 'We want the King, we want the Queen.' Bemused, the Royal couple came out on the balcony seven times altogether; the King, spare, dedicated and, beside him, his caring Queen.

Until it got dark the people, their faces pressed against the Palace gates, cheerfully went on shouting their thanks. 'We have only tried to do our duty during these five years,' the King said, speaking for them both with typical modesty. But they had been inspirational. Together, in peacetime, they would try to put heart back into a worn out people.

They were joined on the balcony by their daughters, Princess Elizabeth, nineteen and gravely self-possessed in uniform, and Princess Margaret, nearly fifteen and on the threshold of a destructive love affair. Wanting to share in the elation on the Mall, the Princesses ran from the balcony. The Queen looked worried, but the King gently reminded her: 'Poor darlings,' he said, 'they've never had any fun yet.' His daughters were hardly worldly, so he insisted they should have an escort of young naval officers and sent one of his equerries, Group Captain Peter Townsend, along too.

In that highly charged, euphoric atmosphere the Palace party waved back up at the King and Queen. It was an incredible moment even for the Princesses to see their parents so rapturously appreciated as they joined crowds and the dancing. 'It was,' Princess Margaret recalled, 'very gay. Everybody was knocking everybody else's hats off, so we knocked off a few too.' In the heady excitement of that evening, it would be surprising if Princess Margaret, an impressionable teenager, had *not* begun to fall in love for the first time.

Fifty years later on 8th May 1995, the Queen Mother stood on the balcony at Buckingham Palace for the VE Day jubilee celebrations to make one of her rare speeches, and without notes. Dressed in pale lilac, pearls and diamonds, her voice was strong. Only friends and family knew the effort she was making to overcome failing sight and frailty.

Not a baby cried, nor a sound was heard as her voice carried to a crowd of some 150,000 people, a mixture of veterans, disabled people, young families, those who remembered the war years and those who did not but just wanted to be there.

It was a day when she broke two of her own rules: never to speak in public and never to show emotion in front of other people. 'This day will bring back many memories to many people ... God bless them all,' she said in a personal message to the brave men and women.

Then, when Vera Lynn, the 'Forces' Sweetheart', began to sing 'White Cliffs of Dover' it was a bit much and a rogue tear rolled like a marble down a well-powdered cheek.

Just before her ninetieth birthday, the Queen Mother had gone back to the East End. Standing on a spot where a bomb had killed many people, a survivor paid her the highest compliment. 'We always felt,' he said, 'that she was one of us during the war; as Queen she wasn't afraid to come out among the people.' And he added simply, 'She's a great old girl.'

CHAPTER 15

A Ten Shilling Note

The King and Queen were coming to terms with a Labour government and inviting Cabinet ministers for 'dine and sleep' weekends at Windsor Castle. The King, who considered that the new Government might do away with the monarchy, was pragmatic. 'Before long,' he declared, 'I shall also have to go;' and he was shrewdly cutting back on lavish expenditure. But there was a chance now for life at last and he showed a certain gaiety, though worn out by war and a diet of powdered egg.

Hugh Gaitskell, when Labour Chancellor, once complained that the royal couple were 'both extremely conservative in their views', but the Queen had made him uncomfortable in the post-war years by implying 'Everybody was in a very bad way ... poor, dispirited and not happy.' She wondered what the new Government planned to do about their plight. She herself might have had the answers. Although very much head of the family, if there was a problem the King would say often, 'You must ask Mummie.' 'Your mother,' he told Princess Elizabeth, 'is the most marvellous person in the world.'

It was not uncommon after dinner to see in the drawing room at Windsor Sir Anthony Blunt, later the disgraced custodian of the Queen's pictures, in the act of miming a hippopotamus, or Sir John Pope-Hennessy trumpeting like an elephant. 'Sardines' could be another minefield, not much to the taste of academics or aesthetes, and Vita Sackville-West's son, Ben Nicolson, was appalled when he ended up under a piano and discovered that the soft cushion he was prodding was the Queen's bosom. All great fun, but mortifying for those who had not spent their childhood delving into the dressing-up chest of a Scottish castle.

Unsympathetic politicians, distinguished worthies, friends and courtiers were all expected to join in Charades, Murder, Sardines and other parlour games. The royal family loved them. For newly elected Labour ministers however, lacking that public school willingness to make fools of themselves, the games could be agony. Churchill, although a royal favourite, was in the Queen's bad books because he refused to play.

'Oh Bertie, let's do the Parada.' This was a heart-stopping signal for dignified Cabinet ministers and members of the Household to gamely line up and goose-step past the King, who would take up a position by the fireplace and stand stiffly to attention. Surprisingly good at this send-up of high-kicking Nazis was Sir Stafford Cripps, whose tenure at the Exchequer was for years a byword for austerity. Normally rather stern, he for some reason relished marching with a pair of fire-tongs on his shoulder in parade before his King. Comically childish, this game succeeded in breaking down social barriers.

Card games were easier. Guests could not suddenly be dragooned into playing bridge but would not be excused a round of Racing Demon or Canasta. The Queen played fast and well, once outwitting 'Bobetty', the fifth Marquess Lord Salisbury, an old friend with a lisp who famously wailed, 'Oh, Ma'am, I am suwwounded by howwible, howwible queens.'

There was a lot of laughter now, the atmosphere was gay. Excitable young Guards officers smoked and lounged around, applauding a little too enthusiastically if one of the Princesses added a piece to the many jigsaws on the green baize tables. Humming 'Daisy, Daisy' the King's daughters skimmed along the long corridors, carefree, stopping only to wind up the gramophone to play another foxtrot. The Queen loved being surrounded by young people. Life had been far too serious.

Sometimes the King was tetchy because the illness that would kill him had already begun its insidious infiltration of his body. But, adoring his daughters, he tried to conceal any irritation at the rowdy parties. When not out shooting, he preferred to relax doing fretwork or laughing at ITMA on the wireless with Tommy Handley's fast cracks and Mona Lott's lugubrious 'Can I do yer now, Sir?' Princess Elizabeth may have been his 'Pride' but Margaret was his 'Joy' and could keep him entertained for hours at the piano playing Chopin and jazz or singing music hall favourites.

An old friend of the King recalled 'how very lovely Princess Elizabeth was at this time,' and how the King had begun to rely on her, perhaps with prescience about the brevity of his life. In many ways they were alike: stalwart, with a belief in doing what was right whatever the cost, yet behind the solemn formality both had a dry, observant humour. At times, the King may have found his daughter more compatible company than his wife, with the Queen's zest for life and gaiety, and who would now happily dance the hokey-cokey to Maurice Winnick and his Band until the small hours.

A gently ironic description of one of these dances was given by John Gale, an officer cadet in the Coldstream Guards and later a journalist with the *Observer*. The 'small dance' to which he was invited at Windsor Castle began at nine o'clock in the evening. It proved one of the lighter moments in his short life. Instructed by his adjutant to get a haircut and to take a gold cigarette case even though he did not smoke, his first impression was how 'surprisingly small but comely the Princesses were in their brocadish dresses'.

After a few glasses of 'refreshing Hock cup' he asked the future Queen of England to dance. Consulting her card, with its 'serpentine list of names', she murmured that for the next ten dances she was not free, but 'perhaps later'.

Persistence eventually won him a dance with the Princess but no conversation. At between two and three in the morning, more sherbets gave him the chutzpah to approach the Princess again. Claiming he could not dance a step, he recalled: 'I put my arms to her and then, saying nothing, we swayed and rocked to the music.' Eventually the silence was broken by the Princess' clipped inquiry, 'Are you at Sand'ust?' to which Gale replied, 'No, Ma'am, Mons.' And that was the end of his dance with the Princess, who seemed baffled by Mons, the name at that time for a National Service training ground near Aldershot, when most young bloods in royal circles attended Sandhurst, the prestigious Berkshire military academy.

Her mother would have been more fun. When the band struck up 'Hands, Knees and Boomps-a-Daisy' he noted how 'the Queen enjoyed this very much' and 'several times our bottoms boomped. Later she sat on the arm of a chair and talked to several of us. She laughed constantly: no doubt she guessed we felt out of place.' The young sprigs were charmed by the Queen, who had 'enormous magnetism'.

Throughout the evening the King had looked tired; his face was 'heavy with orange pancake makeup ... and his head was small.' The Queen, in spite of all the gaiety, constantly worried about him. Dulcie Grey was struck by how 'very much' she loved him.

The Queen had enjoyed seeing the actress in 'Queen Elizabeth Slept Here' and thought it 'fun'. They became friends. She loved the theatre and the company of actors. The rest of the royal family enjoyed musicals and were fans of Danny Kaye, Mae West, Frank Sinatra and of Jimmy Edwards in cabaret. When the Shah of Iran was visiting, the Queen asked him if he had enjoyed the hit show 'Annie Get Your Gun', but he misheard and panic-stricken replied: 'No Madam, I 'ave not got my gun. I 'ave left it in my room. I will send somebody to get it.' The Shah had been married three times. The Queen Mother particularly liked the reason given by his first wife for divorce, citing 'the altitude of Tehran, 8,000 feet up, too high'.

The royal calendar was back on course with ten weeks at Balmoral starting on 12th August. The King was often disappointed that first summer after the war when the bag seemed never to include grouse. An average shoot might produce three rabbits, a heron and a mountain hare. The Queen never followed the guns, preferring to sit in the Tower garden sniffing 'dear old Albertine' roses and reading French poetry, especially Ronsard's 'very touching and poignant' *Les Lilas et Les Roses*.

Princess Elizabeth, increasingly attracted to Prince Philip of Greece, a young naval officer, was growing apart from her loving family. She first set eyes on him in July 1939, when she was thirteen and he was eighteen, during a royal visit to Dartmouth. They shared lemonade and ginger nuts. A cadet at the Royal Naval College, this flaxen-haired young man struck the King, at first, as a bit of a show-off.

His uncle 'Dickie', Lord Mountbatten, remembered: 'Elizabeth stared at Philip for the rest of the day and followed him everywhere.' He had rowed dangerously near the Royal Yacht

Victoria and Albert after all his fellow cadets had obediently turned back. It reduced the King to one of his 'gnashes', while his daughter blushed crimson at this old-fashioned romantic gesture. A shyly maturing teenager, Princess Elizabeth was at that awkward, gawky age and 'rather large-mouthed', according to her governess Miss Marion Crawford, who proved to be an embarrassingly close observer of this unappealing stage of adolescence.

Hardly precocious in the way thirteen year olds are today, yet already trained to observe, the young girl was struck by something special about Prince Philip, who spoke his mind and talked about the need for change. He was born in Corfu on 10th June 1921. His father, Prince Andrew of Greece, a drifter and a charmer, was a younger son of King George I of the Hellenes. His mother, Princess Alice, was the eldest daughter of Prince Louis of Battenberg and a sister of Lord Mountbatten.

A frugal childhood began in earnest in December 1922 when the entire Greek Royal Family, forced into exile in Europe, scrambled aboard HMS *Calypso*. The baby Philip was unceremoniously bundled out of the country in a cot made from an orange crate.

An only son, Prince Philip was fond of his virtually stateless playboy father, who split his time between Paris and Monte Carlo spending whatever he had on sybaritic pastimes. He would complain: 'I don't think anybody thinks I had a father ... Most people think that Dickie is my father anyway ... I grew up very much more with my father's family than I did with my mother's. And I think they are quite interesting people.'

Related to sixteen Oldenburg kings, seven Russian tsars and six Swedish kings, Philip had family connections every bit as grand as the Queen's. This was his Almanach de Gotha, royals who once were symbols of a grand *ancien régime* until most of them were overthrown by revolution.

Although Philip was a great-great-grandchild of Queen Victoria and this link should have made him acceptable, he still was not the King's first choice as a husband for his eldest daughter. Prince Philip was poor but the Queen, who liked good-looking young men, thought well of him.

Prince Philip, now more mature and a lieutenant in the Royal Navy, carried off a surprise encounter with his future father-in-law in the shrubbery at Windsor. On a warm summer's day the King, in his gardening clothes, emerged from behind some bushes wearing a large bearskin. Prince Philip was not to know that he liked to garden wearing Brigade of Guards' dress headgear to familiarise himself with its weight for Trooping the Colour but did not bat an eyelid. It was an early test the young man carried off with aplomb.

The King did admire Philip's war record, appreciated that he had not had a privileged upbringing, and also found his down-to-earth attitude refreshing. He protested that there was 'nothing wrong with Philip', but secretly had misgivings. He argued against the couple becoming engaged on the grounds that Princess Elizabeth was too young for marriage and had not yet met many young men of her own age. He rather hoped she would choose a home-grown aristocrat.

Princess Elizabeth, however, had her father's quiet determination. Discreetly, without any 'scenes' with her parents, she would get her way, believing as firmly as she later did in the Commonwealth that she had found herself the right husband. Prince Philip was quite unlike the young men in her circle, solid symbols of settled decency, landowners secure in the knowledge of their place in the world with a tendency to throw bread rolls at hunt balls.

The Prince, on the other hand, had no land. He had been brought up by a disciplined mother who later, disillusioned by the vicissitudes of her charming but garrulous husband, became a nun. His father left him an ivory handled shaving brush and two suits when he died in France in 1944.

The Queen, who always steered a diplomatic course, was quietly supportive of both her husband and her daughter, but she distrusted Mountbatten's influence in the royal family, particularly after the King's death. Saddened by his assassination by the IRA in Ireland in 1979, she nevertheless had always felt apprehensive about his ambition and the sway he held over Prince Charles, who adored him and once joked: 'He is my Falstaff.'

In February 1947 the King and Queen were to attend the opening of the Union Parliament in Cape Town and then do a tour of South Africa. The King insisted that Princess Elizabeth, by now moodily in love, should accompany her parents and her sister. She was not at all keen. The King hoped that she had not thought him hard-hearted when he asked her to wait until she was twenty-one before becoming engaged. Princess Elizabeth understood the importance of their appearing as a strong, united Royal Family in the difficult post-war years at home and in South Africa. Even then, duty came first with her, but a bargain was struck with her father privately: he would agree to her engagement to Prince Philip on their return. Secretly, the King hoped she might be diverted while abroad.

He had misgivings himself about a visit to the sunny Cape. He worried that it might conjure up provocative images of the royal family basking in the sunshine while, at home, coal was rationed as Britain endured one of its coldest ever winters: flooding, power cuts and over two million people out of work. Standards of living were miserable, luxuries unobtainable and almost everything else on ration or in very short supply. The King feared the tour would be seen as an insensitive royal jolly.

For Queen Elizabeth that 1947 tour of South Africa was the last as a family. The next time she went abroad, it would be alone and as a widow.

Prior to the visit, the Queen and her daughters, in a pleasurable flurry of activity, ordered clothes from Hartnell. Hardly a day passed without the couturier's distinctive striped boxes being delivered to the Palace. More and more creamy silk and cotton flounced dresses in colours called called 'Pale Mealies' and 'Rhodesian Gold' arrived in layers of tissue paper.

There was thick snow on the ground as the royal party left Buckingham Palace for Waterloo. At Portsmouth, they boarded HMS *Vanguard* where the royal family's seven-bedroomed, five-bathroomed suite was equipped with its own telephone exchange and historic furniture from the old *Victoria and Albert*. 'It's like being stroked,' was the Queen's sensuous reaction to the calm seas that succeeded the storms after days of Biscay buffetting.

In South Africa, where there were strong feelings of republicanism, the King was tense but the Queen eased much of the stress during the two-month visit. Gently tugging his arm, 'Oh Bertie do look ... those people behind that little fence ...' She spotted a group of excited, leathery faces beaming at this little family. 'Only four', they said to each other, and 'so fresh and white'.

'That is Mr King and next to him is Mrs King; then just behind, Princess Elizabeth King and Princess Margaret King,' a policeman instructed children waiting for the royal visitors on board the celebrated White Train.

Wherever they went, the Queen behaved as if in the fulfilment of a dream, but never overplayed the moment, just appearing genuinely pleased that anyone should turn out. 'Oh Bertie, do you see, this is Hicksdorp! ... I expect they are the Bantu choir. How kind. We must wave, Bertie,' she said as they arrived at another small undistinguished town in the South African veldt.

Even when the train stopped at some uninspiring outposts, the Queen was never caught out. There she was, cool in steam heat, wearing lavish hat, pearls and diamonds, and waving brightly at a sea of African faces. And it mattered how she looked. People were never disappointed, though occasionally she was asked 'Mrs Queen, Mrs Queen, where is your crown?'

Her *forte* was in calming situations, defusing potential rows. A Boer told her that he could never quite forgive the British for having conquered his country. Queen Elizabeth, a fervent supporter of the white regime in South Africa, replied with a smile: 'I understand that perfectly,' and went on reassuringly: 'We feel very much the same in Scotland.'

The royal family spent thirty-six nights on the White Train. There was little privacy. 'It was doubly hard for Bertie,' the Queen explained, 'he was worried about things at home and, finding it a particularly exhausting trip, was easily irritated. If there was any slovenliness or the smallest alteration to a timetable, he "blew up".' All those moments the Queen would take his wrist and smilingly pretend to take his pulse ... This calmed him, although sometimes it was the Queen herself who had brought about one of his 'gnashes' by being late, but as soon as she appeared, he would smile. Royal advisers noticed how he could 'never take his eyes from her'.

In the Queen's luggage there was not one pair of sensible shoes amongst the charming biscuit crêpe suits trimmed with feathers and cream frocks with matching picture hats. Watching the Queen trying to climb Matopos to see Cecil Rhodes' tomb, the King shook his head as she teetered along a rocky path. Princess Elizabeth, with a quick glance at her father, whisked off her own shoes, saying briskly: 'How like Mummie – typical', and handed the shoes to her before padding off in stockinged feet. 'At least they were not planning an assault on Table Mountain,' one of the royal party suggested thankfully.

A royal tour is a minefield of potential disasters to be avoided. A royal 'recce' party, as the Palace staff who go out ahead are known, are sent to fix every minute in the visit, to assess how long it takes to walk to the royal car, how much time should be allowed for waving, and how long a speech should last. But the outraged shriek of a poor ostrich at a farm in Oudtshoorn had not been anticipated.

The King had snipped off more than a token feather from the unsuspecting creature's behind, but the Queen swiftly stepped forward and soothingly confided, 'We do a lot of gardening at home; the King is good at digging and weeding and it is I who concentrate on the secateurs.' The ostrich, still with its head in a sack, was no longer so agitated as the Queen deftly snipped a feather and admired it. Ostrich feathers trimmed many of her hats, though she had not expected to see the owner of this priceless haberdashery trim at such close quarters.

Tireless and indefatigable, the Queen's example prompted Townsend to have a 'heart to heart' with the King and to ask if the Princesses could be more giving, more like their mother in public? Young and inexperienced, they could not of course have the Queen's touch. Besides, the King was exceptionally proud of his daughters and thought they were doing rather well: Lilibet 'competent and classic', Margaret 'pretty and dashing'. And if anything went wrong, they could not be expected to have their mother's presence of mind in that enervating heat.

The royal party had to recover from an incident on the tour which had potentially been frightening. A villager at Benoni appeared out of nowhere, loped alongside the slow-moving royal car and muttered ferociously. This so alarmed the Queen that she seized her decorative Winterhalter-style parasol, under which she had smiled so winsomely in the white heat of the Rand mining towns, and cracked it firmly on the assailant's head several times, breaking the parasol in two. The man collapsed. The Queen, who feared the King was going to be attacked, remained composed and 'within a second was waving and smiling as captivatingly as ever'; that beatific smile concealed a remarkable strength.

The King was upset when he heard later that the would-be assassin had actually been loyally chanting 'My King, My King' and only trying to press a ten-shilling note into Princess Elizabeth's hand as a 21st birthday present.

The high point of the tour was the Princess' birthday, when she offered her life 'to the service of my people'. Her voice then had that note of privileged precision, but today it is much mellower. Increasingly our Queen's Christmas broadcasts seem warmer and more in touch with modern Britain. But the birthday reminded the King of the burden his elder daughter was facing. Watching her when she had wandered off on her own, he turned to his wife and said, 'Poor Elizabeth, already she's realising that she will be alone and lonely all her life; that no matter who she has by her side, only she can make the final decisions.'

Princess Elizabeth's best birthday present was the King's formal consent to her marriage. Prince Philip had shaken off the Schleswig-Holstein-Sonderburg-Glucksberg-Beck ancestral family name and became a British citizen on 28th February 1947. He was now a Mountbatten, but would lose this in a bitter battle after the King's death when it was decided that the family name should be Windsor.

On the eve of the wedding, Prince Philip was created Royal Highness and Baron Greenwich, Earl Menioneth and Duke of Edinburgh and a Knight of the Garter. The King remarked, 'It is an awful lot to give a young man all at once.'

The Queen was delighted. Softly conciliatory, never putting her foot down, always leaving the unpalatable decisions to her husband, she could see her daughter was now truly happy.

CHAPTER 16

For Valour

The King watched the newlyweds being pelted with rose petals and drive away in an open landau, the bride with her hot water bottle and 'Susan', a favourite corgi. The Queen put her arm through his and he smiled, hearing the lilt of that familiar voice at his elbow. They walked under the archway into the Palace.

If there had been any anxiety about Princess Elizabeth's choice of husband, the King was generous now. He told her in a touching letter: 'Your leaving has left a great blank in our lives ... I can see that you are sublimely happy with Philip,' but added 'Our family, us four, the royal family must remain together ... with additions, of course, at suitable moments.'

Princess Elizabeth Alexandra Mary Windsor married her naval Prince, Lieutenant Philip Mountbatten, at Westminster Abbey on the 20th November 1947. In the austere post-war atmosphere, their wedding provided welcome pageantry but was not ostentatious. They were a striking couple, and it is easy now to forget how attractive the Queen was as a girl, that creamy complexion, pretty eyes and quick smile which lit up her whole face. Her husband was blond and athletic. Their wedding would fill scrapbooks and be the stuff of memorabilia.

A little lacklustre amongst the 3,007 wedding presents, which included Sheraton furniture, a horse, Aubusson rugs, cigarette cases studded with cabochon emeralds, diamond necklaces and tiaras, was a piece of grey homespun cloth from Mr Gandhi, the Indian independence leader. 'What a horrible thing', Queen Mary exclaimed, convinced it was a symbolic loincloth. Prince Philip gently explained it was a great honour because it had been personally woven by the Mahatma.

The Queen gave her daughter a sensible present, an engraved tray with salt cellars, mustard and pepper pots and a toast rack. Relishing the wedding day, even its air of mild panic, she soothed the princess who was suffering a touch of bridal nerves. Her bouquet, a spray of orchids, had gone missing. It was found in a fridge, where a nursery footman thought it best to keep the delicate flowers fresh. Then the 'something borrowed', one of the Queen's own sunray diamond tiaras, snapped; more panic. 'We have two hours,' the Queen reassured. 'There are other tiaras,' she told the harassed bride, in something of an understatement.

Two forgotten strings of pearls had to be collected from St James'; then the Queen did a quick personal check that each of the hundred and fifty guests' plates at the wedding breakfast had a bunch of white heather and myrtle from Queen Victoria's wedding bouquet. At last she could go off and change into in a favourite, draped-style apricot and gold brocade dress.

After the wedding, trying to cheer up the King as the newlyweds left for their honeymoon at Broadlands, Lord Mountbatten's home in Hampshire, the Queen philosophically reminded him: 'What a wonderful day it's been ... They grow up and leave us and we must make the best of it.'

The Princess enjoyed being a naval wife. Retired sailor Tommy Gardner, who used to look after the Duke's car, recalled that when they were stationed on HMS *Glendower* at Pwllheli, Gwynedd, how Prince Philip would say, 'Wash my car Tommy, I'm off to see Lizzie at the weekend.' Those early years were probably the most carefree time for Elizabeth II in her long marriage.

The love the King and Queen bore each other was obvious and had strengthened through their trials, so now they looked confidently to peaceful years ahead and to celebrating their Silver Wedding in April 1948.

However, by the following October the King was plagued by cramps in his legs, but he took no notice, believing firmly in the royal family maxim: 'Never give in to illness, duty first, health later.' If you have a headache, the Queen Mother says to this day, 'take an aspirin.' He had always been a heavy smoker, on at least twenty-five cigarettes a day.

A second warning came in the summer when cramps cheated him out of a favourite walk by the Palace of Holyroodhouse in Edinburgh. Irritated, the King tried to climb the hill to Arthur's Seat, but it was difficult and his usual long decisive stride was gone. 'What's the matter with my blasted legs?' he grumbled. 'They won't work properly.' Sir Morton Smart, the Royal Physician and Manipulative Surgeon to the King, diagnosed arteriosclerosis. After a further consultation with another surgeon, Professor James Learmonth, the Queen was told there was a danger that they might have to amputate the right leg.

A year later, the King seemed better. However his left foot often became numb and it gave him considerable pain. He was operated on in the Buhl Room at the Palace, now turned into a temporary operating theatre, on 12th March 1949. The doctors pleaded with the Queen to persuade the King to rest: 'He may pay more heed to you, Ma'am, than to his doctors.'

Princess Elizabeth, now expecting her first baby, was living at the Palace with Prince Philip, while waiting to move to Clarence House. The Queen, protectively, refused to tell her how ill the King was because she was so attached to her father. The anxiety could affect her pregnancy.

Prince Charles was born at the Palace at 9.14 pm on 14th November 1948, a cheerful distraction. The King and Queen rushed to the Buhl Room, now converted into a maternity suite, to see their first grandchild. Prince Philip had been playing squash so was still in tennis shoes; the Queen hugged him and the King ordered champagne. The 'enormously proud' young mother was kissed and congratulated.

The baby was circumcised, breastfed, christened with water from the Jordan and admired by a formidable posse of royals. His great-grandmother Queen Mary even smiled a little at this small creature wrapped in royal lace christening robes. His father thought he looked 'like a plum pudding'.

The King enjoyed the Ascot week ball at Windsor in June 1949, though he had to keep resting his foot in between dances. He knew how much these occasions meant to the Queen and how she loved dancing, and this evening she was 'magnificent in a white satin semi-crinoline with the Garter and splendid rubies'. While keeping up a show of gaiety, she noticed how the King often looked apart, at times forlorn. He had never properly regained his strength.

For Scotland, the King had designed himself a harness with a halter attached to a horse. This ingenious pulley hauled him through the glens so he could shoot and keep the strain off his legs.

The first public telltale sign that all was not well was when George VI went to the Trooping the Colour ceremony sitting down in an open carriage. In 1987, the Queen also went in an open landau; not because she was unwell or because she was sixty-one but because her horse 'Burmese' had grown too old to be ridden.

A second grandchild, Princess Anne, was born on the 15th August 1950 at 11.50 am at Clarence House. Prince Philip became a Lieutenant Commander the day his daughter was born. He was posted to Malta to enjoy his first command, HMS *Magpie*, and Princess Elizabeth went with him; the children stayed behind with doting grandparents.

In the early summer of 1951, on 3rd May, the King opened the Festival of Britain from the steps of St Paul's. The family then went to Balmoral, which usually worked its magic but not this time. The King was worn, had 'flu and was depressed by his inability to 'chuck the bug'. The Queen had to deputise for him. She received their old friend, the amiable King Haakon of Norway, at Westminster Pier, and managed to look 'sublime'. Chips Channon's admiration brimmed over yet again as he watched her host a state banquet for the Norwegian King. He was one of her greatest fans.

Princess Margaret's twenty-first birthday celebrations were at Balmoral. The King went out with his son-in-law Prince Philip and the Earl of Dalkieth, an admirer of Princess Margaret's, and bagged three hundred grouse. He enjoyed the evening celebration, but the thump-thump of the music wearied him. He appeared in his dressing gown in the early hours of the morning, saying fretfully, 'Won't those bloody people ever go to bed?'

Not long after the hectic succession of parties and dances for Princess Margaret, the King travelled overnight by train from Scotland to London for X-Rays. 'Now they think there's something wrong with me blowers.' He was always gallantly dismissive about his health. The result of these tests was an exploratory operation, again in the Buhl Room, on 23rd September 1951 when an inoperable malignancy on the left lung was discovered.

Unsuspecting, the King had been suffering from lung cancer for six months. The Queen was told. Now all that could be done was a lung resection which weakened the King's voice.

'The King is esteemed by his people ... to the point of tenderness,' the novelist Rebecca West observed when a National Day of Thanksgiving was held (ironically for his apparent recovery) on 2nd December 1951. The King may not have known how long he had to live but there was a moving quietness about his courage in this last struggle, a touching determination to recover, although he had lost a great deal of weight quickly, at least twenty-one pounds.

Churchill, who admired him now more than ever, said 'The King ... walked with death ... as if death were a companion whom he recognised and did not fear.' After the Day of Thanksgiving the royal family moved to Sandringham.

For Princess Elizabeth, who adored her father, the most urgent test of her courage was when she had to go to the King's room the night before she and Prince Philip left for a tour of Kenya, Canada and America. She curtsied, spent time at his bedside and both acknowledged that she would carry in her luggage the Draft Accession Declaration that would be required if the King died while she was abroad. Often during the tour, the Princess appeared pensive and preoccupied. She had a special bond with her father; nobody could ever replace him in her life.

The Queen never allowed her anxiety to show. When Princess Elizabeth telephoned her parents from North America she would keep up a pleasant banter: 'Are you smiling enough, dear?' The reply was an impatient 'Oh, Mother, I seem to be smiling all the time.'

One of the doctors, dismayed and apologetic at the inability of the medical profession to do anything more to save the King, was amazed at the way in which the Queen '... spread balsam ... Friar's balsam if you'll forgive the medical expression'. Her secret grief would take a toll; the strain of this serenity would destroy a part of her emotionally, but make her more inviolable in the future.

It was hard for her to stay calm and reassuring, as she watched her husband grow more frail and thin. A doctor said, 'You could pick him up in two hands.' The illness accentuated what Cecil Beaton described as the 'raw, bony, medieval aspects of that handsome face'.

After Christmas at Sandringham, the King seemed to rally and his doctors allowed him to go out to shoot, though he had to wear specially heated boots, gloves and waistcoat. By 28th January 1952, he had insisted on travelling to see Princess Elizabeth and Prince Philip off to Australia and New Zealand. The night before, the family had gone to Drury Lane to see *South Pacific*, the last time they would all be together.

It was bitterly cold at Heathrow Airport on 31st January 1952. The King stood on the tarmac in an icy wind: hatless, shoulders hunched, his hands in his pockets, face taut and distress in his eyes. The world was given an uncomfortable glimpse of a grief so personal it should have been private, but was caught by a news agency photographer as George VI watched the Argonaut carry his successor into the grey sky over Middlesex. Princess Margaret stood miserably apart.

The King liked the Keepers' Day shoot at the season's end. It was a chance to be with friends and tenants of the Sandringham estate. February 5th, 1952 was a glittery, brilliant blue icecream day. The King, 'as carefree and happy as those about him had ever known him', tramped through the pinewoods and over the stubble.

'A good day's sport, gentlemen,' he said, as they totted up the bag of 280 hares before heading back towards the house. 'I will expect you here at nine o'clock on Thursday,' were his parting words to these old friends. The King then stopped at the kennels to see a golden retriever which had picked up a thorn in its paw.

Reassured by the King's good spirits, the Queen had gone with Princess Margaret to see a favourite artist, Edward Seago, at Ludham that day. They had a charmed lunch, went by motor cruiser for tea with mutual friends, and excitedly brought home some delicate landscapes of Sandringham which they had commissioned.

They had a 'truly gay dinner', swopping stories about their pleasant day. 'How wonderful,' the Queen thought, 'the King was once again his old self.' In this tranquil mood, the King, Queen and Princess Margaret all felt more hopeful, deluded by calm normality. All would be well, surely?

They listened to the wireless and heard how Princess Elizabeth and Prince Philip had gone to stay at Treetops, a game lodge by the Sagana River in Kenya. Princess Margaret played the piano; in relaxed mood the King went to bed at half past ten, saying, 'I'll see you in the morning.'

His room was on the ground floor to save climbing the stairs, which were now too much for him. He had been brought a cup of hot chocolate and just before midnight he fiddled with a faulty window latch and turned his light out. In the morning, at half past seven, his valet James MacDonald tapped on the door with a tray of tea but got no reply from that familiar slow, husky voice. When he went in the King was dead.

'I never knew a woman could be so brave,' was the stunned if chauvinistic reaction of Equerry in Charge, Sir Harold Campbell, who had the task of telling the Queen of the King's death. Her maid, Gwen Suckling, had brought tea to the Queen at the same time as it was taken to her husband. Elizabeth's first reaction, touching in its immediacy, was: 'I must go to him,' expressing almost the same frail hope as when in the past she had rushed to the King's bedside, summoned by anxious doctors, but then somehow, he had rallied.

No longer Queen, but still in command, she gave instructions: 'The King must not be left.' She ordered a vigil by his open door and went to comfort Princess Margaret. Mother and daughter were 'hammered senseless' by sadness and by shock.

Although it had been known that the King would not live long, that happy last day as a family had been cruelly deceptive. Had the King gradually become weaker, if they had been spending long days with him in a sickroom, with talk in whispers and increasingly gloomy bulletins by the royal doctors, this might have cushioned them against the suddenness of his death. That evening the Queen Mother came downstairs to see her grandchildren Prince Charles and Princess Anne. 'I've got to start some time,' she said, 'and it might as well be now.'

The children's mother became Queen aged twenty-five, sitting in a *machan* on top of a fig tree watching rhinoceros in the Aberdare Forest. The news of the King's death reached Kenya at 2.45 pm. London time was 11.45 am, Prince Philip told her when he took her out for a walk along the river bank. Almost immediately they left for the airport.

Awed by the vulnerability of this slight young woman who had changed from a safari shirtwaister into black mourning clothes, Africans lined the roadside to Entebbe, chanting 'Shauri mbaya kabisa – the very worst has happened.' A trail of red dust fanned out behind the car taking the Queen and her husband to their 4,127 mile turbulent flight home through tropical storms.

The Queen arrived in London at 4.19 pm on Thursday, 7th February, the day the King had hoped to shoot again at Sandringham. On Friday, 9th February, after her Accession Declaration at ten o'clock in the morning, the new Queen excused herself. 'My heart is too full'. In the privacy of the royal apartments, her head on Prince Philip's shoulder, she wept.

'Her old grannie and subject must be the first to kiss her hand.' Queen Mary, at eighty-five, was rigidly aware of protocol whatever her own sadness, but as she rose from a deep curtsey, she rebuked her granddaughter: 'Lilibet, your skirts are much too short for mourning.' It was a moment which made the Queen smile.

A painful reminder of the Abdication, and of the Queen Mother's belief that it shortened the King's life, was the arrival of the Duke of Windsor from New York. Queen Mary received him.

The King's body lay in the family church of St Mary Magdalene at Sandringham for the weekend, guarded by estate workers. Then the coffin was placed on the royal gun-carriage and taken to Wolferton station, followed by the King's personal servants, his valets, and his detective. Here it was put on the train for London and Westminster Hall for the lying-in-state and the remorseless panoply of a royal funeral, to be attended by seven kings.

Royal women do not often show emotion in public. The King's widow, his mother and his daughters presented a dry-eyed composure behind black gauzy veils. They stood together in Westminster Hall by the King's coffin which was made of oak from Sandringham. At each corner stood a motionless Guardsman. By the third day, 300,000 people had filed past, many queuing for three and four hours. The air was sweet with the scent of spring flowers, hyacinths and primroses in the waxy warmth of the tall candles standing sentinel.

Just before midnight on the eve of the funeral, Queen Elizabeth slipped in by the East door of the Hall and stood in the shadows. Dressed in black, hatless, she wore a favourite diamond leaf clip from 'her dear husband' on her lapel. Even this last, quiet moment was hardly private. There was the presence of the Lord Great Chamberlain, the Marquess of Cholmondeley, tactful, solicitous and watchful, and the young guardsmen, their eyes rigidly ahead, fearful of a breath too loud in this grieving quiet. Her vigil went on for two hours.

The funeral was on 16th February at St George's Chapel, Windsor. The coffin was draped in the red, gold and blue Royal standard, borne out of Westminster Hall by naval ratings in white gaiters, and placed on top of the green gun carriage. Big Ben tolled fifty-six times, once for each year of the King's life. The cortège moved along the Mall, the Imperial State Crown carried on a purple velvet cushion with the insignia of the Order of the Garter and the Sceptre.

'Here he is,' Queen Mary said, standing tall and straight at a window at Marlborough House. The Queen, her mother and Princess Margaret leant forward in their carriage to acknowledge the old lady's words, but as the procession moved on Elizabeth reached for the hand of Lady Airlie, sensitively aware that Queen Mary's 'dry eyes were seeing beyond the coffin, a little boy in a sailor suit. Past weeping, wrapped in the ineffable solitude of grief ... I could not speak to comfort her. My tears choked me, the words I wanted to say would not come and we held each other's hands in silence.'

In St George's Chapel it was the young Queen who needed support from her mother, as she was almost overcome by the poignancy of the bagpipes, 'The Flowers of the Forest' lament and, above all, the moment when all the trappings of monarchy were removed from the coffin. Then the flowers were placed on it by guardsmen 'with hands as gentle as girls'. The Queen and Princess Margaret mourned 'Darling Papa'. The Queen's own special flowers carried a message from 'your sorrowing Lilibet'; her mother's, a posy of white, grieved for 'a great and noble King'. Churchill's eloquent handwritten note said 'For Valour'.

For the Queen, the hardest moment, even though now she was more composed, was taking earth from a gold bowl and sprinkling it on the coffin as it was lowered into the vault.

Later, when congratulated on being so brave, the Queen Mother would reply softly: 'Not in private'. Writing afterward to a friend, she said her husband had 'a sort of natural nobility of thought and life' and that 'he was too young to die'.

There was a lunch for the royal family after the funeral, but the Queen Mother insisted the Duke of Windsor be refused an invitation.

CHAPTER 17

Luminous Courage

In the autumn of 1952 Edith Sitwell received a letter from the Queen Mother in Scotland in which she thanked the bejewelled, beaky poet for an anthology she had sent her called *A Book Of Flowers*. Explaining how much she appreciated 'such a delicious book', the Queen Mother described how she had 'taken it out and started reading it sitting by the river ... I felt a sort of peace stealing round my heart; such lovely poems and heavenly words'. She confided that, as she read, she found a hope in George Herbert's poem. 'Who would have thought my shrivel'd heart could have recovered greenness? It was gone quite underground.' Her thank-you letters were always special.

Acknowledging 'how small and selfish sorrow is ... it bangs one about until one is senseless,' the Queen Mother remained heartbroken and found neither Scotland nor poetry could help restore her. Spiritualism did give some comfort, although there was embarrassment at the Palace in case this reliance on the spirit world leaked out. George VI once revealed, 'My family are no strangers to spiritualism;' and still it worried Sir Winston Churchill and others outside the family circle.

Her background, a mixture of mythology and descent from a long line of Scottish kings with a solid belief in an after-life, prompted the Queen Mother to turn to Mrs Lilian Baylis, a celebrated London medium. Telephoned, out of the blue, at her home in Wembley, she was asked to go to a house in Kensington where she was blindfolded and then taken on to a mystery address. The normally imperturbable, silver-haired medium felt she was being kidnapped. Although she claimed psychic powers, she had no idea where she was going or with whom, but would always remember the rustle of skirts at the start of the seance.

Was she unnerved? 'Not a bit', claimed her son-in-law Gordon Adam, a former director of *Psychic News*. 'My mother-in-law had dealings with all sorts of people like Chiang Kai-shek and the King of Greece, and had been with them at vulnerable times in their lives. So she did not feel intimidated by royalty; it was all in a day's work to her.'

When the seance was over and Mrs Baylis came out of her trance and the blindfold was removed, she looked around and found the Queen Mother, the Queen, Prince Philip, Princess Margaret, Princess Alexandra and the Duke of Kent sitting in a circle on gilt chairs.

Slowly coming to terms with her loss the Queen Mother, who had been so long strong for the King but now suddenly felt fragile, was bewildered by the intensity of her grief and still needed to telephone Mrs Baylis at home. Then, quite suddenly, the calls stopped. Mrs Baylis was pleased, hoping that perhaps that she had helped. Summoned for one last visit to Clarence House, the Queen Mother said softly: 'You know we do not have many possessions but I would like you to have this,' and taking a brooch from her own dress, stood on tiptoes to pin it on the shoulder of the statuesque medium.

Just as many who are widowed will hark back to the happiest days in their married life, the Queen Mother now pined for her time as George VI's trusted confidante. 'The King always told me everything first,' she said to a friend wistfully, 'I do so miss that.'

Her importance now her daughter was on the throne was as mother of the Queen and grandmother of a future king. Subconsciously, even at that fraught stage, she was not going to settle for being a widowed, royal granny existing in the shadows. 'Queen Mother' had too cosy a ring to it, so she invented a more impressive title. In future she would be known as Queen Elizabeth, the Queen Mother. This grand title was announced on 14th February 1953 and was unique. It spoke volumes for her psychological strength and complemented the extraordinary role she would carve out for herself.

The brutality of succession meant that the Palace was speedily cleared of the Queen Mother's possessions. She was expected to move to Clarence House, but she hated the idea and was reluctant to leave as it emphasised her newly diminished role. As Dowager Queen she was no longer vital to the business of monarchy. It was all so depressing, swift and necessary. Yet the new Queen Mother knew how important it was for the Queen to be installed at the Palace with proper royal authority.

Now, as she faced her daughter's Coronation and the traumatic move from Buckingham Palace, another link with the King was broken with the death of his mother at Marlborough House on the 24th March 1953, aged eighty-five. Typically, Queen Mary had insisted that should she do anything as inconsiderate as dying, her granddaughter's Coronation must go ahead as planned. During George V's reign, when the death of a public figure upset the royal schedule, Queen Mary grumbled: 'How inconvenient of him to die in the middle of the season.' Nobody was more of a stickler for protocol, even in death.

The Queen Mother was grateful for another timely bout of 'flu, which gave her an excuse not to attend a dinner party for twenty-eight on the night of her mother-in-law's funeral. The royals behaved like Jesuits who celebrate the death of one of the order with a festive supper. She had been extremely fond of Queen Mary, and had forged a remarkably warm bond with the royal matriarch who could appear formidably frosty.

The Coronation was at Westminster Abbey on a typical summer's day, 2nd June 1953: icy winds, grey skies, cherry blossom blown on the pavements. The Queen's George III gold State Coach was drawn by eight Windsor greys. Already in the Abbey were world leaders, seven crowned heads, stalwart squires, diplomats, European royal relations, members of the peerage, all admiring the grace of mother and daughter.

With innate dignity, slowly, faultlessly, the new Queen moved forward in her white satin Coronation robe studded with the floral symbols of the Empire including the thistle, the shamrock, the wattle and the Tudor rose. Eyes were on the mother too. 'Dear Mr Hartnell' surpassed himself with a magnificent dress trimmed with a border of golden tissue and dotted with elaborate embroidered, jewelled feathers.

The Queen Mother's luminous courage was evident as the small, motherly figure walked slowly into the Abbey 'glittering from top to toe, diamonds everywhere, a two-foot hem of solid gold on her dress', to give a 'superb performance', playing second lead as beautifully as she had played first.

Displaying faultless composure and never looking down to negotiate a step, with a look of combined pride and sadness, the Queen Mother took her place to watch her daughter being crowned. At twenty-six the Princess became Elizabeth Her Most Excellent Majesty, Elizabeth II (by the Grace of God) of the United Kingdom of Great Britain and Northern Ireland and her other Realms and Territories, Queen, Head of the Commonwealth, Defender of the Faith.

As she bore the Crown of St Edward effortlessly on her head, the Queen admitted, 'Yes, it does get rather heavy.' Her mother thought of the King and his hours of practise with an equivalent weight of books. Knowing, too, how perilous these moments could be, she smiled, recalling how 'Bertie' had been plagued by clumsy clerics at his Coronation.

A welcome distraction for the Queen Mother was her grandson Prince Charles, in satin rompers, who spent most of the time under the pew, searching for soothing barley sugar in his grandmother's handbag.

Later the Queen, still pale and earnest, brightened when given the news at the Palace that Mount Everest had been conquered. On its summit was a Union Jack, a triumphant symbol placed there by Hunt, Hillary and the great sherpa Tensing. These were Elizabethan heroes for the old King's shy daughter on that daunting day.

By the end of Coronation day, the *Jackmanii* clematis and the *Etoile d'Hollande* roses at the Palace were wilting, but not the Queen Mother. With 'her enormous presence' she had stunned those who feared the day would be too distressing for her. Cecil Beaton was euphoric about her air of 'radiance'. Also, because she was his benefactress, she arranged that he should take the Coronation pictures. Prince Philip had favoured his friend, court photographer 'Baron' Nahum, a playboy. The two men enjoyed socialising and night-clubbing together. Beaton, sensitive and aesthetic, felt the Duke's antipathy was perhaps due to his inability to crack 'Navy-type jokes', but the Queen and her mother disapproved of Baron because they thought he led Prince Philip astray.

Sir Winston Churchill had feared that the Queen Mother might become more reclusive and feel she no longer had any useful role to play. Now, seeing how superb she had been under pressure, he cajoled her skilfully: 'Don't lead too quiet a life.' He added, 'Your daughter the Queen needs you. The people need you.' The Queen Mother listened, still not convinced. He promised her an allowance, the use of The Royal Lodge and Birkhall in Scotland for her lifetime and Clarence House to be redecorated. The Queen Mother still wavered. She was not grasping, but relatively speaking it was not a great deal to offer and she would always be quite short of money. 'I was going to throw in Big Ben,' Churchill quipped. In the end he won her over and good to his word, Clarence House was soon filled with whistling workmen glad to brighten the place for their favourite royal.

After all her misgivings, Clarence House would become another happy place. Over the next forty years the Queen Mother continued to display what Noel Coward described – after the two had enjoyed bullshots, curry served in coconuts, and strawberry and rum pie on the terrace of his home in Jamaica – as 'that infinite grace of mind, charm, humour and deep-down kindness. In addition to which she looks enchanting.'

For a long time after the King's death, though, she was 'engulfed by great black clouds of unhappiness and misery.' Those who had once wondered if her marriage had been a love match now had no doubt. The King was only fifty-six when he died; much of their married life had been sacrificed to duty. Happy, fulfilled years together had eluded them and the Queen Mother felt cheated. Advisers and courtiers who had been close to the King rallied to try and comfort her. Jolly Group Captain 'Mouse' Fielden, formerly of the King's Flight, could make her laugh by reminding her of his escapades in Occupied France during the war. One friend said: 'he was awfully helpful, talking about the past and just listening.'

Close friends who saw how 'dreadfully shattered' the Queen Mother was felt helpless. Then a lady-in-waiting and former bridesmaid, Katharine Seymour, had an inspired idea and suggested to trusted friends Commander Clare Vyner and his wife that they should invite Queen Elizabeth to stay with them in Caithness during Ascot week. The King had never liked the North coast of Scotland much, so this would be new ground for his widow without any sad associations. The invitation was accepted.

Years later, Commander Vyner, who was a younger son of Lord Alwyne Frederick Compton, explained how he and his wife had viewed the proposal with misgivings. A man of wry humour, he said they liked to live simply, but this was exactly what the Queen Mother wanted. The Commander's wife, formerly Lady Doris Gordon-Lennox, a delicate-boned beauty and daughter of the Duke of Richmond, had done the London 'season' with Lady Elizabeth. The girls had married within three weeks of each other.

As he talked, Commander Vyner, a sprightly widower of 94, glanced from time to time at the two Sargent sketches on either side of the drawing room fireplace, one of his wife and a charming one of the Duchess of York in 1934, who he remembered all those years before as having been 'tiny, so very attractive and full of laughs'.

Sitting in his house by the water's edge in Ullapool, watching the Klondyke herring ships glide by heading for shelter under the bracken covered cliffs, the Commander constantly referred to the King's death as 'the Queen Mother's disaster', saying quietly, 'nobody quite realised how she was dreadfully broken up.'

His view was quite the opposite of the popularly held belief that the King was the weaker character of the two. 'People were wrong,' the Commander was emphatic, 'The reason Queen Elizabeth collapsed so completely was because she had relied completely on the King. He was the strong one and the organiser, he ran the show.'

He knew, as did all her close friends, that the Queen Mother would always remain a widow though there were any number of eligible Establishment figures who would have loved to marry her. But as one friend said, 'Remarry? When you have been married to the King of England, you do not marry again.'

The Vyners were the friends who gave the Queen Mother one incalculable gift: the discovery of the Castle of Mey and a first step towards a new life.

CHAPTER 18

Blowing the Cobwebs Away

To begin to understand the Queen Mother it helps to visit the Castle of Mey. Perched on a Scottish cliff, it is wildly bracing even on a hot summer's day. It gives a hint of the Bowes-Lyon strength that underlies what people fondly think of as Neapolitan icecream charm.

The Queen Mother would fall in love with the uncompromising vastness of the huge Caithness landscape. It gave her a feeling of freedom and peace and she loved its 'apartness'.

The Vyners, sensitive, supportive friends, were delighted that the Queen Mother was coming to stay with them at their white House of the Northern Gates on Dunnett Head, but stressed that they could not cater for her in the grand manner. 'We had only one servant so we requested, "Please, no large entourage". Queen Elizabeth,' the Commander said, 'happily acquiesced and flew up to Scotland with just Betty Somerset, the Duke of Beaufort's mother, a royal footman and a detective. That's all.'

It was June, the place was filled with wild flowers and the red and white doors of the stone crofts were staying open late at night. On a good day, the Arctic almost glittered, seeming barely over the horizon; at night the lights of seven lighthouses flashed.

While the crofters huddled in their cottages as the sky turned inky dark, the Queen Mother would put her head outside the Vyners' front door and murmur 'Ooh, the air'. When others wilted, she would pull on wellingtons and her battered fishing hat, with its enduring feather, to go for another long, solitary walk in this remote north-east corner of Scotland.

After about four or five days in this revitalising but relaxed atmosphere, she agreed to undertake a public engagement. Commander Vyner, who had set up a factory canning lobster and crab asked diplomatically: 'Ma'am, would you ever think of coming to the fish factory? They'd adore to see you.' The Queen Mother, now much more cheerful, agreed.

Commander Vyner remembered it as a happy day but how that undemanding visit had worn her out. 'As we drove off the staff gave her a cheer. I was using my car, a very ordinary saloon, Betty was next to me and Queen Elizabeth was in the back. In those days she used to get awfully tired. Well the name of her driver in London was Hurl and at one stage she must have almost dozed off because she woke up saying, "We'll go home now Hurl." '

Another gentle expedition a few days later would be momentous, when the Vyners and the Queen Mother drove past a small sixteenth-century castle on the John O'Groats peninsula. This was Barrogill, a fort originally built to repel Scandinavian sea wolves, where often the only sound was from the skeins of swooping grey geese. Soon after seeing the small derelict building, which had virtually no roof (it had been blown off by a vigorous wind) the Vyners took her to tea with the owner, Herbert Terry. 'It was rather amusing, with a bumbling butler shuffling about tapping everyone on the shoulder,' the Commander recalled. Later, the Queen Mother heard the castle was going to be pulled down and thought, 'It might do for me ... It must be saved.' Much helped by Commander Vyner, the little ruin became hers for £25,000. She liked to refer to this Scottish family castle as her 'bothy' and returned it to its original name, the Castle of Mey.

While the Castle was being renovated – it needed bathrooms, electric light and altogether twelve months' work – the Queen Mother visited Caithness thirteen times, through all seasons, including those daunting winter months when it got dark as early in the afternoon as Norway, the kingdom of her dear friend.

Mey was new, absorbing and would become a true home. Tramping along the spectacularly deserted beaches softened only by waving bunches of lyme grass like distrait ballerinas, she grieved, planned, was tearful, lonely and elated by turns, brightening as the Northern Lights flickered over the Pentland Firth.

The resident wind had bent the 150-year old sycamores, ash and hawthorn bushes into deferential crescents and would buffet her along the silvery turf path leading down to the sea. It sent the curlews shrieking and whipped the woolly, 'buttery-coloured' curls of the Cheviot sheep trying to shelter at Longoe Royal Farm.

Somehow the idea of the Queen Mother as a farmer was not really convincing, but Longoe Farm at Mey was run efficiently and profitably. She tramped about in a kilt, designed by Hartnell of course, and twinset with a walking stick, and made comments like a true Scotswoman with a shrewd eye for the health of her sheep. She asked technical questions about their 'muzzles' and commented: 'Mm, a good long body, meat in the right places on the hips and plenty of character in the head'. Practical and with a farmer's eye to an animal's potential, she was never sentimental about her herd of sheep if they had to be sold, although one farmer near Inverness who bought one of her pedigree beasts was amused to receive a telephone call from the Queen Mother's stockman three weeks later, asking how it was settling in. Not all Scottish farmers are as concerned about the well-being of their animals once sold and the money in the bank.

Restoration at Mey was well under way by the spring. Southerners were made anxious as great whirling waves of rain slapped against the castle doors and called it a hurricane, but the Queen Mother would simply say, 'Just look at the yellow of the gorse.'

Another antidote to her grief was the fun of choosing her colours and furniture. There was no need to defer to the Ministry of Works now, Mey was her very own. The whole atmosphere was light – ivory white walls and pretty pastel fabrics counteracting the wildness outside. In her bedroom with its four-poster bed in piped chintz, there was a tiny pale marble fireplace with a heart medallion, a gift from the King. It was moved lovingly to Scotland along with dog baskets, walking sticks, fishing rods and deck chairs, and the Queen

Mother's distinctive blue and biscuit coloured raincoats with hoods, one of her few concessions to the climate.

In the drawing room, on the piano beside a piece of elegant Caithness glass, were piles of frayed sheet music. Cole Porter, Jerome Kern and Noel Coward numbers: 'Now that Sir John Gielgud can't sing any more,' the Queen Mother would say, 'I'm the oldest person alive to remember all of Noel's songs.' The bookshelves were brimming with biographies and walls covered with landscapes by local artists bought at the Thurso exhibition every summer.

There were old gramophone records from the 'Forties and enticing beaded footstools and china cats guarding the fireplace; above all, there were lots of clocks, her passion; not that time mattered much at Mey.

Ignoring all the gloomy warnings about the potential damage which could be done by one whoosh of wind, the Queen Mother successfully grew some of her favourite coppery pink roses and the cramoisy Silver Jubilee which all blossomed bravely but seemed slightly out of character. You expected to find potatoes and the odd resilient cabbage, but a romantic garden flourished behind the castellated low stone wall. In summer it was a riot of pink petunias, dark blue lobelia, sweet white alyssum, begonias threaded along a border like a pink ribbon and buddleia for the more intrepid butterflies. A rustic trellis covered in clematis and honeysuckle was optimistically set up against the wind. It had the charm and dreamy escapism of a Beatrix Potter watercolour.

Her friends thought it a typical triumph of will. Every morning the Queen Mother would walk round her garden with Sandy Webster, the gardener, planning how best to cheat the northern gales which could reach ninety miles an hour.

The kitchen garden, full of rosemary, marjoram, fennel and thyme, could provide enough fruit, strawberries, raspberries and plums for summer entertaining.

Mey was for long rambles and 'riotous parties'. Lunch was always a picnic – but elaborate. A servant would set out with at least six hampers with excellent food, egg and lobster mayonnaise, and drink. 'It was,' one guest observed, 'almost impossible to get a glass of water.' Days were spent fishing for mackerel and hunting for crab unless it was salmon run time, when salmon and trout were landed in the rivers and burns of Caithness and, deliciously fresh, cooked the same night.

In the evenings, before a candlelit dinner, a fire of logs and peat crackled in the dining room and a glow on the bronze firescreen lit up the 'Willie Weet Feet' sandpipers and the Royal Yacht *Britannia,* engravings by good friend Lord Charteris of Amisfield, the Queen's Private Secretary from 1972-77 and later Provost of Eton. Also on display was a tapestry of the Queen Mother's coat of arms designed by Stephen Gooden. It took three girls three years to embroider it and the effect was charmingly medieval.

Dinners were never before nine; guests were an informal mixture of the Queen Mother's Household and friends from London. Bowls of 'Pink Iceberg' and 'Glenfiddich' with golden whisky-coloured petals, favourite roses from the garden, decorated a highly polished table. The food as at Clarence House and The Royal Lodge was fatteningly delicious and imaginative: fresh salmon, vegetables from the kitchen garden such as peas and broad beans beautifully cooked with a scattering of herbs. If artichokes were served, the Queen Mother would urge her guests to savour 'the taste of rusty nails' by drinking some local water with the last mouthful. Bowls of strawberries and large golden gooseberries were inevitably accompanied by great jugs of cream. She preferred champagne after dinner.

The talk would be of old times and values, which in Caithness seemed comfortingly unchanged. Relaxing after dinner if it was a balmy August night, and in the summer it stays light until eleven, the Queen Mother would lead her guests out under the stars to dance the conga or a reel until the moon came up over the neat pointed haystacks of the coastal farms.

It was a bit rugged for some of her Household, who used to organise trips to Orkney for its comparative sophistication. Many of the elderly courtiers and old friends were not always as enthusiastic as she was about the bracing outdoors. She loved the touch of salty foam from the insistent leaping waves, as the spray splashed elderly faces. The Queen Mother sang 'Speed, Bonny Boat' or Sir Walter Scott's 'Ca the yowes to the knowes', cheerfully calling over her shoulder with cosy nanny incentives: 'Come along, this is blowing the cobwebs away.'

They marvelled at her resilience underneath that goose-down feathery softness. The only time the Queen Mother stopped was to gather shells, which she loved and found enough to create several white paths in the gardens of the Castle.

When the courtiers had all gone back to London, the Queen Mother would invite Mrs Christianne Bell, the rector's widow, and other locals to dinner. She liked their quiet dignity, which was not at all subservient; they accepted their royal neighbour quite naturally. They were never intrusive so the Queen Mother could go shopping freely in Thurso, calling on Hattie Munro in her little antique shop or on grocer Hamish Cameron. He earned a royal warrant over the door. Thanks to the Queen Mother's house-parties, he would now happily stock more Veuve Clicquot than McEwan's Ale for the regulars.

Keen on local life, the Queen Mother always liked to get her copy of the *John o' Groats Journal* 'wherever I may be – at home or overseas', and she enjoyed stories about the paper's founder, the son of a Pultneytown fishcurer. The *Groat's* most illustrious reader called into the offices on the paper's 150th anniversary celebrations, looked at old back numbers, reminding the group around her that a bar of Fry's chocolate cost 2d in 1934, and was amused to read that a woman was fined seven shillings and sixpence for throwing out her rubbish at an 'untimeous hour' in 1886. 'We don't like litter,' she remarked, sailing from advertising to editorial. 'It's like one big family ... so nice to have everyone doing their own thing,' she remarked. If only those cheeky tabloids of the nineties could be more like the 'dear Groat'.

When the Queen Mother first wanted her hair done at the Castle of Mey, thirty-three year old hairdresser Malcolm Steven received a summons at his 'Northern Lights' salon in Wick's main street. Apprehensively he packed his brushes and scissors but did not use them. Instead he had 'a nice chat' with the Queen Mother, who occasionally, patting her grey curls, inquired casually if he knew anything about the Marcel wave. Well, young Malcolm had always loved the old movies of the twenties and thirties and could talk confidently about this dated technique.

Discreet and well-mannered, he passed the initial test and had an old-fashioned set of hot tongs to crimp her hair. He was summoned to Mey again and did such an effective soft Marcel wave that he was asked to travel to Balmoral when the Queen Mother joined the rest of the family after her summer break.

'She was a lovely lady with a very good head of hair,' he recalled. As he combed and brushed, they talked of flowers and gardening, a passion they shared. He was always a bit nervous but this pleased him because, in his forthright Scottish way, he said it prevented him from becoming too 'saucy'.

After the King's death the Queen, who had given her mother the use of Birkhall with all its sybaritic comforts, was puzzled by all the excitement about the little house called Mey. But in the way that families indulge the bereaved, shortly after the Queen Mother bought the Castle, the Queen and Prince Philip agreed to stop at the small fishing port of Scrabster on their family holiday cruise round the coast. They had some misgivings. The Queen loved Scotland too, but she hardly knew Caithness. On that first visit the weather, no respecter of royal visitors, was stormy, creating rough seas. But as if it was a Mediterranean day the Queen Mother, in a hat which magically did not fly off, waited serenely for her daughter and grandchildren to come ashore.

It was all low key. The Vyners were there, a few locals and a couple of corgis. The whole party, including Prince Philip's mother in her nun's veil and now quite deaf – she lived at the Palace with the Queen who was devoted to her – went to Mey for tea. This visit became a tradition each summer, with fires, and flares and fun, and from the Royal Yacht fireworks as mother and daughter said goodbye. The Queen Mother would go up to her bedroom to watch *Britannia*, splendid if slightly incongruous in that rough unfashionable harbour, plough out through the white surges of the Pentland Firth. Then, with a warm feeling, the Queen Mother would change for dinner.

In 1987 there was a departure from the routine and locals were pleasantly surprised to see the Queen stepping out of a green Land Rover to attend the modest Mey Games, a mini-version of the more famous and fashionable ones attended by the royal family at Braemar. The Queen has rarely looked so happy and relaxed, laughing at her mother's exultant urging on of the Castle team to win the tug o'war.

The Vyners left their House of the Northern Gates and moved from Caithness after the death of two of their children.

'It became so depressing. Every rock told a story; we had grown very fond of it,' the Commander said. Later as a widower (his wife died in 1980) he lived alone in a gabled house in the wilds of Ross-shire.

He relied on young New Zealanders and Australians to help on his farm. When the telephone rang a cheery, easy-going 'G'day' would often amuse the Queen Mother when checking on her old friend's health. 'Don't mix in those circles now – haven't got the right clothes, but always remember how good the food was at Clarence House,' the Commander recalled, the year before his death in a car accident near his home at the age of ninety-five.

In September, the Castle is always shut down and barred against winter storms. The gardener's wife, Jane Webster, will tidy away the picnic hampers, the rugs, the dog leads, wellingtons and walking sticks for another year. Outside her husband tries to stake down the enduring roses and shrubs.

The cannons on the wall stand sentinel through another winter. The Queen Mother was very taken with them and liked to tell guests how they were intended for use against Napoleon. Even Napoleon, her London friends would think, might have been chastened, not by the ancient cannons but by the weather.

A favourite time at Mey for the Queen Mother is spring, 'when the celandines are out and the salmon run'. In the garden, snowdrops and daffodils welcome her back and the little wood nearby grows bright with primroses and violets. Mey was her extravagance and she has always loved it for restoring her.

CHAPTER 19

Reaching for the Cream

After a tremulous, unwilling start, the Queen Mother returned to public life and became one of the most cherished members of the royal family.

Gone was her mood of despair, the feeling that at fifty-three her life was worthless. Even in this downcast mood, though, she had not cared for the idea of being just a Dowager Queen. Once her title had been satisfactorily established, she could shine in her own right and selflessly devote her life to her country.

What made her achievements all the more remarkable was that, by nature, the Queen Mother had been neither a doer nor a lark – in fact she had a tendency to a little self-indulgence. Unlike the Queen, she did not long to be out on the gallops at seven in the morning, preferring to stay in bed reading the racing pages.

Coming from a privileged pre-1914 background when women hardly ever worked, she was not by nature industrious and had to drive herself to be dutiful. On her desk there is a crystal triptych. Etched under 'Duties' is a foundation stone, a microphone and a speech. 'Pleasures' include a fishing rod and a book of poetry.

If there was a struggle with the sybaritic side of her nature, her conscience nagged and always won. Driven by some inner voice, she believed in filling Kipling's 'unforgiving minute' and this has been her mantra throughout life.

Her niece Lady Mary Clayton explained, 'She never gave way to personal feelings if they interfered with duty,' and she sent abrasive notes to herself. A private keepsake reminded her, 'Labour well the Minute Particulars, attend to the little one's.' Her niece said, 'She has the happy knack of a combined sense of fun and duty.'

The move to Clarence House had been painful, but quickly it became much more than an official residence and instead a royal home of exceptional charm. Inevitably she brought with her many treasures accumulated over the years at Buckingham Palace, all evidence of an appreciative eye and abiding passion for beautiful things.

As the Queen Mother settled in the Queen arranged for significant State visitors, like the Emperor of Japan, the Queen of Denmark or the President of the United States to call on her for tea. It was a clever way of keeping the Queen Mother involved in the monarchy.

These important guests were conducted along the corridors of Clarence House, lined with Brussels tapestries and cabinets of lustrous blue and white Hanover porcelain, before being ushered into 'the Presence'. Smiling, the Queen Mother welcomed them into the chandeliered Nash double drawing room with its Florentine busts and unfinished Landseer of a young Queen Victoria on horseback. They could check their punctuality by Louis Seize clocks and catch their reflections in decorative white and gold Rococo glasses before taking their seats on Chippendale. This interlude at Clarence House, seeing such exceptional furniture and paintings, was always memorable for visitors. In addition they had a charming, knowledgeable and hospitable guide.

To see the Queen Mother's own favourite paintings, especially her French Impressionists, guests are taken to the more informal morning room: Augustus John's portrait of George Bernard Shaw, *A View of Sandringham* by Prince Charles and Sickert's *A Lady in a Pink Ballgown Seated with a Gentleman in Green* over the chimneypiece. What made it so enjoyable was the sight of such a clutter of treasure in a private home. Here you find no minimalism – no single major work on a sterile white wall. Many paintings were propped against the walls awaiting a decision on where they should hang.

On private occasions, one might be invited to her sanctum, her eau-de-nil silk sitting room adorned with lots of laughing photographs of the royal family in oval frames on Sheraton tables or cherrywood stands made by her grandson, Lord Linley.

Free from Palace edicts, the Queen Mother indulged her fanciful taste and created for herself a green and gold Italianate bedroom. She always appreciated the elaborate Bacchanalian Renaissance carvings above her four-poster bed, saying, 'Rather a lot of pomegranates, don't you think?' This was where she could retreat, eat chocolates, read poetry or dream of winning the Derby.

Her own Household, 'my little family' she called them, was quickly installed. They began sifting through the invitations which came flooding in for her. It was advisable to send them a year ahead, to be expected with the Queen, but now her mother was in equally popular demand. If accepted, an aide and the Queen Mother's detective will do a 'recce', 'walk the course', check on the people to be presented and note the name of the child with the posy of flowers. People are often surprised how the royal family seem to remember names so easily and from years back, but the answer is great attention to detail.

A royal visit is meticulously timed but this always has been difficult with the Queen Mother, who happily ignores timetables and refuses to be hurried when there are 'real people' to meet.

No longer a decorative satellite of the King, she could set her own pace. Disregarding Palace advice, 'When visiting a hospital, you need only pause Ma'am at every third bed,' the Queen Mother would stop by every one. She did it her way, and people loved her for that and for her warmth. No respecter of royal guidelines, she changed the usual stiff intimidating atmosphere of royal visits. The trouble was that she thought of the whole population as her extended family and 'saw no danger as people surged towards her,' her Personal Protection Officer, Superintendent John Kirchin, explained.

Even in her very early royal days, when she was first married and going on few engagements, she was always natural, a smiling Duchess with no stiffness, so unlike straight-backed Queen Mary and her awkward daughter the Princess Royal. Towards a young mother, embarrassed because her child was howling, she was reassuring: 'I'd cry too if some strange woman stared at me when I'd just woken up.'

A man working his allotment heard a light voice at his elbow: it was the Chairman of the London Gardens Society advising, 'I always find horse manure is best for roses, don't you?' This spontaneity is not remarkable by today's standards but was refreshing royal behaviour half a century ago.

She had a rare gift of making everyone feel they were unique in her eyes. Joe Gormley, President of the National Union of Mineworkers from 1971-82 commented, 'When you are chatting together, you forget the social differences, me a miner, she a Queen.'

The real spark which would set off her tumultuously varied way of life was an invitation from the University of London to become their first woman Chancellor in 1955. In her Chancellor's robe of black silk damask trimmed with gold and a mortarboard with a bobbing gold tassel, the Queen Mother was popular with the students. She listened to their ideas, was impressed by the 'very big subjects' they were taking, shared their jug of wine, danced with them, understood their hopes and sympathised with their grievances.

They appreciated her humour, her calm and her wisdom, that she made time for them as well as the dons, her vitality and her keen sense of the ridiculous. When complimented on one of her hats and told, 'It looks lovely from the back, Ma'am,' the Queen Mother replied, 'I suppose I'll now have to walk backwards.'

In 1980 it was time to hand over. The students paid her a handsome tribute when they thanked her for 'all the joy you've given us'.

The precise letters which go out from Clarence House before engagements carry the advice, 'Yes, Her Majesty would appreciate the offer of a drink.' The Queen Mother is never averse to a restoring 'G and T', and this was another thing that makes her seem so human. Knowing the trouble taken before a royal engagement, she understands the nervous anticipation. On a visit to the Women's Institute at Sandringham when she was respectfully offered tea she replied, 'No, if you don't mind I'd like a drop of whatever that is hiding behind the curtain.'

It was always a flawless performance, whether awarding the 'best lettuce prize' at a country show or presenting the Dambusters, No. 617 Squadron of the RAF, with their original standard in 1959. Every engagement, no matter how small, is given the full effort.

She was hardly a supporter of feminism, yet in 1933 she became Patron of the Career Women's Advisory Service, believing that women who wanted to work needed a voice and support. Fifty years later on a cold November afternoon, she attended the Golden Jubilee celebrations in Russell Square, London. Some of the older women in subfusc outfits thawed visibly when their Patron arrived; she was the very antithesis of their own severe style. 'So lovely to be here.' She stood beaming in the doorway, dressed in purple velvet, long grey gloves with pearl buttons and grey high-heeled shoes to match. There were violets on her hat and diamonds in her ears and on her lapel. 'How good to see you all.'

'Are those lions eatable?' the Patron inquired as she cut the fiftieth anniversary cake decorated in gold lions with whiskers and bright eyes. 'Oh what a lovely cake!' It was as if she had never seen an iced cake before and the career women surrounding her, the architects, engineers and accountants, seemed to believe her. 'I've never seen anything so marvellous in all my life.'

Devoted as she was to her father-in-law, the Queen Mother never shared George V's view, 'Abroad is awful, I know because I've been there.' Remarkably modern and adventurous, long before the days when 747s made long-haul flights easy, the Queen Mother was the first member of the royal family to fly round the world.

'Incredible', she told Concorde pilot Captain Brian Walpole, who looked as proud as if he were carrying a planeful of Battle of Britain heroes, when he whisked the glittering octogenarian along the flight path on Concorde 001 Alpha Foxtrot in 1985. Sitting close to the controls, in chiffon and pearls, rather frivolous-looking in this functional interior, she watched the mach meter and when they broke the sound barrier continued with her salmon and strawberries. 'What a great thrill,' she said, reaching for the cream.

Her first trip abroad alone and as a widow was in the autumn of 1954 to the United States and Canada. The Americans were quite taken by the grace of the widowed Queen. At a banquet at the Waldorf Astoria she was presented with a gift in memory of George VI. She was remembered as 'a noble Queen, whose quiet and constant courage in time of great stress sustained a nation and inspired a world ...'

The late Mrs Rose Kennedy, matriarchal head of the Kennedy clan, who lived more years than perhaps she might have wished to see her son John F Kennedy become President of the United States and then be assassinated, and his brother Bobby also murdered, spoke movingly of the Queen Mother. 'I've met in my lifetime quite a number of great ladies. Queen Elizabeth the Queen Mother of England would be at the top of my list, anybody's list.'

In New York, the Queen Mother went sightseeing, visited several art galleries and shopped for souvenirs for the royal family. 'I'd like them to be very American,' she said emphatically to the assistant at FAO Schwartz on Fifth Avenue, 'I'm interested in toys for a six year old boy and a four year old girl.' She bought Prince Charles a steam shovel and Princess Anne a tea-set and chocolate drink mixer. Then to Saks, for jewelled cashmere sweaters for the Queen – size twelve – and Princess Margaret a size ten: 'I'm afraid I'm buying too much.' For Prince Philip there was a magnetic bottle opener and for The Royal Lodge a scrabble set on a turntable, always a favourite game.

Americans thought her like a southern belle and praised her extravagant, puffball dresses. Of course the Queen Mother played to this, nobody enjoys dressing for the grand occasions more. Well-remembered too was the moment when in diamanté-studded evening dress at a gala ball in her honour, head on one side, she asked the band to play 'Hernando's Hideaway', one of her favourite numbers. The merry widow got everyone to their feet.

A taxi driver who saw her arriving on Broadway to see *The Pajama Game* commented, 'If she wasn't a Queen there's many a man who'd like to marry her. She'd be a pleasing handful at playtime.' If you asked the Queen Mother what her secret was she would simply say: 'I love people.'

In Canada, they called her QE II. She loves Canada for its wholesome, decent values. The feeling is mutual and she was always rapturously received. In the summer of 1987, as Colonel-in-Chief of the Black Watch for now more than half a century, she went to Montreal for the 125th anniversary celebrations of its affiliate, Canada's Royal Highland Regiment. She was the first member of the royal family to visit Quebec for eleven years. The French Canadians were beguiled. The Queen Mother had been in hospital twice the previous year and there would have been no surprise if the visit, her tenth to Canada since 1939, had been cancelled.

Her procession sped like an American presidential cavalcade from Dorval Airfield into Montreal at rush hour. By 4.25 pm she was making her first speech, unruffled, serene, smiling, 'So lovely to be here.' Jet lag was for younger women.

For months the troops had drilled in preparation for the big day at Montreal's Molson Stadium and some nearly toppled over on the astroturf from fatigue. But they soon learnt a trick from their Colonel-in-Chief: the secret, she told them, was to spread the weight more evenly on the balls of the feet and not to use their heels.

Wilting briefly, the Queen Mother sat down for just a fraction of a second. It was a remarkable performance for an eighty-seven year old, standing for two and a half hours, attending three receptions, wading in to shake outstretched hands on walkabouts, handing out fifty-four awards and making three speeches in French. That evening she reassured a nervous young officer of the Regiment as he escorted her into dinner, 'I am sure everything will be splendid.'

'She's a great lady with a lot of courage,' remarked Frank Flory, an eighty-seven year old First World War veteran.

That summer in temperatures soaring above eighty-five degrees, the Queen Mother went to Berlin for celebrations marking the city's 750th anniversary. She apologised for her poor German but was moved when the mayor replied: 'Through your many years in the service of your people your presence has invariably been serene, good-humoured and optimistic ... You embody the continuity and all the charm of the British monarchy.' It took a foreigner to give the Queen Mother this sort of bouquet. It was what people at home felt about her but, naturally reticent found hard to express. Perhaps the simplest and best accolade is the warm 'The Queen Mum – God bless her', when her name is mentioned.

There have been so many memorable moments. As Colonel-in-Chief of the Irish Guards she liked to pop in on informal visits. Once on a chilly day she walked past a tall Guardsman who was snuffling and desperately trying to muffle a cough during a parade rehearsal. The Queen Mother looked in her handbag, fished out a cough sweet and popped it straight into his astonished mouth – a direct hit. Lord Kingsale who was in the Regiment at the time said: 'It was a marvellous moment. We all adored her.'

CHAPTER 20

Her Imperial Ostrich

Group Captain Peter Townsend was amusing, attentive and had a certain glamour. In 1953, the year following the King's death, the Queen Mother appointed him Comptroller of the Household at Clarence House. Married, the father of two boys, a former equerry of the King's and member of the royal Household, he appeared ideal. Princess Margaret dryly observed, 'My father became very fond of Peter. They both stammered and that was a bond.' In retrospect, it does not sound much of a compliment.

Self-deprecatingly, he made light of the heroism which had endeared him to George VI and now the widowed Queen Mother. A Battle of Britain fighter pilot, he liked to portray himself as a simple airman, who knew nothing much except how 'to pull back the throttle and zap a few Germans' during World War II. Yet he was a polished courtier and could also dance well which appealed to his new employer.

In royal circles, it is hard to get a balanced view about the romance between Princess Margaret and Townsend. There are those who still cannot forgive him for his audacity in even setting eyes on the King's younger daughter. When Prince Philip first heard about the relationship, he said, 'What cheek!' and added scathingly, 'Equerries should look after the horses.'

This was a classic case of a girl, not terribly mature or worldly-wise, attracted to a dashing, substitute father-figure. The Queen Mother, usually so solicitous and particularly close to the Princess, should have been aware of this growing infatuation. She was wrapped up in her own sorrow, which enveloped her and made her determined to lurk in the shadows and stay apart. Neither saw much of the preoccupied Queen.

Townsend claimed to be surprised that the Princess, 'so completely in love with life ... surrounded by friends who were both eligible and available', should have turned to him, but the Princess was aware of her love for Townsend long before it was reciprocated. He was quite unlike landowning aristocrats. With his slight figure, greying hair, he had a touch of the Leslie Howard matinee idol. He did find her receptive, and said that more than anyone else she knew how to make him laugh. She was also rather beautiful.

The Princess was not interested in any of the eminently suitable Establishment admirers, not even in that civilised brace, the Earl of Dalkeith and Cohn Tennant, who later became Lord Glenconner. He would give the Princess land in Mustique, an island he owned in the West Indies. As a wedding present he built a house for her, Les Jolies Eaux. It cost £250,000, and became a special refuge for her. He remained an exceptional friend.

It was not until they were left alone one afternoon in the red drawing room at Windsor Castle in the spring of 1953 that Townsend declared his love for the Princess. Freshly divorced, his wife Rosemary had been given custody of their sons, Giles, eleven and Hugo, aged eight. Two months later Rosemary married John de Lazlo, whose father Philip was a distinguished portrait painter.

Townsend and Margaret now spent time together in the royal homes at Birkhall, The Royal Lodge and Clarence House, riding out in the mornings through the woods at Windsor Great Park. There never was any real privacy, however, and watchful eyes were everywhere. 'Poor dears,' Noel Coward remarked later, 'I hope they had the sense to leap into bed a couple of times at least.'

Townsend recalled the Princess' love as 'dazzling as well as devouring' in those early days. She once demanded that he should carry her up the stairs at Clarence House. He demurred. What if the Queen Mother appeared on the landing? No excuses were accepted. 'Peter, this is a royal order.' Townsend obeyed.

Although loving her daughters deeply, the Queen Mother in her continuing mood of unhappy introspection failed to notice how a sorrowing Princess Margaret suddenly seemed buoyant and positively glowing. There were other things on her mind; this was Coronation year and besides she was absorbed in the restoration of the Castle of Mey – as demanding as any wilful daughter.

Once she knew about the romance, her first reaction was one of incredulity. Much as she liked a Townsend, the Queen Mother felt this could never have happened in the King's lifetime and that he would not have approved of such a marriage. Her daughter's besottedness with this divorced member of her Household, who was not even aristocratic, was too nightmarish and made her miss the King even more.

As always she was caring and understanding, but her hope was that if she did not make a fuss or take any notice, the problem would go away, resolve itself. She was displaying what Sir Alan 'Tommy' Lascelles, Private Secretary to the Queen and before that the King, contemptuously referred to as 'Her Imperial Ostrich stance', unwilling to act as many mothers might have done, even if it meant losing a daughter's love temporarily. Her way has always been one of gentle non-interference. Lord Charteris once said of her, 'What she doesn't want to see, she doesn't look at.'

Was she indifferent or just wrapped up in her own grief? The King's death had undoubtedly altered her; from now on she would gracefully sidestep anything unpalatable while remaining ineffably solicitous.

At the Coronation on 2nd June 1933, Princess Margaret had never looked better, 'superb, sparkling, ravishing', Townsend thought. Afterwards, joining him, she picked a piece of fluff off his uniform, a stray feather perhaps from some passing plume. This possessive gesture alerted the world's media and the ill-fated couple became the focus of insatiable attention.

There was no point in issuing a denial, it was too late. The secret was out. 'You must be mad or bad' was the splenetic splutter of Lascelles when Townsend told him about his hope of marrying the Princess. Princess Margaret always countered: 'Had he said we couldn't get married, we wouldn't have thought any more about it.' Lascelles never cared much for the Princess but was devoted to the Queen.

The problem for the Queen was that, as Governor of the Church of England and Defender of the Faith, although she longed for her sister's happiness, she could not consent to her marrying someone divorced. They had a bitter exchange.

Princess Margaret would complain: 'Nobody bothered to explain anything to us.' No one took the trouble to point out that the Royal Marriages Act of 1772 demanded the sovereign's consent if the prince or princess was under twenty-five.

Instead of talking to the couple and making the Queen's position clear, the immediate reaction amongst the elderly Palace advisers was to get rid of Townsend for a few years. Things had gone far enough, 'get the fellow out of the country.' At first he thought they were joking – this was almost medieval. Townsend had a choice: deportation to Singapore, Johannesburg or Brussels.

'It was a hefty come-down after the commands I had previously held in the RAF and my nine years in the royal Household,' was Townsend's reaction to these unattractive options. He chose to become Air Attaché in Brussels. The Palace mandarins' solution had the ruthlessness of a Tudor court. They saw Townsend as a bit of a bounder who had had the temerity to fall in love with a King's daughter. 'Booted out of England', he took up what he considered 'an obsolescent post' which virtually finished his RAF career.

Like two fairly innocent lambs, neither Townsend nor the Princess had any say in their destiny. They believed the sentence of exile, though 'harsh', would last only a year. At this stage their relationship was far from over.

The Queen Mother always loved Rhodesia, and on 30th June 1953 was relieved to go there on a sixteen-day tour, with a reluctant Princess Margaret who hated it. The 1,500 miles by road and train were therapeutic for the mother, traumatic for the daughter. The Queen Mother's legendary calm and good nature eased some of the emotional tension, as she waved from the train to Gwelo and looked up at the triumphal arches which proclaimed: 'Greeting great White Queen and great White Princess'.

On a bright morning in Umtali, on a sightseeing tour high in the Vumba mountains, the Princess heard that Townsend had been told to leave England before their return on 15th July. She collapsed with 'flu and had to be flown to Salisbury immediately.

That autumn, on 22nd October 1953, Princess Margaret went to stay with the Queen and Prince Philip at Windsor Castle and after hours of talking and in a state of 'great distress', she telephoned Townsend, 'the loneliest man in Brussels'. They both, without saying anything, knew the relationship was over.

The Princess then went to see the Archbishop of Canterbury at Lambeth Palace and with historic words which still move romantics, spoke to him calmly: 'You can put away your books Archbishop, I am not going to marry Peter Townsend. I wanted you to know first.'

Dr Fisher, everyone's idea of an Archbishop with his white hair and aquiline features, was clearly relieved at no longer having to find a loophole that would enable the couple to wed. 'What a wonderful person the Holy Spirit is,' he declared. The Princess looked suitably nonplussed.

Retreating to The Royal Lodge she found refuge in the unquestioning, warm protectiveness of a mother who did not once say, 'I told you so.' There were never any recriminations.

'The Queen Mother,' Townsend recalled, 'was always wonderful, always there being kind,' and he 'blessed her for her exquisite tact,' when she left the couple alone in her sitting room at Clarence House for a few last moments to say goodbye.

Long after Peter Townsend and Princess Margaret broke up and were married to other people, the Queen Mother met him at a reunion of HMS *Vanguard* in 1976, the ship which had taken the royal family to South Africa. 'Hello Peter,' she beamed with her head one side, wagging her finger at him in the way she did when the band struck up. 'It had always been her signal that she wanted to dance the hokey-cokey,' he recalled with a smile in Paris years afterwards. For the Queen Mother it was as if nothing had happened in the intervening years.

Together, the unhappy couple, weary and devastated by the wrangling of Church, Parliament and public opinion, worked on a statement at Clarence House. 'There was a wonderful tenderness in her eyes,' Townsend recalled – neither could admit that they both felt a sense of relief.

To this day there are those who could forgive Princess Margaret anything, recalling her grace and how, like a tragic Donizetti heroine, she lost her love. 'Ah poor Margaret,' they will say and forgive her occasional *grande dame* moodiness, her Hanoverian hauteur, 'what a sad life.'

Not really; she has a tremendous sense of her own history and has always loved being royal. 'I can't imagine anything more wonderful than being who I am.' The family think she has survived 'marvellously well'.

However in October 1959, a letter to the Princess from Townsend explaining how he was to marry Marie-Luce Jamagne, a Belgian girl from a rich family was an emotional betrayal. Their secret understanding about not remarrying no longer held, snapping a thread which for too long held the Princess in an unsuitable love.

Princess Margaret has never been sure how she would have coped as Mrs Townsend, with a couple of step-children and not much money. Once the chemistry had waned, it might have been a pedestrian lifestyle for a King's daughter who knew no life except that of being royal.

Years later, talking about his life at his home in Paris, Townsend did not give the impression of a man heartbroken because he had been unable to marry the Princess. His wife Marie-Luce, a taller, slender version of Princess Margaret, had model chic. It was a happy marriage and they had three children, two girls and a boy.

Townsend had lunch with the Princess at Kensington Palace three years before his death from stomach cancer in June 1995. He asked that his ashes be scattered in France, but 'if the wind, the south wind on which the swallows ride, blows them on towards England, then let it be, I shall never know or care.' France had become his real home.

Years later, the Queen Mother and Princess Margaret burnt papers and letters – some relating to Townsend, others to the Abdication and some from the Princess of Wales when she was unhappy in her marriage. A picture emerges of mother and daughter sat by a fire at The Royal Lodge, Windsor, sifting through letters, now smiling, now nostalgic. But they were ruthless in this emotional cull of papers too personal to be left to the nation, and were deaf to the pleas of historians who bitterly lamented the loss.

Princess Margaret became secretly engaged in December 1959 to Anthony Armstrong-Jones, that 'nice young man', the Queen Mother said, who had taken such charming photographs of her daughter for her 29th birthday. Both were thirty when Armstrong-Jones proposed to the girl he called 'my pet' or 'ducky'.

'I'm so pleased you are going to marry Margaret,' the Queen Mother told the young man. 'Sssh, I haven't asked the Queen,' replied the well-mannered photographer. The Queen, who was now expecting her third child, Prince Andrew, to be born in 1960, liked 'Tony' from the start. He may have been happier looking into a lens than along the barrel of a shotgun on the grouse moors but she liked his work. She was particularly appreciative of his discretion when the marriage ended in divorce.

Antony Armstrong-Jones was talented and witty. Princess Margaret was now being introduced to a new bohemian way of life and the Queen Mother was invited to the couple's hideout in Rotherhithe, where they cooked for her and took her on expeditions round the East End, playing at being 'Ordinary'. Sometimes the couple raced around on a motorbike and ate in Chelsea bistros.

The Queen Mother had much more fun with this son-in-law than Prince Philip, whom she liked but treated with caution. Once, invited by Armstrong-Jones to visit a weekend country cottage he was restoring, and not above a bit of self-mockery, she performed a send-up of an opening ceremony with a plastic bucket on her head as a crown.

On Friday, 6th May 1960, their wedding day, there was an enormous fund of goodwill for the Princess, who wore a 'ravishing' romantic white silk organza dress and diamond tiara. By October 1961 Princess Margaret's husband had earned a title and became the first Earl of Snowdon, Viscount Linley of Nymans.

In the beginning, a friend recalled, 'They couldn't keep their hands off each other, even with other people there, it was a terribly physical relationship.' The marriage was genuinely good for about four years. It liberated the Princess from the horsey world and she met a mixture of raffish, creative people in the theatre and the ballet. New friends would include the Irish writer Edna O'Brien, Derek Hart, an entertaining television presenter, Rudolf Nureyev the ballet dancer, actor Peter Sellers and the other Goons.

There were two children, adored by both parents. Viscount Linley – christened David in the Music Room at Buckingham Palace – was born at 10.45 am on Friday, 3rd November 1961, and Lady Sarah Armstrong-Jones on 1st May 1964. Then things began to go wrong for 'Tone' and 'Pet' as they called each other. Lord Snowdon began to spend more time abroad concentrating on his work. The Princess' moods would swing from throaty laughter to petulance, sometimes imperious and at other times emotionally vulnerable and bewildered, consoling herself with flirtations with mutual friends.

The Queen Mother was distressed and wept when she told her Household at Clarence House that Princess Margaret and Lord Snowdon were parting. The eighteen-year marriage ended in divorce in May 1978. Princess Margaret told friends it was 'the saddest thing that ever happened to me'.

Whatever their peccadilloes, both Princess Margaret and Snowdon were excellent parents. Viscount Linley had a successful furniture shop in Pimlico and recalled that he and his sister Lady Sarah, who is married to Daniel Chatto and has two children, had the happiest childhood memories. They were never aware of any tension, just parties, lots of laughs and innovative games designed by their father.

The following December, Snowdon married a grave, slow-to-smile girl with long dark hair, Lucy Lindsay Hogg, who worked in television. Their only child, Lady Frances Armstrong-Jones, was born at midnight on 17th July, 1979. Princess Margaret would refer disparagingly to the new Countess Snowdon as 'that thing'. The Princess openly said, 'I'm no angel and I'm not Bo-Peep either.' She was wretched and unhappy. The Queen Mother eventually persuaded her daughter to consult Andrew Stringer, a psychiatrist.

Princess Margaret's dalliance with a man fifteen years younger than herself, twenty-eight year old Roddy Llewellyn, raised eyebrows from Windsor Castle to Balmoral. 'He seems a nice boy,' the Queen Mother said, as if they were a couple of teenagers, and waited serenely for this phase to pass. She found the attentive young market gardener, son of the late Colonel Harry Llewellyn of 'dear Foxhunter' fame, pleasant enough. The Princess indulged him and bought him underpants with a Union Jack design; she made him a collage which included a bow tie, a feather, a moth and a Dinky Toy. She took him to Mustique where they were photographed on the beach, knee to knee.

But he would be the subject of another row with the Queen. Princess Margaret said she only ever had two arguments with her sister. 'These were probably both about men,' she said with regret.

There was no question of marriage. When Roddy told her he was engaged to an interior designer, Tanya Soskin, the Princess looked relieved and, rolling her eyes, remarked in her eighteenth-century actressy voice: 'I am really very happy for him; anyway I couldn't have afforded him much longer.' The importance of the relationship was exaggerated, a friend suggested. 'Roddy and Margaret went beddy byes once or twice but it wasn't a huge success.'

Lord Snowdon and his fifty-seven year old second wife parted in April 1999. The Countess moved out of their £2 million house in Kensington saying, 'every marriage has its hiccups ... We have suffered from them.' Blame for the break-up was attributed partly to the suicide of Ann Hills, a former girlfriend of Lord Snowdon's. A highly regarded journalist, she killed herself on New Year's Eve 1996 after a relationship with Snowdon had ended. A service was held at the Royal Geographical Society in London where her two young sons welcomed friends and remembered their mother with readings and music.

The Earl, who had always fended off interest in his private life, was further embarrassed at the age of sixty-eight, when it was revealed that another girlfriend, thirty-five year old Melanie Cable-Alexander, who worked for *Country Life*, had given birth on 30th April 1998 to 'a son, Jasper'.

Yet his attachment to Princess Margaret never wavered and his concern for her was in no doubt when she was rushed back to England from Mustique in March 1998 suffering from her first stroke.

The following year, the Princess decided to hand over Les Jolies Eaux to Viscount Linley, now married to Lady Serena Stanhope, the fashion-conscious daughter of an Irish peer. Inviting her son and his wife and a group of special friends to accompany her, the Princess returned to Mustique for a nostalgic visit.

The island no longer seemed lucky for her. Burning the soles of her feet in scalding bath water, the Princess had to be flown back to England, where she was bedridden for several weeks and then needed a wheelchair.

In November 1999 she collapsed again, this time at her apartments in Kensington Palace. The possibility of this being a second stroke, the Princess felt, was unfair since she had been following a spartan regime, drinking only lemon barley water and no longer enjoying sixty cigarettes a day. A practising Anglican, she quoted the Prayer Book to describe her new frugality as 'godly, righteous and sober'. It had been no defence against the body's unpredictability.

The Princess became noticeably slow-moving and subject to bouts of depression; she decided to give up nearly all public engagements. The Linleys were enjoying the arrival of their first child, Charles Patrick Inigo Armstrong-Jones, and put Les Jolies Eaux on the market for £3 million. They bought themselves a handsome property in the South of France.

Although frail, Princess Margaret attended the christening of their five month old son at the Queen's Chapel, St James' Palace in December 1999. It was the Queen Mother who bounced this alert, newest addition to the royal family on her lap. The infant, 13th in line to the throne, clung to the hand of his ailing grandmother as they posed for a four-generation family portrait.

The Princess was determined not to allow ill-health to keep her from the long-awaited gala opening of the restored Royal Opera House in Covent Garden. As President of the Royal Ballet, she insisted on accompanying the Queen and the Queen Mother in December 1999 to one of the capital's starry occasions. The flamboyant, youthful energy of the dancers seemed poignantly to highlight the Princess' frailty and her mother's age, when both had been glamorous and vibrant at an earlier re-opening of the Opera House after the war.

Princess Margaret is philosophical about adjusting to a gentler pace and cutting down on foreign travel, but she was disappointed when she was not allowed to travel to Jamaica to unveil a statue of Sir Noel Coward. When 'The Master', who would have been a hundred on 16th December 1999, had heard the Princess' throaty rendering of 'You Can't Chop Your Momma Up in Massachusetts' he was charmed.

The Princess thinks it unlikely now that she will ever travel on a London bus. It has been a lifelong ambition, but her doctors are dismayed at the prospect of the Princess clinging to the bar of a red double-decker as it hurtles round Hyde Park Corner.

Although she is content to be enveloped by the royal family, her children worry about her being alone and wonder if she should have remarried. There was no scarcity of admirers. As she sponges down the leaves of her camellias at Kensington Palace, the Princess laughs at their anxieties: 'Don't be so ridiculous, old ladies do not get married again.'

Enjoying her own company more, listening to music and reading biographies, the Princess still entertains and loves to line-dance. When in the mood there remains a hint of that old defiant glamour and those blue eyes can still be mesmeric.

CHAPTER 21

The Jewel Pool

Coming from an old aristocratic family and used to jewels, Elizabeth was not acquisitive when she became Queen. Her parents, the Earl and Countess of Strathmore, abhorred any form of flamboyance. It had been typical of the Countess to insist on a modest arch of rosy apples when her son, Michael Bowes-Lyon, married Elizabeth Cator in 1928 at St George's Chapel.

As a child, Elizabeth had worn a coral and seed pearl necklace. Then she graduated to pearls, the standby of generations of well-born or aspiring Englishwomen. In the 1920s the swing away from high, lacy, majestic Edwardian clothes to flapperish long-waisted, pleated dresses suited her unshowy style, which she usually complemented with a string of matchless milky pearls.

For her wedding she wore very little jewellery, just a single row of pearls and orange blossom in her hair. But like every other royal bride, becoming one of the King's daughters-in-law had entitled her to access to suites of diamonds, rubies, emeralds and sapphires, undreamt-of treasure. As Queen, important royal heirlooms, rings with romantic messages – 'Toujours chère', aigrettes, stomachers, bijoux, *bien placé* ornaments for the bosom, tiaras and necklaces cascaded into her modest Scottish jewel box, but on the strict understanding that they were on loan from the Crown.

It was fairytale stuff for this level-headed girl from the Grampians. Her wedding presents included a long amethyst and pearl heart necklace set in brilliants from Queen Alexandra and, from a doting George V, a turquoise and diamond suite;

Queen Mary, not to be left out, gave her sapphires and diamonds. Her husband, the Duke of York, gave her a diamond and pearl necklace and diamond floral bouquet brooch. Almost as precious to the bride as 'Bertie's' brooch and other impressive royal gifts was the diamond circlet of flowers and leaves given to her by her father as part of her trousseau. Its delicacy suited her well, sitting becomingly on her curly brown hair.

Soon after the wedding, the Duchess was spotted at the theatre absolutely '... sparkling ... her wrists twinkling with diamonds'. The Duke continued to buy her jewelled love tokens. Knowing his wife's fondness for flowers, he instructed Cartier in 1928 to design her a leaf brooch. Studded with emeralds, sapphires, amethysts and a ruby, a convincing diamond vein ran down the centre of the leaf. In her early married life, the Duchess liked to wear these flower brooches pinned on her cloche hats.

When King George V died, Queen Mary remained custodian of the royal jewels, a happy task for a zealous collector. Had the new King been married, the jewels would have passed to his Queen Consort. But Edward VIII was besotted by twice-divorced American Mrs Simpson, who had a penchant for glamorous jewellery.

Tut-tutting about her son 'David's' infatuation, Queen Mary's unspoken fear was that the best of the royal heritage could easily be spirited away to the New World by the 'ghastly American'. The Dowager Queen had already lost weight, a stone during the Abdication crisis. Now she felt the urgent need to catalogue the 'Crown' jewellery. By nature she was methodical and loved listing furniture, her porcelain, and now the royal jewels.

No matter how proprietorial an eye she kept on the royal jewels from her eyrie in Clarence House, nothing could have stopped the King lavishing some of the treasure on Mrs Simpson. When designing some of the more spectacular pieces for her, Alexandre at Van Cleef & Arpels recalled how the King would arrive with 'pockets full of gems', mouth-watering yellow diamonds, rubies and emeralds, gifts from Indian maharajas, African potentates, a 'grateful people' in the colonies, all in homage to their King Emperor.

This could not happen today when every gift received on royal tours is meticulously catalogued and put in the 'jewel pool'. During his brief reign, Edward VIII commissioned a great deal of bold un-English jewellery: lolling panthers, birds with long tails studded with brilliants and serpent necklaces. He obviously saw Mrs Simpson as an exotic creature. Her cabochon emeralds, her rubies, canary diamonds and suites of sapphires, were outrageously big, the size of carbuncles. Rivals admired them but declared hopefully that they must be fake 'dressmaker's jewels'. Mrs Simpson enraged them further with quips about the 'Wallis Collection'.

All this was very different from the Duchess of York's pearly demureness; Wallis liked gentle aquamarines, but in common with her *bête noire*, she had a penchant for platinum and Elizabeth quite liked rubies too.

After the Abdication, with a new King and Queen on the throne, there still was a reluctance to hand over all the 'Crown' gems. The implicit suggestion was that Queen Mary was not passing on to her 'darling daughter-in-law' all the royal treasure to which she was entitled but keeping back some of Queen Alexandra's jewels and her own Indian collection.

One of the great royal foreign tours was the Delhi Durbar in 1911, when George V and Queen Mary were given an enchanting reception in India and the princes showered them with jewels. In one state alone, received by the libidinous Maharajah of Patiala's wife, the Queen Empress was presented with 'a large square of emeralds ... engraved and set in diamonds, and a necklace and pendant of emeralds, set in rosettes of diamonds'. Queen Mary particularly liked the message read out by the Maharani explaining that while the ladies lived in purdah, they were no strangers 'to that mighty process of evolution which manifests itself beyond the limits of its four walls'.

'Felt very sad at parting,' Queen Mary, a real connoisseur, lamented that the jewels in her appreciative care since 1910 were handed on eventually to the new Queen. Despite her great affection for her daughter-in-law, the theory is that the Dowager Queen simply 'bagged all the best bits for herself,' according to Lady Pamela Berry, an observant political hostess.

As Queen Consort, Elizabeth was not about to challenge her formidable mother-in-law's inventory. She could not know to how much she was entitled, so was hardly bothered by the apparent sparseness of her cache of royal jewels. A few years later however, when asked if she could put on as much jewellery as possible for a formal portrait, the Queen said with a knowing smile: 'The choice isn't very great, you know.' This was not strictly true. Even if Queen Mary did temporarily salt away some of the royal jewellery from Crown possessions, fearing that it might end up gracing an unsuitable X-Ray thin throat, Queen Elizabeth still inherited a handsome collection.

For the Coronation, she wore the great Koh-i-Noor diamond. Apprehensive beforehand, stunned by the 'intolerable honour of monarchy', the Queen wept but admitted afterwards that she had felt an extraordinary calm when the brilliant Regal Tiara holding the 'Mountain of Light' diamond was placed on her head.

Elizabeth had her ears pierced for the Coronation in order to accommodate a pair of drop earrings from the royal collection. She has always loved earrings – usually pearl and diamond and preferably flower-shaped.

After the Coronation, her style became confident and elaborate. Chips Channon was impressed by her at a ball at Windsor, 'a vision in white satin wearing pearls and rubies'. Gone was her *jeune fille* fringe, and with it the end of carefree days. Had Queen Victoria been alive, it would have been compulsory to get rid of it: fringes she considered 'frightful' and thought they made girls look 'like poodles'.

Under a crown or a tiara, the Queen wore her hair off her forehead, sometimes with a centre parting. The public must always be able to see the Queen's face. But she wore diamond flower bandeaux low on her forehead and flower and star-shaped jewelled clips in her hair. All this was quite different from her days as a debutante, when she liked to put fresh flowers in her hair.

Elaborate tiaras were still being worn at the Palace for receptions, banquets, balls and even dinners. Edward VII rebuked Consuelo, Duchess of Marlborough, for wearing a pretty but inadequately formal diamond crescent instead of a tiara at a dinner for the Prince and Princess of Wales. King Edward, normally more fun than many of the royals, asked her crossly, 'The Princess has taken the trouble to wear a tiara, why have you not done so?' The Duchess answered quickly that she had been delayed in the country and the bank had been shut by the time she got to London. Gradually tiaras spent more time in the bank in the increasingly harsh economic climate of the late Twenties, but in royal circles they have never lost their lustre.

Always fond of tiaras, a sign of her approaching recovery after the King's death was the Queen Mother's order for a new tiara from Cartier in 1953. It was surprisingly modern and made from South African diamonds given to Edward VII in 1901. Elizabeth was the first Queen Consort to perch a tiara directly on her hair, rather than use her predecessors' method of weaving ornaments into great dry wodges of false hair. For 'grand dressing' the Queen often chose Queen Victoria's diamond fringe tiara, as seen in a Winterhalter painting. This charming sunray of diamonds made in 1830 from stones belonging to George III was versatile, since it doubled as a necklace. A lucky symbol, it was worn by the present Queen for her wedding in 1947, though it snapped hours beforehand. Princess Anne wore it too for her first marriage in 1973 when she was one of the more stunning and tiny-waisted royal brides.

The responsibility of wearing such treasure seemed not to daunt young, high-spirited royal women who thought them decorative but cumbersome. Princess Marina, the Duchess of Kent, thought them 'a nuisance, far too heavy and out of keeping with the times'. Once, when King George V and Queen Mary had retired to bed, the Duchess handed her tiara to bandleader Tommy Kinsman, who put it on the piano so she could dance unencumbered for the rest of the night.

As Queen Consort, Elizabeth really enjoyed royal jewellery 'just to sparkle' and without any spine-tingling sense of royal ancestry which burdened women of royal blood. Nor was she overawed by the grandeur of the royal collection: the great stomachers stretching from bust to waist or the heavily ornate armlets, but she was greatly relieved she was not expected to wear Queen Victoria's Emerald Girdle made from Ranji

Singh's horse trappings. It is Queen Victoria's Regal Indian Tiara with its 2,678 diamonds in flower and ruby setting which has long been one of the few pieces of jewellery she really cherishes.

Less is best is not one of her maxims. A three-strand pearl necklace held with a ruby clasp; large pearl earrings and diamond brooch would be her idea of low-key dressing for lunch.

In common with other royal women, the Queen Mother loves brooches and three enduring favourites which are seen regularly are Queen Alexandra's flirty Victoria tassel brooch, Queen Victoria's diamond bow brooch (a wedding present from her beloved Albert) and Victoria's Jubilee pearl and diamond brooch given to her by her Household in 1897. A replica of 'Albert's brooch' – made for one of his daughters – is dearly loved by the Princess Royal today.

Some of the Queen Mother's impressive jewellery has come not from the royal vaults, but from Mrs Ronnie Greville. Famous for her intimate dinner parties (never more than forty guests) the fashionable sneered at her vulgarity as she presided in her jewels and black lace – but they flocked to her table.

Mrs Greville had lent her home, Polesden Lacey, to the Duke and Duchess of York for their honeymoon and she had been very supportive at the time of the Abdication. She was a shrewd judge of character and the Queen always liked her. Upon her death in 1942 Mrs Greville left all her jewellery to the Queen: her Marie Antoinette diamond necklace, her magnificent pearls, a diamond ring shaped like a playing card and a spectacular set of rubies, all 'with my loving thoughts'. As this was a personal legacy these do not have to be put back in the royal coffers, already quite full enough anyway to cope with the needs of the next couple of generations.

As she got older, the Queen Mother had a plumpness that enabled her to wear jewellery better perhaps than some of the more craggy older royal women. Although she is only five foot two, Queen Alexandra's festoon necklace with teardrop pearls sits so well it might have been specially commissioned for her. It was Queen Alexandra who helped inspire her love of Fabergé. An aunt of Nicholas II, last Tsar of All the Russias whose mother Dagmar was her sister, Alexandra brought a number of these charming Russian porcelain boxes and jewelled Easter eggs to England. The Queen Mother has one of the best collections of Fabergé in this country. Some of the pieces were found at Wartski's, one of her favourite jewellers, imported to the West after the fall of the Romanovs. These days she turns to Halycon Days for eighteenth-century style enamel boxes with personalized messages.

Neither the Queen Mother nor her daughter ever felt the need to have their jewels reset and modernised. 'Things were very nicely done in Papa's time,' the Queen likes to say, echoing her mother's faint distaste at too much preoccupation with jewellery. They would both have been appalled if their husbands had presented them with the 'panthers rampant', tiger lorgnettes, frog bangles with ruby eyes or crouching snails of the type so enjoyed by the Duchess of Windsor.

When George VI died, the Queen Mother passed on all the Crown jewellery to her daughter, the new Queen, then twenty five years old, except for one royal heirloom she has always loved, the Regal Indian Tiara. As Queen she did have it altered slightly in 1937, adding an extra row of pearls to a diadem studded with clusters of diamonds to symbolise the thistle of Scotland, the rose of England and the Irish shamrock.

The present Queen is happy to let her mother go on enjoying her great-great-great grandmother's tiara for the rest of her life. 'Mummie,' she says, 'will give it back one day.' Few things are so certain.

16. As the King was being crowned on 12th May 1938, the Queen prayed that he would be granted 'not a lighter load, but a stronger back'. Here the newly crowned King and Queen pose with the Princesses with quiet assurance.

17. Even with the traumatic move to Buckingham Palace, the King and Queen and the Princesses remained a close, happy family and their dogs were an important part of their relaxation.

18. There was nothing the Queen Mother liked more than cheering up the elderly, although at ninety-eight she was probably older than most of the chairbound group here.

19. Two of the young royal cousins, Zara Phillips and Prince William, with fair good looks, appear uncomplicated and not too scarred by the divorces of their parents. Seen here with Prince Charles and their great-grandmother at her ninety-eighth birthday celebrations, Zara Phillips hides the diamond in her tongue, fashionable maybe but not a way of wearing jewellery the Queen Mother could quite understand.

20. It was fondly believed that the Queen Mother had helped Diana, Princess of Wales in the early days of her marriage. But rumours of this friendship have been greatly exaggerated. The Queen Mother, dismayed by the Princess' refusal to conform to the Palace dictates, thought her too wayward for a royal wife. The Princess treated the Queen Mother warily.

21. Black has always suited royal women, but it is a colour they rarely wear. The Queen Mother on Remembrance Day enhances it with a red poppy and diamond brooch.

22. The Queen Mother has a way of outshining those younger than herself. In eye-catching shimmering chiffon with Princess Margaret a few paces behind, the Queen Mother smiles at the cameras before going in to a charity gala at the London Palladium in 1990 in honour of her ninetieth birthday.

23. The Irish Guards and their Irish Wolfhound mascot have always had a special place in the Queen Mother's heart. On St Patrick's Day, 1995, she distributed shamrocks to the 1st Battalion Irish Guards at London's Chelsea Barracks and Cuchulain, the Irish Wolfhound, seems confident that the Colonel in Chief may have some Good Boy choc drops in her handbag.

24. The Queen always gives a special bow to her Mother at Trooping the Colour. The Queen Mother seen here with Princess Margaret will say with pride: 'My daughter, the Queen you know, isn't it exciting?'

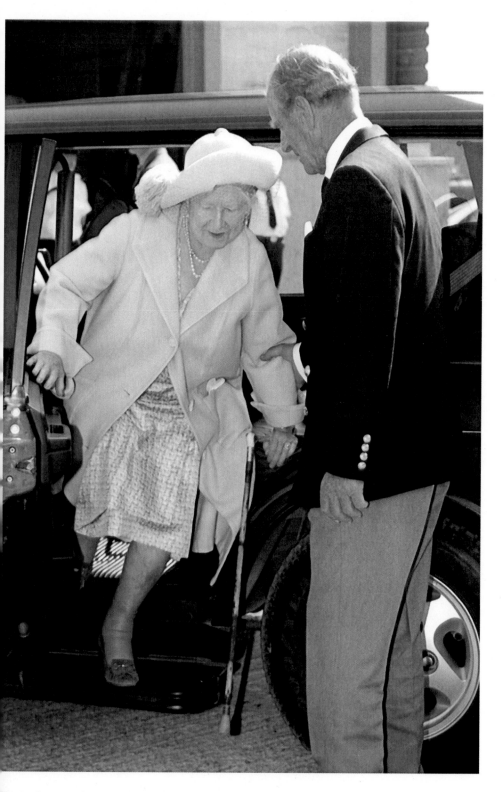

25. Scrabster Harbour was the port for the Castle of Mey. When they had the Royal Yacht Britannia, the Queen and Prince Philip visited Mey every summer although they thought the Caithness countryside rather rugged. The Queen Mother and Prince Philip are fond of each other, although she thinks him too abrasive and he finds his mother-in-law a bit frivolous.

CHAPTER 22

A Beleaguered Royal Family

Grief in the royal family is intensely private, even amongst one another. Emotion is an unwelcome visitor. The family were at Balmoral when Diana, Princess of Wales, was killed in the early hours of 31st August 1997. The thirty-six year old Princess had been in a speeding S-280 Mercedes when it crashed in the Pont de l'Alma tunnel in Paris. Her latest companion, Dodi Al Fayed, was killed too, and also the chauffeur.

Prince William and Prince Harry were told the news by their father, Prince Charles, at quarter past seven in the morning. Hours later and at Prince William's request, they joined the Queen Mother and royal family for the usual eleven o'clock service at Crathie Church. The vicar, Robert Sloane, had not been instructed to change the service in any way, so he talked about moving house and threw in a few Billy Connolly jokes, rather painful for the princes who would shortly be moving out of Kensington Palace, the home they had shared with their mother. Stiff-necked, adhering to routine, the Queen and royal family appeared to be insulating themselves from the momentum of the tragedy.

With her enviable ability to create a protective canopy, the Queen Mother instructed her servants that morning to turn off the television sets for fear the continuous news about the Princess' death would upset her house guests. But there was no hiding from the pain of those she loved. The young princes had lost a spectacular mother, and Prince Charles anguished over the wife he had never been able to love. The Queen's usual imperturbability was visibly shaken, although this daughter-in-law had herself created unimaginable waves for the royal family in her lifetime.

In those still, end-of-summer days, the world reverberated with a sense of loss even greater than that following President Kennedy's assassination in 1963.

Millions mourned, but at the time it did not seem mawkish. Young men with shaven heads and explicit T-shirts, grannies, office workers, actors, young families, diplomats, the disabled and the famous stood together, silently, motionless outside Kensington Palace and Buckingham Palace, where people had pinned favourite teddies to the railings.

Londoners became gentler; strangers helped each other, sharing flasks of tea and coffee; some had travelled huge distances to keep candlelit vigils. A young policewoman broke down and cried on duty. Commentators, especially Americans, found it refreshingly unlike the 'Olde England of the stiff upper lip'.

Emotional messages were scrawled on bunches of flowers for a caring Princess who had moved them. Her gaiety had made them laugh and her beauty had brightened their lives. A minority found this 'mob sentimentality' distasteful, disliking the huge wave of emotion now sweeping over a normally phlegmatic country. 'Queen of Hearts,' they sniffed; the Princess had been teased when she had said this was her ambition.

The Queen's continued remoteness in Balmoral, when flags were flying at half-mast everywhere in the country except Buckingham Palace, was beginning to appear callous. Routine, the royal family's salvation in the face of any human catastrophe, made them appear as inflexible as the dolls in the Fortnum and Mason clock in Piccadilly: appearing on the hour, to be stared at by a curious crowd, then disappearing until the chimes heralded their return. If there was a blip in the mechanism, the figures momentarily jolted, but creaked on.

Not appreciating the depth of feeling about the Princess, the Queen planned to miss only one afternoon on the grouse moors by travelling overnight to London on the royal train in time for the funeral on 7th September, returning that day to continue her summer holiday. Old-guard Palace courtiers, who had always mistrusted the Princess' popularity, failed now to advise the Queen how things were in the capital, outside her own home.

Even her Private Secretary Sir Robert Fellowes, whose job was to inform and be informed, was preoccupied. Married to the Princess' sister Jane, who was of course devastated by the news, his priority was his wife as she prepared to fly to Paris with Prince Charles to bring back the body.

It was difficult for the Queen. Far from insensitive to the pain in Diana's life, despite much that is assumed, she was sad about this lively daughter of her old friend Earl Spencer whom she affectionately thought of in lighter moments as a 'highly strung racehorse'. This overwhelming outpouring of feeling by a normally stoic people, however, bewildered her.

Although she had such a happy upbringing with an openly affectionate mother, the Queen rarely shows emotion, though there was a tear when saying farewell to the Royal Yacht *Britannia* in 1997. Urgent calls for her return to London well before the funeral could no longer be ignored. They were being made not in an aggressive or ugly way, but politely in Establishment newspapers and from behind a sea of flowers. Later this would be known as Britain's Floral Revolution; how English, how effective.

Though a mistress herself of the art of crowd-pleasing, the Queen Mother was dismayed to see her daughter being subjected to such insistent public pressure. Having lived through a century when the monarchy was largely revered, this call to the Queen by her people was unprecedented.

Prince Charles was astute enough to sense the public mood. Confrontation was avoided. He and the Prime Minister, Tony Blair, were both aware of the pulse of an increasingly feverish people. The Prime Minister talked emotionally about The People's Princess and, with Prince Charles' influence, liaised successfully with the Palace over the funeral arrangements.

The Queen responded with grace and spoke sparingly and movingly on television about the Princess, referring to her as 'an exceptional and gifted human being'. The Palace Union Jack flew at half-mast and, in the most dignified tribute of all, the Queen bowed before the coffin bedecked with the royal colours as it passed the gates of Buckingham Palace.

The Queen Mother wanted now to be a rock for a beleaguered royal family. Everyone would have understood had she not felt up to attending the Princess' funeral, but she insisted. It was on with the black of mourning which suited her so well, a large diamond clasp on her lapel. Unaided, the Queen Mother did the long walk up the aisle at Westminster Abbey, leaning on a stick, poignant in the frailty of her own great age but magnificently determined.

In all the adulation for the Princess, it would be only human if she did not begin to reflect on her own popularity. The emotional grandeur and dignity of the Princess' funeral and the maelstrom of public grief must have made her wonder if she had moved down a notch or two on the scale of 'the best loved person in Britain'.

Cherished, venerated scion of the royal family, she had lived longer than any other British King, Queen Regent or Queen Consort. Her life had spanned a century, a generous run, while the Princess died young with so much more to contribute.

That summer of 1997, people felt sad and disillusioned. The Queen Mother's matriarchal serenity shaken, she worried now about a tarnished monarchy, so her comfortable twilight days were filled with a new determination. 'She is indomitable,' Prince Charles said. The Queen Mother, with an acute sense of history behind the sweet smile, feared the death of the Princess could herald a renewed resentment against Prince Charles and his mistress Mrs Camilla Parker-Bowles, though she cared less about her feelings. At the time of his divorce from the Princess in 1996, questions about his suitability as King had been raised. To the Queen Mother, this was too reminiscent of the unease created by the Abdication in 1936 when the monarchy reached its lowest ebb, before the King, with her support, restored it to triumphant heights.

Once again she felt needed. Prince Charles had always been special. He was the son she never had, her first grandchild; there was between them an indestructible bond.

She had seen him through the early difficult years when his parents were often abroad and he was at Gordonstoun, Prince Philip's old school, renowned for its rigorous regimen on Scotland's uncompromising north-east coast. The Queen Mother thought it a 'dreadful place' and far too harsh for that 'poor dear boy'.

'It's near Balmoral ... your grandmother goes up there to fish. You can go and see her,' Prince Philip told Charles airily as he flew him to Lossiemouth on 1st May 1963 for his first term. In a fatherly farewell gesture, Prince Philip dipped the wings of the aircraft over Gordonstoun on the way back to London and secretly hoped this stern academy would toughen up the heir to the throne.

The Queen Mother never confronted Prince Philip about his choice of school; it was not her way. Their relationship has always been one of guarded respect. His mother-in-law is one of the few women who has baffled him, her willpower and her strength filling him with admiration, but her frivolity discomfits him. Prince Philip was a demanding father, but the Queen Mother understood his attitudes were partly in keeping with the grooming of princes for the twenty-first century.

In the meantime she would comfort Charles all she could, knowing the way to a small boy's heart. 'Now do have another buttery,' she would say over tea at Birkhall, plying her homesick grandson with Scotland's answer to the croissant. During that first term, he had been bullied unmercifully, whacked at night with pillows as other boys shouted abuse, 'sponger' or 'bloodsucker'; dunked fully dressed in baths of cold water and made to empty the dustbins. Treated, in fact, like any other 'new bug' – but it was still a rude shock for a cosseted prince, the first not to be educated at home. The Queen Mother could give him the warmth and affection his own mother had been unable to provide, preoccupied as she was and perhaps over-zealous about her duties as Queen.

Thanks to his grandmother's sympathetic but deliberately restrained ear, combined with butteries and Black Bun, a rich Highland cake, the glum boy cheered up by the end of that first term and saw that being Prince of Wales could be exciting. You could do most things – play polo, hunt, fly your own plane; perhaps be managing director of the royal family Firm while Mother remained chairman.

Charles listened; he usually took his grandmother's advice. Her influence in the family was never heavy-handed, but subtle and valued. Charles would decide against joining the Freemasons, unlike his grandfather, George VI. His abhorrence of modern architecture owed much to his grandmother's view that it 'was best seen upside down'.

'This very gentle boy ... with a very kind heart,' was her description of him. He reminded her of the late King, though perhaps not so much in later years when his private life was in disarray. But even then Charles could do no wrong; she could forgive him anything. Once a photograph appeared of the Prince cheekily captioned 'With the Woman he Loves'. The prurient were disappointed to find him holding the hand of the Queen Mother and not that of his mistress.

In the circles in which the Queen Mother moved throughout the century, royal mistresses had always been accepted. During a row with the Princess, Charles once snapped: 'Do you really expect me to be the first Prince of Wales not to have a mistress?'

A true Edwardian, the Queen Mother understood better than most about royal mistresses and her grandson's need for the motherly, warm maturity of a woman like Mrs Parker-Bowles, which continued the security of the nursery in a lonely childhood.

The Queen Mother was ten when King Edward VII died. His mistress, Mrs Alice Keppel, 'La Favorita' with her luxuriant head of hair, big blue eyes and 'ripe curves', sobbed and cajoled her way to the King's deathbed. After his death and in later years, she had 'lost all bloom' but retained what Virginia Woolf described as the 'extensive, jolly, brazen surface of the old courtesan'. These two women could not be more opposite. Surprisingly, the Bloomsbury writer who had a virtual '*ménage blanc*' liked the 'old grasper, whose fists,' she said, 'have been in the money bags these fifty years.'

Mrs Keppel's great-granddaughter, Mrs Parker-Bowles, fair-haired and Sloaney, revelled in the connection. Famously she would remind Prince Charles about their shared, racy background when they met in 1970, she a far from shy twenty-three year old debutante.

'My great-grandmother used to have it away with your great great-great-grandfather, and she saw it as her job to curtsey first and then jump into bed. So how about it?' Prince Charles, then a diffident twenty-two year old naval officer, goggled at this come-hitherish remark accompanied by a game smile.

Not as exotic as Mrs Keppel, Camilla lacked the voluptuousness so appreciated by Edward VII, but both women shared the same capacity to flatter and be good humoured, understanding and unquestioningly available to their royal lovers.

Prince Charles, greatly attracted to Camilla Shand, never got round to proposing. Tired of waiting, this feisty girl married Major Andrew Parker-Bowles, a former escort of Princess Anne. They had two children, Laura, and Tom, who later would cause anxiety and parental guilt because of his addiction to cocaine and friendship with Prince William. The Queen Mother knew the couple socially, for they shared her love of horses and racing.

The Parker-Bowles were divorced in January 1995, ending a jaded twenty-one year old marriage. He had never been known for his commitment to hearth and home, but was always discreet. Later he became a Brigadier and was given the honorary title of Silver Stick in Waiting. He had to put up with predictable jokes about there being no greater honour for a man than that he lay down his wife for a future king. He has since remarried.

Mrs Parker-Bowles bought a house sixteen miles from Highgrove, Prince Charles' Gloucestershire home, for £850,000, though the Brigadier had only a modest army pension of £27,000 a year. Increasingly she was to be found at St James' Palace or wherever the Prince happened to be.

The Queen Mother had an unswerving belief in the sanctity of marriage and asked Prince Charles not to appear in public with Mrs Parker-Bowles. She hated scenes and liked to make things easy, however, so offered them a haven at Birkhall with its 'delicious' garden, a riot of blue and white nutty scented phlox and larkspur, perfect for romantic summer trysts.

As the Prince of Wales' marriage difficulties became more public, there was an increasing wariness between the Princess and the Queen Mother. The Queen Mother had known Diana since she was a child, but now she hardly recognised this shy little creature from Sandringham days who had taken off like a bird of paradise. This was not the sad, vulnerable granddaughter of her old friend Ruth Lady Fermoy, who often talked of the heartbreak at Althorp when her daughter, Frances Shand Kydd, Lady Diana's mother, had bolted, abandoning the four small Spencer children who cried themselves to sleep. But it is not true that these two old ladies engineered the match. They were both too wise.

Lady Fermoy warned her starry-eyed granddaughter before any engagement how difficult it would be marrying into the royal family and told her, 'Darling, they are not like us'; prophetic words. Another mistaken, happy belief was that the Queen Mother had taught Lady Diana Spencer all she needed to know about being royal when she stayed briefly at Clarence House before her wedding at Paul's Cathedral on 29th July 1981, which was watched by a billion television viewers.

The romantic image was of an elderly Queen Mother gently initiating the untutored granddaughter of her greatest friend in the art of tripping lightly through the labyrinthine ways of royal life, but the bride-to-be said she saw hardly anything of her elderly hostess in those hectic pre-wedding days. 'The Queen Mother was meant to help me, to teach me, but she did not do anything at all.'

The Queen Mother, out lunching, dining at parties, was celebrating. It looked as if the marriage would be 'the stuff of which fairytales are made,' as Archbishop Runcie said when he married them.

Dismissing the Princess' theory as unkind, a friend later explained, 'The Queen Mother would never tell anybody what to do; you learn by watching her.'

The Princess did learn, too well perhaps for her own good. She shared with the Queen Mother the same warm ability to brighten the lives of the people she met. Maybe they were too alike to get on really well. Her allies, she felt, were few. Diana, without much help, acquired poise and, with her compassion, quickly outshone Prince Charles. Her popularity, ironically, would work against her in the royal family but, finding them cold and remote, she was unrepentant.

The Princess later bitterly expressed the unpopular view that the Queen Mother was 'tough and interfering', had 'few feelings' and was not 'as she appears to be at all'.

The Queen Mother had created her own frothy public identity and had always been careful never to outshine the King. She thought it a pity that Diana had not tried to be more of a traditional low-key royal wife. Ironically the Princess did identify with one royal wife, Queen Alexandra, but, unlike this other sad, beautiful and neglected Princess of Wales, Diana, as a girl of the nineties, made her own unhappiness known to the world. By their eleventh wedding anniversary on 29th July 1992, the Wales' marriage had deteriorated beyond hope.

The Queen Mother would always be firmly on Charles' side, even when in 1994 he confessed on television to his adultery with Mrs Parker-Bowles – leaving twelve million viewers in no doubt about his twenty-five year affair with his forty-five year old mistress.

What upset people most about the Prince's 'Let's be honest campaign' was his admission that he had never loved the Princess, yet it was well known how depressed he had been even before his wedding. For him it was a marriage of convenience, medieval. People felt he had let them down, and besides, the country had grown more attached to the Princess than ever he or the rest of the royal family realised. Charles won no sympathy when he pleaded that he had tried to stay faithful to his wife, and spoke of the 'total agony' of a situation which had all the ingredients of 'a Greek tragedy'.

The Queen Mother knew how royal marriages 'often ran into difficulties, but couples soldiered on,' she said, even the choice of words implying an endurance test.

Recovering from her first hip replacement operation in November 1995, the Queen Mother was horrified to see the Princess talking tearfully on television about the breakdown of her marriage. Admitting her love affair with Major James Hewitt, Diana never claimed to be a paragon, but was still seen by most as wronged and vulnerable. The Queen Mother was unashamedly partisan. Appalled by the Princess' revelations, she saw them as retaliatory and any early delicate bond between them was now severed. Saddened by the final breakdown of the marriage, the Queen Mother inevitably sided with her grandson – even if the 'dear boy' had been a trifle unwise.

The Princess now complained: 'His grandmother is always looking at me with a strange look in her eyes ... It's not hatred, it's sort of interest and pity mixed in one.' The Queen Mother was wary of her, and never forgot the moment when she saw the pregnant Princess, in a tantrum, throw herself downstairs.

The Princess and the Queen Mother were rather alike and understood each other almost too well. The Princess was sensitive to atmosphere, but no more so than the Queen Mother with her intuition – 'the wee giftie' from childhood. Both came from aristocratic backgrounds, but the Princess showed less reverence for the royal family. Having grown up with them at Sandringham, she saw them as fallible. This irked the Queen Mother. Both could be manipulative, had terrific charm and were hypnotic in their effect on people.

The Prince and Princess of Wales were finally divorced on Wednesday, 26th August 1996, both relieved after the emotional exhaustion of the bitterness and several years of acrimonious tit for tat. By the summer of 1997, they were beginning to rebuild their lives. The Prince felt he could gradually bring Mrs Camilla Parker-Bowles into the public eye and gave a large party for her fiftieth birthday at Highgrove. Camilla's friends, who had worried that she would be relegated to the shadowy role of being another royal mistress, were relieved. Before the Prince's divorce, Mrs Parker-Bowles had been living like a recluse and had suffered the indignity of having bread rolls thrown at her in a Wiltshire supermarket.

That summer, the Princess too seemed more settled and happy. There was her latest flirtation with Dodi Fayed, son of the wealthy Egyptian owner of Harrods. There were playful holidays aboard the Al-Fayed yacht *Jonikal* in the Mediterranean. She joked with friends about the ostentation, but enjoyed the luxury and the spare-no-expense pampering.

'I'm having a wonderful time,' the Princess told Lady Annabel Goldsmith in a telephone call from France but added, 'the last thing I need is a new marriage.'

On Saturday, 30th August, when the yacht was moored off the coast of Sardinia, the Princess was cavorting in a leopardskin swimsuit with a golden tan and blonde hair cut like a model's. She had never looked better.

The Princess was canny and young Fayed provided a light-hearted distraction for the summer. Glamorous photographs of her were clouding any attempt by Mrs Parker-Bowles to gradually emerge from the shadows with her motherly, Lady Thatcher-style bustling walk.

On Saturday, 30th August the Princess flew to Paris to buy Prince William and Prince Harry presents. She knew she would be seeing them before they went back to school for the Autumn term.

And then she died.

CHAPTER 23

A Private View

A credible 'private view' portrayal of the Queen Mother has always seemed maddeningly elusive, defying the finest artists. The face turned towards them and the world is one of benign roundness, the mouth turned up at the edges as if its owner has never known a moment's peevishness or grumpiness.

Portraits seldom do her justice. Most artists find it difficult to focus on any one strongly defined feature. An awkward subject, the Queen Mother appears good humoured, smiling serenely, with a fine skin, a bit crinkly now, and eyes still shining with that hint of 'Celtic summer blue'. The distinguished Italian sculptor Fiore de Henriques struggled for a year to capture some essence of his subject; the result was a striking bronze for the *Ark Royal* but showed more firmness than the Queen Mother's admirers wished to see.

Portraits are an inevitable part of royal life. As Queen, her own preference had been for sketches, rightly thinking they had more charm and expression. She understood the need for formal portraits, so she would sit for fashionable painters Philip de Laszlo, Sir James Gunn, Gerald Kelly, J S Sargent and the Russian artist Savely Sorine. They all thought her a dream sitter, so unlike other royal women, some so difficult and stiff in their great jewelled stomachers, staring 'frozenly and unsmilingly ahead'.

Augustus John described the Queen as 'angelic' but still he failed to turn up for a first sitting, sending a curious telegram to Buckingham Palace saying he was suffering from 'the influence'. This was immediately understood by the Queen who, charmed by the eccentric John, persuaded him to return.

In spite of the string quartet that played soothing English music, and sherry and brandy discreetly placed in a nearby cupboard, he still found the Palace atmosphere icily inhibiting. John abandoned the commission, and later spoke of this half-finished work as 'the most endearingly deficient' picture of his life before hurling it into a cellar. Twenty years later, in 1961, it was unearthed and presented to the Queen Mother.

In one of her special handwritten notes, she told the artist 'what a tremendous pleasure it gives me to see it again ... It looks so lovely in my drawing room and has cheered it up no end! The sequins glitter and the roses and the red chair have a fine glow and I am so happy to have it.' A few months later, Augustus John was dead.

It now hangs in the Garden Room at Clarence House. Her Household always liked its misty, elusive quality. On the other hand, they have never cared for Graham Sutherland's portrait, commissioned by London University in 1960, seeing it as a hard, severe 'Queen Elizabeth' with a thin slash for a mouth. It is consigned to a corridor.

The Queen Mother conveyed such a sunny composure in public that only in repose was there a glimpse of a strong-willed, politically astute character. 'You ought to know that she is adorable, but quite tough and resourceful too,' Lord Charteris advised, but this never came through in portraits.

Sir Roy Strong, a long-standing friend, dared to express the unpopular view that he thought Sutherland had actually caught the real Queen Mother: that 'typically upright posture ... alert turn of the head and eyes – together with the determined set of the lips' which revealed a robustness behind a perpetual 'beguiling mask of humorous charm'.

People were outraged by the artist Alison Watt's attempt to probe the amiable Florentine mask with her eighty-ninth birthday portrait, which shows a long-faced, bitter-sweet Queen Mother with stubby nails and chunky hands. The art critic Brian Sewell thought it made the nation's adored grandmother look like an ancient pensioner waiting for her 100th birthday telegram from the Queen, and that 'her hair looks like an unwashed perm.'

The Queen Mother had posed hatless for the six sittings. Without her props, those grand scalloped oyster hats, her wispy, long, grey hair could not be disguised. The young Scottish artist had been determined to get beyond the 'sugary image' and, 'seeing a very strong character', said 'I did not want her to come across as a wee waif,' a dry reference to the meltingly coy watercolours of the Queen Mother over the years.

This uncompromising portrait hangs in London's National Portrait Gallery. Curator Robin Gibson argued at the time that it was a 'picture of a dignified elderly lady at home' and that in years to come, it would be appreciated as a refreshing change from the more usual 'candy-floss'.

'An old lady with really white hair ... with ... a deep, croaky, posh voice' was how children invited to Clarence House in 1998 saw her. 'The Queen Nanna' they called her. The children, from St Matthew's Primary School, Leeds, noticed how she 'kept putting her neck on the right', a typical Queen Mother gesture as she listens. A child's view, so simple, brutal in its accuracy.

When the artist Johnny Jonas said he would like to show the Queen Mother's love of racing for a portrait commissioned by the Carlton Club for her hundredth birthday, the Queen Mother was delighted. The sittings got off to a fine start as she posed happily with binoculars and a fluffy white parasol. During the five sittings in all, the corgis were never far away.

Artist and sitter got on famously. Struck by her 'alertness and the empathy', Jonas suggested that the best way of viewing her portrait was through a mirror as this was how the Queen Mother was used to seeing herself.

'I have had my portrait painted many, many times,' the Queen Mother told Jonas, 'but you are the first artist to explain this to me.' Reaching out, she took the offered handmirror to study her portrait and saw herself in a sea of blue with matching cartwheel hat, pearls and a restrained smile.

Had it been unflattering, the Queen Mother would not have been bothered, but she was highly critical of many portraits of the Queen, dismissing most as 'amateurish and hideous'. Princess Margaret fared better, altogether more luminously photogenic.

With her keen, artistic eye and frank about the Queen's lack of interest in art, the Queen Mother blamed Buckingham Palace for failing to spot exciting new artists. However it was announced in 1999 that the Queen would sit for Lucien Freud, an artist whose incisiveness could make Graham Sutherland's portraits appear kittens-and-ribbons schmaltz.

Happily the Queen lacks any real personal vanity and with equanimity faced Britain's finest living painter, who claimed, 'I'm really only interested in sitters as animals.'

Even Freud, celebrated for his remorseless eye, might have difficulty getting beyond the Queen Mother's carapace of sweet calm, this perennially pleasant face obviously irritating to some. Frances Partridge, last of the Bloomsbury set and a keen and normally kind diarist, thought her face 'a little like Harold Wilson's' as she sourly watched the Queen Mother at the King's Lynn Festival, 'radiating charm ... and ... tittupping along on pig's trotter shoes'.

Even Spitting Image caricaturists have been kind in their failure to portray an unlikeable Queen Mother. Towards the end of the century, when a national pastime was the stripping away of illusions and getting below the cuticles of the famous, no dark secrets about her emerged. Like the rest of the human race, she experienced events in her long life which made her sorrowful, disappointed, even a hint bitter. It is true that she harboured a distaste for the Duchess of Windsor, but she was not venomous. As the Queen Mother crushingly explained, she 'would never demean myself to hate her'.

There were those who thought her ambitious; the late Sir Isaiah Berlin admired her but claimed that as Duchess of York she drank champagne all through the Abdication Crisis. He told the historian Andrew Roberts that 'She was terribly excited at the prospect of becoming Queen Empress.' This view is in sharp contrast with Sir Cecil Beaton, whose lens did not reflect an image of a calculating woman when he took formal photographs shortly after the Coronation. Instead he saw a bemused 'pretty child in a new party dress' as the Queen watched her reflection in the long looking-glass. It was that 'fragile mixture of ... child and great lady' which made her unique, hiding as it did impressive moral strength.

That child-woman was to become one of the most remarkable Queen Consorts ever. Anti-monarchists had to admit that she was an enhancer, bringing lustre to a dull royal house. Being royal for her was never a chore, rather as if she has been rehearsing all her life for this role. There was something of the great actress about her, and nobody could match the artistry of her arrival. It was believed that she had taken acting lessons, her entrances were so much better than those of any other member of the royal family.

She has a sunny ability to generate a lighthearted anticipation. Tension dissolves as the whisper goes round, 'She's here, she's here'. The Queen Mother's eyes travel round a room, mentally photographing faces which she enters into a prodigious memory, putting people half her age to shame. Her eyes rest on someone and with an air of approachability, she shows a readiness to be amused, interested, sympathetic.

She has never forgotten the importance of being royal, but her warmth touches those around her. When a member of her staff was in trouble and broke down in tears, she did not hesitate but went forward with arms impulsively outstretched; spontaneity is rare in royal circles.

In the gossip that circulates about the royal family's peccadilloes, there has never been a whiff of scandal about her. Broadminded, rarely condemnatory, even with her own high standards she has always been tolerant of the indiscretions of friends. She showed understanding even when those of a former admirer, Viscount Findhorn, came to light in recent years.

Her own life has been devoted to family and country. Although a Bright Young Thing of the Twenties, able to make sophisticated worldly men feel chivalrous and witty, remarriage never crossed her mind. The King of Norway might have been eminently suitable and he proposed several times in the years following his wife's death in 1954. There was a touching moment in Oslo in 1983, during his eightieth birthday celebrations, when the Queen Mother was applauded warmly at the concert house as they entered the royal box together. 'You see, my dear Elizabeth,' he said kissing her hand, 'how much my people love you. What a wonderful Queen you would have made for them.' They remained the best of friends until his death in 1990.

Intensely patriotic and loving things for being 'so English', she particularly regretted the end of white supremacy in Africa and pined for a disappearing Empire.

When the Queen Mother was being entertained at the Carlton Club and viewing the finished Jonas portrait, members chuckled when she asked them if they knew why 'the British Empire had lasted so long?' They shook their heads. 'Cricket,' she said triumphantly, 'it had great value in sticking everyone together.'

Of the vintage and background to be unwaveringly right-wing, she has not been at all fond of Socialists, and worried about the fate of the House of Lords, 'An institution that I venerate.'

Her ideal politician was Harold Macmillan, Earl of Stockton. When asked if it was really true that Harold Wilson, of all Prime Ministers, had known the best personal relationship with the Queen she replied: 'I don't really know him, but he is a frightful little man. I am only going by what my daughter says.' She disliked Shirley Williams because she did away with grammar schools; liked Sir Edward Heath; was against the ordination of women but never seriously dallied with the Roman Catholic church. She was too Scottish for Popery. However she did have a fleeting brush with one of the Princes of Rome when she was at the Travellers Club in Pall Mall, where she ran into the late Monsignor Gilbey, then ninety-five years old. In good spirits, the Queen Mother said pleasantly to the Brideshead Catholic priest from the famous gin family, 'Excuse me, I believe I'm a year older than you are.' The elderly cleric, who had always wanted to meet the Queen Mother but failed to recognise her, retorted in Alice in Wonderland vein, 'You can't be, there is only one woman a year older than me and that's the Queen Mother,' looking past her with glazed eyes.

She has a gift for friendship. An easy guest, she was famous for making her host feel that he uniquely had found what would please her most. Sir Frederick Ashton loved the pavane as a choice of aperitifs was reeled off. 'Campari, champagne, Dubonnet ... ?' Only when a 'Dry Martini?' was mentioned would there be a responsive glimmer, her hand resting on her neck as if no one had ever before offered such an entrancing possibility. 'Mmm, that would be lovely.' Her own hospitality is legendary: the Martinis are large, the claret excellent and sometimes strong men have had to hold on to the backs of chairs but she never appeared squiffy. That Scottish fibre had imbued her with admirable self-control.

Generous and gregarious, her lifestyle is a mite indulgent, her standards *haute* Edwardian. When the artist David Shepherd, who had been working on yet another portrait of her, turned up wearing a suit at Clarence House, the Queen Mother teased him for being so formally dressed, saying, 'But it is only us today and the Duchess of Gloucester', with an airy wave of the hand. Even so it would have been unwise to turn up in jeans even for a picnic lunch where the Queen Mother, a stickler for correct dress, always wears a hat and pearls. Her apparent easy informality could mislead the unwary.

Not generally intolerant or dogmatic, one would not hear from her lips that she did not care for coffee, cats, divorce, platitudes, early mornings, smoked salmon, social climbers, turbans, abstract art, bad posture, bumptiousness, jersey, irksome security, government cuts in the Health Service, flat shoes, malingerers, navy or brown, bores or anyone who upset the Queen.

The Queen Mother has a clever, sprightly mind. She enjoys classical music, ballet, theatre and has read more than most in the royal family: Belloc, Thomas Hardy, Galsworthy, Evelyn Waugh, especially *The Loved One*. Quietly and behind the scenes, she stepped in with a generous donation to save Britain's oldest art school – the Heatherly School of Fine Art – which included Lewis Carroll and Evelyn Waugh among its former students. Many modern novels she thinks 'vulgar' except those by Barbara Pym, Dick Francis and Dorothy L Sayers; all are enduring favourites as is P D James, but, she finds, 'it takes me two months to finish one of her books.'

She loves P G Wodehouse, sending a 'What ho' message to the society that honours the creator of Jeeves and Bertie Wooster; just her sort of characters, that vanished world of impeccable butlers and languid young men who consider 'work' an important piece of art or literature.

The Queen Mother is a happy person, even jolly. The word 'gay,' for her, means 'bright and merry'. There is something old-fashioned and innocent about her: the pleasure she gets from hearing her piper play; wearing her floppy pea-picker hat; a taste for scrambled eggs; singing 'I'll See You Again' in the back of her Rolls-Royce; listening to Puccini and Verdi; plaice and mash; Viennese waltzes; Bendicks Bittermints; jugs of sweet peas; big breakfast-sized cups for tea; tapestry; solitary walks, and her corgis. There is a sweetness about her which is not cloying. She is often regarded as very funny and the best company.

Well into her nineties, she loved proving she was mentally and physically spry, enjoying midnight films at Sandringham at a time when her great-grandchildren were yawning; but perhaps because her choice might be a re-run of 'Yes, Minister' rather than *Reservoir Dogs.*

Over these last years her friends have been 'gathered' at a dismaying rate. The actress Dorothy Dickson, star of *Cooee* and *The Cabaret Girl,* 'inconsiderately slipped away aged one hundred and two.' But the Queen Mother does not pine to be young again, as hers has been such a fulfilled life. She never dyed her hair, went to Health Clubs or chased serums to puff up wrinkly if exceptional skin. Her great age has become a matter of increasing pride. Perhaps artists have found this tranquil acceptance bland. You never hear her complaining or being downhearted. 'A splendid old bird', said a friend.

Always 'looking forward, never back', she has been sustained by an inner strength. No artist ever quite caught that intangible lightness of spirit.

The Queen Mother likes to say, 'I'm not as nice as you think I am.' Everybody waits for confirmation of this, but it has yet to come.

CHAPTER 24

Pink, White and Polished

A true Edwardian, the Queen Mother runs her homes on sleekly benevolent, old-fashioned lines: a Fabergé bell for service, a footman behind nearly every chair. As she presides at any gathering, her tiny size three-and-a-half feet resting on a tapestried stool, there is always a half bottle of vintage champagne in a silver ice bucket within easy pink-nail-polished reach. Over the years it has been English country-house style at its best, privileged pre-1914 graceful living.

As one house guest said, 'Staying with the Queen Mother simply made any other royal hospitality feel like a boarding house.' Clarence House is particularly pleasant, a jewel of comfort, with its porcelain, antique silver and peerless service. Her collection of paintings and distinguished eighteenth-century furniture made a visit there as enjoyable as a day at the Wallace Collection or the Frick in New York, her possessions beautifully chosen and harmonious.

Her Household has a certain style, maintained into the new century. Next to the Queen, she has the biggest personal staff, fifty including housekeepers, butlers, footmen, ladies' maids, cooks, gardeners and chauffeurs. Her Household, her courtiers, are a shrinking band, 'old cosies', as she has called them; many might be frail, but all have been dedicated to keeping up her sybaritic standards.

When the unwelcome spotlight beamed in on the Queen Mother's financial plight in March 1999, revealing an overdraft of £4 million with Coutts bank, it was suggested that she might like to send a few *objets d'art* to the saleroom.

Outraged, one of her advisers responded: 'You can't have the Queen Mother being asked to send a picture to Sotheby's every week.'

Things are maintained as if the King were still alive, indeed better. As soon as you ring the bell at the discreet black doorside entrance of Clarence House, a footman in blue tailcoat, white tie and medals answers with a huge smile, showing you into the drawing room. It is a source of slightly bitter amusement among staff at Clarence House that they always have to wear formal white tie and medals. One caustically remarked, 'The other day I saw Princess Anne's butler and he was in jeans.'

There was once an engaging shabbiness about Clarence House but it has been renewed and freshened up, so anybody anxious about the future of the establishment would be in no doubt. It has high security squawk boxes, intercoms, panic buttons, electric typewriters and computers in the 'girls' office, as the secretaries are known whatever their age.

Rooms are filled with freshly-cut flowers bought in dawn forays to the New Covent Garden Market, where royal footmen mix with designers, restaurateurs and party planners. Flowers are changed each morning, cars polished daily.

Hard work behind the scenes is disguised by an elegantly convivial air. Depending on the time of day, you are offered tea, coffee or Bovril. You never expect to see the 'the Presence', as the Queen Mother is known, before eleven o'clock in the morning when she appears in some floaty creation and a sunny mood. By a quarter to twelve there is a pressing invitation to the 'grog' cupboard for nice old establishment drinks – sherry, or gin and tonic. For her, a decent measure of gin and Dubonnet is mixed expertly by a manservant. In the afternoon for tea there is the joy of scones freshly baked, chocolate cake and Earl Grey poured from an eighteenth-century silver bullet-shaped tea kettle decorated with the Bowes crest. Everything is turned into an occasion.

Much of the credit for the professionalism of the Queen Mother's public image is due to the enthusiasm and touch of military meticulousness of her Household. It was Sir Martin Gilliat, her Private Secretary for thirty-seven years, who helped generate an atmosphere of genial efficiency. His background,

Eton and the Greenjackets, made him an ideal courtier. When his older brother died in India in 1935 after being mauled by a tiger, he inherited the family acres in Hertfordshire, a county much loved by the Queen Mother. A bachelor and a prisoner of war in Colditz, he was also an engaging and humorous companion, and shared with the Queen Mother a devotion to the turf. He was also a master of tact.

There was about his office at Clarence House a deceptively casual atmosphere; a desk was piled high with wickerwork trays brimming with invitations and the odd Teddy Bear; a huge exercise book with parchment pages acted as the royal diary. This relaxed air masked a professionalism very different from the tautness of Buckingham Palace, where the role of Monarch's Private Secretary was once described as 'dignified slavery' by Harold Laski.

'We were expected to be on our toes, to be competent, but then Queen Elizabeth was always so appreciative.' Sir Martin Gilliat explained why it had been such a pleasure to work for the Queen Mother and paid her the best compliment. 'In all the years I worked for her, I don't think I have ever heard a cross word ... or seen a sign of grumpiness.'

If there was a hiccup, she was never sharp. When a member of her Household once forgot her speech, he was asked if he could scribble another in the back of the car. After it had been delivered, the Queen Mother said, 'Now I thought we did that rather well.' Royal handbags rarely hold much more than a short speech and a handkerchief. Once the Queen Mother's bag fell open on a parade ground and out tumbled her favourite chocolate violet creams.

When a valet failed to answer the bell as he had nodded off on duty, the Queen Mother tiptoed to the kitchen to get her own glass of water and pinned a note on the somnolent lackey's lapel: 'I have got it myself, thank you. Have a good night.' Just the hint of a rebuke, but a gentle one.

When Sir Martin died of cancer in 1993 aged eighty, he was replaced by Sir Alastair Aird who at sixty-eight became her Private Secretary. Brisk, questioning and precise, he is an altogether different personality. He has brought a healthy hint of abrasiveness to the Clarence House he understands so well from his previous days as Comptroller. Married, he and his wife are valued friends of the Queen Mother, joining her for picnics and jaunts.

Sir Ralph Anstruther, another old Etonian whose military background was in the Coldstream Guards, was her Treasurer for nearly forty years. The Queen Mother does have a weakness for Etonians. When he was seventy-seven, and after forty years, it was felt Sir Ralph should step down, but the Queen Mother hated to see him go and said, 'Why not keep a desk in Clarence House,' so he became her Treasurer Emeritus. Sir Ralph, a friend with a house not far from the Castle of Mey, was also a bachelor. The Queen Mother has sometimes been teased about being surrounded by so many unmarried men. She took Sir Woodrow Wyatt to task when he suggested that her good friend, Osbert Sitwell, a bachelor, must be homosexual. 'Lots of people say that about people who don't get married,' countered the Queen Mother, 'but it isn't always true.' She had grown up in an era when unmarried 'boys' left over from two World Wars were ideal companions; they just had never found the right 'gel' to marry.

In 1998, a new Treasurer, the Hon. Nicholas Assheton, who had a sound financial background, took over from Sir Ralph Anstruther. He would handle the scrutiny of the Queen Mother's accounts, knowing the kitty needed another £2 million a year to fund her taste for racehorses, new hats, designer clothes and opulent living. His father-in-law was Air Chief Marshal 'Bomber' Harris, which endeared his wife to her.

Her ritual has been as predictable as the seasons, gliding between Clarence House in winter, Mey in August, Sandringham at New Year, Windsor at Easter, Birkhall in summer and an overnight at Walmer Castle in Kent where she is Warden of the Cinque Ports. Each move involves a stately procession of personal footmen, chauffeurs, ladies' maids and chefs. 'We are off for the Easter court,' they would say, merrily climbing into a Daimler and heading off to Windsor to add the personal touches possibly overlooked by the resident staff.

In the nineties, comparisons have been made between the Queen Mother's privileged living and Britain's needy pensioners facing the prospect of selling their hard-earned homes to pay for institutional care.

In 1999, her wealth was estimated at £26 million. Like many she was rich on paper, but owned only one of her homes, the Castle of Mey. Her ten racehorses cost £120,000 in training fees. The others were on loan from the Queen. The Queen Mother's annual £643,000 Civil List payment, which will be reviewed in the year 2000, has been just enough to pay the salaries of her senior Household.

Ladies-in-waiting, vital in her public life, fortunately usually have a private income. The custom dates back to William the Conqueror's wife Queen Mathilda, and is seen as an honour, meriting only a token allowance. But modern ladies-in-waiting are expected to do far more than sit around sniffing nosegays and listening to madrigals. Self-effacing, discreet, dressing quietly, never outshining the star, they act unobtrusively behind the scenes, 'oiling the wheels'. They share the Queen Mother's love of needlework, racing, fresh air, gardening and music.

Once there were twelve, although recently she has been limited to half a dozen: Lady Angela Oswald, wife of trainer Michael Oswald, often seen at race meetings with her; her niece, the Hon. Mrs Rhodes, formerly Margaret Elphinstone, a daughter of the Queen Mother's sister May; Miss Jane Walker-Okeover; Mrs Michael Gordon Lennox, a daughter of Lord Aldenham, formerly Jennifer Vicary Gibbs, from an old Hertfordshire family; The Lady Margaret Colville and the serene octogenarian Dame Frances Campbell-Preston, daughter of the 2nd Viscount Cowdray. In the hierarchy, 'they are all expected to do all the chores.' They work out a rota between them and at changeover time their names appear in the Court Circular.

They deal with day-to-day arrangements like organising helicopters, special flights, train tickets and chauffeur driven cars. The Queen Mother's travelling expenses for a visit to the 1st Battalion of the Black Watch in September 1997 at Fort George were £12,507; a two day visit to the Queen's Royal Hussars at Catterick by royal train in June 1997 cost £15,001.

Correspondence is demanding as about one hundred and forty letters pour into Clarence House daily. Every one, 'some quite potty and prolific', merits a reply in a cream parchment envelope with the embossed red Clarence House crest. A happier task for ladies-in-waiting is to hunt round Chelsea and Knightsbridge looking for small, tasteful Christmas presents from the General Trading Company or Peter Jones for many of the five hundred people who also received handwritten Christmas cards. Personal letters always have her initials on the corner of the handwritten envelope.

Because of the Queen Mother's great age, some of her more elderly ladies-in-waiting had to almost beg to be allowed to retire, but were told, 'I have to go on – so why shouldn't you?'

Some of the Household found it a bit hard to keep up, wondering occasionally if she would consider slowing down, but, one said wearily, such a suggestion would have been sheer provocation. 'Her Majesty would only have taken on more.' It was a cheerful grumble, even if her ladies-in-waiting occasionally longed to rest their thin, capable legs, and get on with stitching another kneeler for a Norfolk church.

The Mistress of the Robes is a seventeenth-century title and, along with Laundress of the Body and Mistress of the Sweet Coffers, might imply washing and starching but in fact is the grandest of all. It has 'Head Girl' status and is usually given to a duchess who accompanies the Queen Mother to State occasions but is never actually in-waiting. When the Dowager Duchess of Abercorn died in 1990, there was no replacement Mistress of the Robes.

Also special and almost as rarified are the Ladies of the Bedchamber. There are two, Lady Grimthorpe and the Countess of Scarbrough. Lady Grimthorpe, daughter of the 11th Earl of Scarbrough, knew how sad King George VI had been, as an enthusiastic Freemason, when illness had prevented him installing her father as Grand Master after the war. Her sister-in-law, the 12th Earl's wife, Countess Scarbrough, a daughter of the Earl of Dalhousie, was also a personal friend of the Queen Mother. They too appear only 'for the smartest occasions' at Buckingham Palace.

An extra Lady of the Bedchamber is the nonagenarian Lady Elizabeth Basset, serious and of a generation like the Queen Mother, educated at home. Deeply spiritual, she shares with the Queen Mother a devotion to Julian of Norwich and has written books about this favourite saint as well as edited poetry.

The Queen Mother's closest friend in the Household was Ruth, Lady Fermoy who had been with the Queen Mother since both were widowed. They shared a love of music, Scotland and high moral standards. Once a concert pianist, Ruth Lady Fermoy was founder of the King's Lynn Festival. She lived quite frugally in a small flat in Eaton Square, estranged from her daughter and granddaughter. She had taken a strong line against her own daughter, Frances Shand Kydd, when her first marriage was breaking up. Lady Fermoy disapproved and sided with her son-in-law Viscount Althorp, later Lord Spencer. She gave evidence against her daughter in a bitter custody battle for the four children. Mrs Shand Kydd, whose second marriage had also failed, found it hard to forgive her mother: the bitterness lasted for years.

There had been a rift, too, between the Princess of Wales and her grandmother. A friend said, 'Ruth was appalled by what she saw as Diana's refusal to put duty before her own wishes'. She saw it as a betrayal of her own long service to the royal family. But the Princess, who admired her strong-willed grandmother, was devastated when she heard she was dying of cancer and visited her several times at her Belgravia flat and also in hospital, asking for her guidance.

Lady Fermoy was eighty-four when she died on 6th July 1993. It is rare for members of the royal family to attend funeral services but the Queen Mother insisted on venturing out for her old friend on a damp, drizzly day to the little church of St Margaret's Canon in Norfolk. Lady Fermoy had planned the simple funeral ceremony and chosen the music, Cesar Franck's Adagio and Bach's Fantasia and Fugue in G Minor. 'The music was especially wonderful,' the Queen Mother said afterwards. She always tries to be positive.

Pink, white and polished is the requirement for an equerry, Eton and the Brigade of Guards preferably. They are on an Army salary, and are chosen occasionally for their personality rather than blue blood. It helps if they are amusing, have the ability to recite a line of poetry at dinner, can handle a decanter with ease, dance well and are unmarried. After a congenial spell as equerry to the Queen Mother, a posting to a war zone in Bosnia, Northern Ireland or Kosovo is something of a contrast.

The only thing missing in this pleasant attachment for these equerries is the company of girls of their own age. 'Young women', the Queen Mother once claimed, are a 'nuisance to amuse'.

Socially, she does not relish the presence of women of her own age either. Men of the same vintage are always welcome. The Queen Mother was always a man's woman and her equerries leave once they marry.

An intrinsic part of the Queen Mother's success has been her cosseted, well-ordered life. Beneath the wafting softness, there is self-discipline. If she got to bed at two o'clock in the morning after a party at Clarence House, her early morning tea is still served at half past seven the following morning. There is a light tap on the door, and a curtseying maid carries in a white wickerwork tray with a bone china teacup, pink roses and the newspaper. A light breakfast follows, fruit, toast and sometimes a free-range boiled Buff Orpington egg at nine o'clock.

As she sips, reads the *Daily Telegraph* and listens to the wireless, her corgis – Rush, Mini and Dash – are taken out by her Steward, William Tallon, who at sixty-five is still known as her Little Dog Boy. He has walked generations of corgis, carrying them up and down aircraft steps, making sure their little camp beds are made up daily and their pillows plumped. Tallon was given the bijou lodge at the gates of Clarence House as a reward for fifty years of thoughtful care, sharing one of the most prestigious addresses in London.

He began work at the Palace when he was seventeen, having written to King George VI asking for a job. Soon afterwards at the Ghillies Ball when the royal family democratically danced with the servants, Tallon, partnering the Queen, was asked, 'What do you do?' He replied, looking into those incredible periwinkle blue eyes, 'I wait on the servants, Ma'am.' The Queen smiled, 'Ah well, we all have to start somewhere.' Later he became her Page of the Backstairs, an honour with special access to the 'Presence'.

Far from being a rough, outspoken, personal servant as John Brown was to Queen Victoria, Tallon has a desirable address with a fine collection of Edward Seago landscapes and a cultivated taste for ballet and champagne. He knows how to please, putting just the right posy of flowers in the Queen Mother's sitting room on her return from a trying day.

Below-stairs royal staff, lacking a public school education or the right regimental background, rarely make the transition to Household. Few had been resentful but in the 1990s they began to wonder as they watched a social revolution in Britain lifting barriers. Money opened doors; there was a new élite of pop singers, footballers, entrepreneurs and computer kings. So below-stairs pay at the end of the twentieth century does not have the jobless queuing at the ornate gold crested gates of Buckingham Palace or Clarence House.

Among the older servants, Reg Wilcock, 'Dear Reg', a footman and Page of the Presence who had worked for the Duke of Windsor in Paris, might have wished for more security but he is deeply attached to the Queen Mother. Her top Chef, Michael Sealey, is lucky; he can get a job anywhere, such are his skills in creating creamy, calorific dishes which have added handsomely to the girth of the Queen Mother's friends.

Many of the Clarence House staff have been decorated with awards within the Royal Victorian Order. A right royal recompense, but not much help in providing for their old age.

Staff used to be given about £20 each to spend on Christmas presents from the Queen Mother; they would wrap these up elaborately and place them under the tree so she could present them. One royal servant was so pleased with his, he asked if he might unwrap it and show it to her. When the Queen Mother saw her gift she was utterly baffled. Head on one side, she asked, 'But, what on earth is it?' Standing to attention, the retainer replied proudly, 'It's an ironing board, Your Majesty.'

The Queen Mother knows how much her below-stairs fear redundancies should she ever become too infirm to need them or, worse, not be there at all. In 1995, she put the Castle of Mey in trust, so it could not be sold after her death. When her overdraft reared its cheeky head, it was suggested that the Castle should immediately be opened to the public for the entire summer, instead of three days a year.

Clarence House is a happy place. The trouble is the cost. There was a suggestion that the Queen Mother, beautifully looked after and then a spry ninety-eight year old, should go into 'sheltered' accommodation at St James' or Buckingham Palace. The accountants thought it was time to give up her homes and move into a flat. It is true she enjoys being near the Palace, telling guests if she is late 'so sorry … but I have been up the road having coffee with my daughter', but she does not love it so much she wants to rattle around a suite of rooms as Prince Philip's mother did for lonely years before her death.

The Queen Mother is canny enough to know that Clarence House would be an ideal home for Prince Charles and his sons. But they can hardly put pressure on her to move out, since they are beneficiaries of a trust fund she set up in 1995 which takes care of two-thirds of her estate. Prince William and Harry will receive £13 million; the rest goes to the other four great-grandchildren, Princess Anne's son Peter and daughter Zara, and the Duke of York's daughters, Princess Eugénie and Princess Beatrice, each getting a share of £6.1 million.

It has been difficult for the Queen, who loves her mother a great deal but could hardly go on being seen continually funding her splendid lifestyle when the royal family, driven by public opinion, has been forced to cut costs. The Civil List was reduced and Buckingham Palace opened to the public; the Queen herself uses only five of the 650 rooms.

Money worries are not new to the Queen and her family. When her father became King in 1936 and had to pay £25,000 each year to the Duke of Windsor out of his own money, his concern was for the Princesses' financial future. Invoking the help of brother-in-law David Bowes-Lyon's banker, George VI set up trust funds for 'Lilibet' and Margaret Rose from a Civil List surplus. These were not liable for income tax.

The King would have been gratified today by the latest estimates of the Queen's wealth. The figure of £13 billion is misleading, as it includes the value of the royal art collections and crown estates. These are not the monarch's personal property and if there was a revolution, they would be removed from royal custody and enjoyment. None the less, the Queen still has about £275 million in the kitty. Interested in and shrewd about money, she recently dabbled on the Internet, investing £100,000 of her own money, and enjoyed a £900,000 return.

The Queen still takes pride in a certain parsimony, enjoying scrambled eggs and Malvern water rather than lobster and champagne. The Queen Mother's table is one of the best in London.

She has often been teased by the Queen and Princess Margaret about her extravagance, but ironically her overdraft makes shrewd economic sense for a rich old lady, helping to maintain her present lifestyle and merely reducing her personal fortune when she goes.

Who would begrudge the Queen Mother her cheerful way of life, entertaining friends at the Ritz, the Connaught and Le Manoir aux Quat' Saisons in Oxfordshire? It explains how, in the week when her overdraft was being scrutinised in the popular press, she simply went off to Cheltenham Races, carefree and looking a picture in a new pale blue outfit, to watch her horse, Easter Ross, fall at the second hurdle.

CHAPTER 25

A Chiffon Day

Sailing into a party (sometimes the wrong one – 'How lovely,' the Queen Mother would say, 'but I am afraid we are quite lawst') there she would stand in her 'Jewel clothes', her name for her 'grand confection' evening dresses. Her style was unique, inspired by the lushness of Winterhalter with hints of Fragonard's garlanded beauties and old-fashioned pink tea roses.

'Why should I not be known for my style of dressing?' the Queen Mother would ask, smiling, if being teased for wearing her favourite sapphire blue again. 'Well, you see ... it is expected of me.' Besides it suits her fair skin and eyes, compared in their heyday to the blue of delphiniums.

Dressing up was her thank you. 'People have gone to a lot of trouble for me.' 'Dressing up and queening it,' Prince Charles would say affectionately. He thought his grandmother had a theatrical streak and played to her public. A spotlight was installed in her car, shining glamorously on her arrivals; 'Let them have a good look at me,' she would say artlessly.

In her palmy days and again during the vital resurgence in her life during the 1960s and 1970s she might, in a season, happily order fifty daytime outfits and a selection of evening dresses. Her social life is still lively, 'something to do with that sturdy Bowes-Lyon blood', a friend of the same vintage ruefully recalled.

Clothes were important to her. All her life, the Queen Mother interpreted the ephemeral moods of fashion to suit herself. Fashion historians may one day recognise '*L'époque* Elizabeth', a *siècle* of exuberant clothes fanning out from the

Twenties to the end of this century, when men sometimes wear skirts and make-up.

Her self-confidence began with her refusal to conform to fashion dictates. In the 1920s, just after the First World War, you were either a Dream Girl or a Vamp, but she was the Little Duchess. Not for her the '*garçon* look'; instead she preferred demure but becoming frocks on her womanly shape. The just-above-the-ankle look suited her, not the Flapper's flattened bosom. For a while in that post-war era, busts were considered 'common', seen as a symbol of motherly domesticity.

First there were her homemade dresses from Glamis then, from the time of her engagement to the Duke of York, those appealing, slightly uneven, homestitched hems disappeared.

By the late 1930s, as Queen, she began to create her own unusual, floaty style and would stay with it for the rest of her life: in those afternoon tea frocks with crossover bodices, with her simple round necklines, softened only by favourite family pearls, she looked like a 'plump turtle dove'.

They had a saying in the Twenties: 'blondes for weekends, brunettes for keeps'. Unlike the present Queen, who turned her hair a bitter brown with the aid of a rinse called Chocolate Kiss, the Queen Mother never tried to alter the colour of her grey hair. Though it has thinned a little it is quite long and fine, held back with pins as if she has done it herself.

As a young woman, her brown hair was bobbed or economically finger-waved at home. Not for Elizabeth Bowes-Lyon a smart hairdressing salon. Instead, like her other aristocratic girlfriends 'Nanny', or some aged retainer, heated up the curling tongs and there was a smell of sizzling hair and squeals while their charges 'did their faces', a Cupid's bow mouth for the fashion conscious. The Queen Mother would keep the Marcel style 'permanent wave' for the rest of her life. Neither she nor the Queen thought much of soft, natural hair, preferring curls set under old-fashioned hairdryers which could turn even those delicate porcelain rose complexions flame red.

In her day, girls did not wear a scrap of make-up until they had 'come out'; for the rest of her life Elizabeth would never wear more than a little powder and highlighted pink lips. Looking after her skin, she avoided the sun and never allowed herself to get brown.

When it was once suggested that she should have her teeth capped after the Abdication, she replied firmly: 'I'm a Queen, not a glamour girl.' Besides, she was very fond of her little jagged teeth and, like so many people, dreaded dental check-ups. It would be an unusual dentist who could inflict pain on the Queen Mother.

Sir Norman Hartnell was her favourite designer after the triumph of the State visit to France in 1938. He shared with the Queen Mother a distaste for ordinariness, and had no time for the 'dreadful "Who's for tennis?" dresses' of his younger rivals. He thought that upperclass Englishwomen looked best in evening dresses anyway. The Queen Mother, of course, dressed grandly most of the time, a great joy to them both, and the more extravagant the cabbage roses, crystal beading, embroidered hydrangeas and silver bugle beads, the better.

'Oh, I do love those little paillettes,' she would sigh, a finger running lightly over the glittery concave sequins which took hours of painstaking stitching, until they became far too expensive. Hartnell's treasured Miss Edith Read, who spent 3,000 hours hand-embroidering the paillettes on the present Queen's Coronation dress, retired in 1979.

If the Queen Mother did not care for a design or fabric submitted by the couturier, her response would be a mild 'Perhaps another time', but never an unkind downright refusal. Although there was an aura of the *grande dame* about her, the Queen Mother's designers never felt intimidated, whereas Princess Margaret might grumble, 'What was he thinking of when he made this ... ?' If the Queen Mother was being asked to look at samples of dark wool, to her about as acceptable as black leather, she would gracefully pat some silk: 'Perfectly charming, don't you think?' deflecting the couturier in the nicest possible way with a softly murmured, 'Now apropos something becoming ...'

On one occasion Hartnell, bustling importantly to Clarence House wearing a Malmaison carnation tie in the Queen Mother's favourite shades of pink, was convinced he had made her a truly stunning evening dress. Appreciating how her love of sequins could never be over-indulged, the skirt of this latest oyster-satin creation was a riot of mother-of-pearl beads and aquamarine jewels, but when he unwrapped the elaborate dress with a grand flourish, his heart stood still for a moment and he shook like a leaf.

'I do like it,' the Queen Mother said, a bit half-heartedly, adding in a deadpan voice, 'but isn't it rather plain and severe?' Both dissolved in laughter, for the two had had many tongue-in-cheek moments, but still the couturier breathed a sigh of relief.

The Queen Mother has always been sure of exactly what suits her. Those draped lilac, eau-de-nil, ice-blue and silver-grey chiffon and georgette dresses, duster coats and crinolines were her distinctive style but could as easily have been worn by Queen Victoria or Queen Mary. Couturiers were well advised not to stray from three commandments. They could have an utterly free hand so long as a dress had a crossover bodice, sleeves should be loose 'for waving', and any colour as long as it was blue, pink or yellow. Stalwart granny shades were abominated, not that the Queen Mother would ever say so harshly.

She wore yellow, not an easy colour, for her eighty-seventh birthday portrait by Lord Snowdon. A brave choice, because it can be draining on ageing skin. The Queen Mother has never been vain, but knows blue is best on her. Pink is a colour she loves for the evening, aware of how flattering it is for any skin.

Her appetite for 'fun times', as couturiers' visits were known, remained undimmed, whatever the expense. 'Oh, you are a temptress,' she would cry, on being shown some irresistible new silk. 'Am I being too extravagant? But it is so pretty.'

There has been a great deal of affectionate banter between mother and daughters about her prodigal dress bills. 'Clothes, well they are my props,' the Queen Mother would say. The Queen and Princess Margaret in mock disapproval chorused, 'Coutts bank would certainly have folded long ago but for Mummie's overdraft,' laughing when she arrived in a cloud of new chiffon.

It was suggested that she was sluggish paying her bills. The Queen Mother liked to write a personal cheque, so her Treasurer would not know how much she was spending. Unlike one or two newer members of the royal family, she has never asked for favours such as wearing a designer outfit once and then returning it to the salon. Besides she loves her clothes too much to borrow. Row upon row of majestic Queen Mother tea dresses and sequinned evening extravaganzas are beautifully cared for by Miss Betty Leek, her personal maid.

A size fourteen, the Queen Mother loves rich food but has always eaten sparingly. While visitors are pressed to another scone – 'oh do' and 'how about some cream?' – she sips Royal Blend tea, apparently too entranced by the conversation to eat much. In an ideal world, she would have liked to keep her weight at about eight stone. Once at Gray's Inn, dining with the country's best legal brains, the main course was partridge which she felt might be too much for her. Instead of making a fuss, she deftly moved hers on to Sir Dingle Foot's plate, and as her host, he obligingly ate a brace.

Her routine is sensible and she has kept well. Her appendix was removed in 1964; two years later a colostomy distressed her. Ladies-in-waiting would look you in the eye and deny that Queen Elizabeth had undergone this unpleasant operation with its unaesthetic after-effects. Only the Colostomy Welfare Group was pleased. The Queen Mother loathed any mention of illness and people tended to forget about this traumatic surgery; because of it, her life was even more remarkable.

The only illness which could be discussed was when salmon bones lodged twice in her throat, and one had to be removed under general anaesthetic. Afterwards the Queen Mother compared this 'to a feeling of jet lag – that is the trouble with that sort of thing'.

Her two hip replacements were within three years of each other. After the first in 1995, leaving Sister Agnes at the King Edward VII Hospital for Officers, she made a nonsense of surgeon Roger Vicker's fear that the operation might produce a severe shock to the system of someone of her age. She took up Scottish dancing again. After her second hip replacement in 1998, she rarely used her run-about buggy even at Ascot in 1999 and had a small ivory handled walking stick for emergencies.

While the Queen approaches clothes in a businesslike way, for the Queen Mother this is totally feminine time, enjoying the sensuous feel of silk and velvet, talking or listening to the fitters and vendeuses, prompting them with slyly innocent questions. The answers were often a barometer, not so much of the European Central Bank monetary policy, as the cost of a taxi across London.

'Ask the ladies if they'd like a sherry,' the Queen Mother would suggest when she heard the rustling of tissue paper as the dress boxes were being unpacked. What the 'ladies' would often have preferred was that the corgis should be given a bowl of something distracting. They get very excited when new clothes and ankles are about. 'Ranger ... Dash ...' A not very insistent voice ordered the grunting, scurrying animals to 'Come here! they smell Mummie.'

Nothing was quite the same after 'dear' Sir Norman's death in 1979, a witty man, 'so unassuming'. The Queen Mother had been very attached to her fashion team from Hartnell: the dressmaker, the soft tailor who made her silk evening coats and master tailor for wool coats. Mrs Evelyn Elliott, the senior vendeuse who had been with her for more than a quarter of a century, was lured back from a youthful retirement in Kent to go on looking after her at Clarence House.

'Do come and listen to the band!' The Queen Mother loves hearing the Grenadier Guards playing after the Changing of the Guard and would hold the curtain back to give the fitter a better view. 'Oh, Evelyn, do come and look at the magnolia blossom on the lawn,' while the vendeuse or fitter trailed after her with a mouthful of pins, trying to turn a hem. Mrs Elliott was not above advising the Queen Mother on her garden. 'Your Majesty, may I suggest your roses need pruning.' But the Queen Mother – a knowledgeable gardener – would smile, 'I know, but I do love them like that,' reluctantly turning away from the view of billowing, blowsy roses.

Often the radio was on during a fitting and if a recipe or a gardening tip sounded ludicrous the Queen Mother and the team would laughingly shake their heads. If there was some old-time dance music playing, the Queen Mother would sometimes drift off in an impromptu dance on her own, with a few spirited steps, hands fluttering in the air, 'Remember when we were young, doing the Black Bottom.' She asked: 'What must we have looked like?'

At Christmas, presents given to the Hartnell team who have lovingly looked after her clothes over the years include oven gloves or casserole dishes, lamps, handbags, clocks; once, for Evelyn Elliott, an especially elegant piece of Caithness glass and in the 1995 Birthday Honours List, the Royal Victorian Medal.

In the Queen Mother's pale green dressing room there is a sofa table for her hats, each with a name and one to compliment every outfit: royal blue with matching veiling; 'Encore', a feathery green, and 'Pistachio' for a birthday. 'Rare Pearl', 'Imperial', 'Gold Cup'.

'Oh, that will be a great success,' she would exclaim, clapping her hands at some new creation being unwrapped from black and white striped hatboxes. Her hats were originally created by an East European aristocrat, Zdenko Rudolf von Ehrenfeld. The Queen Mother called him Rudolf and he had been introduced to Clarence House by Hartnell in 1965. When he died of cancer in 1980, the Queen Mother asked his partner Joy Quested-Nowell, an elegant woman with artistic flair and private income, if she would continue.

In a corner of her kitchen in a mansion flat at the back of Sloane Square that has a view of some of Chelsea's better rooftops, Miss Quested-Nowell stretches straw into the familiar shapes. 'I'd love a Bersagliere,' the Queen Mother suggested. Miss Quested-Nowell, from years in Tuscany, knew all about this ancient mountain regiment and its plumed headgear. The hats sit on models at her work table and look surreal. The thinnest, most delicate veiling and straw dyed specially in pale blue, lavender and mint green have been selected in Paris. The Queen Mother has never liked turbans or hats which hide her face, making it difficult for photographers. And as for cloche hats, she would ask, 'Did we really wear those funny hats?' but they suited her beautifully as a young Duchess of York.

Coloured trimmings, flowers and feathers are hunted out in rare corners by her discerning milliner, then a bandeau might be fitted inside the hat to go over her bun. Not many nonagenarians could get away with this uncompromising look and the little hint of bandeau above her forehead, but it suited the Queen Mother's singular style.

Although Sophie Rhys-Jones stipulated 'No hats' in the invitation to her five o'clock wedding to Prince Edward, the Queen Mother at ninety-eight felt she could break the rules and wore one matching her pale blue dress and coat. The Queen, in her striking Hardy Amies dress, compromised with a delicate crescent of lilac ostrich feathers.

All her clothes are a source of pleasure. 'Oh, how lovely, I'm going to thoroughly enjoy wearing that!' She never felt they were the same once they had been to the dry cleaners.

Acutely aware of fashion, even in her nineties she still liked to drive along Bond Street and Knightsbridge: 'I saw a very pretty hat in the window', or in Chelsea: 'We were in the King's Road … such a lot of black … all those young girls with short black skirts and long black legs … luckily they were slim.' Not critical or elderly in outlook, the Queen Mother would just be slightly bemused by the Liz Hurley film premiere style with dresses split thigh high to the edge of decency.

High heels are thought bad for the posture, but the Queen Mother is rarely without them, even at race meetings. They give her five feet two inches a little extra height, to make her just a trifle taller than the jockeys. She has numerous pairs of shoes, all made by Edward Rayne, the royal cobbler, but she can never resist just one more pair. Black or, in summer, white, they always get well worn across paddocks and palaces. Her shoemakers however would never express the surprise of a royal cobbler in France who, outraged when a pair of shoes were returned to him by Marie Antoinette, grumbled: 'Ah, but Your Royal Highness, you have walked in them.'

For the last royal wedding of the twentieth century, Prince Edward's, the Queen Mother arrived at the Galilee Door of St George's Chapel, Windsor, in silver two-inch heeled shoes. She quickly shook off the arm offered by Precentor Canon John White to walk unaided to her seat beside Princess Margaret, bespectacled and in a wheel chair.

Her clothes are kept under white covers in her massive wardrobes at Clarence House: a rainbow dream of flouncy evening dresses and day clothes, worn over half a century. You would be hard pressed to get a fine silver cake slice between them. Each tulle and chiffon creation is labelled and tagged with the occasion and date when last worn.

Her wedding dress has been kept separately in a large striped box in the Handley Seymour colours – the staid royal couturier who preceded Norman Hartnell.

When it was once suggested that she might like to donate one or two outfits to a favourite charity, the Queen Mother shook her head. 'One has to be so careful.' Royal women have always been cautious about giving clothes away and make sure they go into the hands of discreet members of the family, who preferably are rarely seen in public. It was hinted that some of the Queen Mother's unworn outfits were burnt.

Unlike many women, there is little preening or fussing, just a quick glimpse in the looking glass and an airy goodbye, 'Oh well, I must be off.' If it is a sombre black coat occasion, the Queen Mother might pat her lapel: 'By the time we've put a little "Mmmm" here it will be very nice.'

Heavy or sensible clothes always invite the 'Mmmm' treatment, which means the addition of a huge piece of jewellery. Typical was a diamond clip the size of a small wild rose on a velvet coat for a National Hunt meeting in January. But the Queen Mother is happiest in summer and on those occasions when her steward taps lightly on her sitting room door before a day's racing and says the words she loves to hear: 'It's a chiffon day, Your Majesty.'

CHAPTER 26

Hard to Know When to Stop Smiling

The Queen, worried that her mother would wear herself out, was always told: 'Work, darling, is the rent you pay for life.'

The Queen Mother still has that strong sense of public duty and a surprising energy. God knows, her place is assured enough as a genuine royal favourite. She continues to appear in the Court Circular, attending a memorial service for a Poet Laureate, presenting a medal, receiving a President. She likes to set an example to fringe royals who seem to pop up only at fun events, royal weddings and the Chelsea Flower Show.

Naturally there has been a gradual reduction in her work load, imperceptible over the years but a relief to her Household, grateful she no longer takes on four engagements in a day: a school in the morning, a hospital in the afternoon, a home for aged jockeys at teatime and a centenary celebration in the evening.

Tireless, keeping her place in the top league of the royal family for so long, her public duties have less been a chore but rather her life. Her instinct is to go on contributing, but these days her diary is not arduous, just a few well-chosen, pleasant engagements, some sentimental.

Part of her secret is her enjoyment of life and the fact that she never thinks of herself as old. Not long after her first hip operation, she saw pensioners waiting near Cheltenham racecourse: 'I've got to go and see the old folk', she said, as if she herself was light years away from a bus pass. Impressive for someone half her age.

People admire her patriotism and compassion. Faces in the crowd watched her with a mixture of affection and nostalgia on 11th May 1999 as she unveiled the first memorial to the 30,000 Londoners killed in the Blitz, in the churchyard of St Paul's Cathedral. The embodiment of the fighting spirit herself, the Queen Mother always acknowledges the heroism of the British people on these 'Lest We Forget' occasions.

The 'most distinguished survivor' of that 1939-45 wartime generation then did what she enjoys most and went out amongst those 'brave London people'. They thanked her emotionally again for staying with them during the Blitz. Some produced photographs of her visits to their bomb-damaged homes. There were smiles, too, when they reminded her of the fruit she brought wounded children in a Lewisham Hospital and how they, because of the war and having never seen bananas before, tried to eat them with their skins on.

Quick to praise others, she was being called Mother Courage at London's St Clement Danes church in the Strand, while she tried to ignore violent protesters shouting 'mass murderer' and throwing red ink to symbolise blood at a ceremony in 1992 honouring Sir Arthur Harris. Hardly used to this kind of thing the Queen Mother, who hates public speaking, was determined to pay tribute to 'Bomber' Harris, chief of RAF Bomber Command, for his part in the Second World War victory.

Ignoring the pacifists' anger about the thousands killed in Germany as a result of the wartime raids which Bomber Harris masterminded, the Queen Mother spoke about 'Sir Arthur ... an inspiring leader who carried the heavy burden of responsibility'. Afterwards, unflustered in pale blue, the Patron of the Bomber Command Association moved serenely amongst RAF war veterans telling them that Sir Arthur's daughter Jacqueline was married to her Treasurer, the Hon. Nicholas Assheton, while the protesters were carried away in police vans.

Patron or President of 300 organisations, the Queen Mother takes patronage seriously and likes to keep in touch. In the late nineties, understandably, she was appearing less on parade grounds, inspecting or taking salutes, although she is still Colonel-in-Chief of eight regiments, including The

Queen's Dragoon Guards, The Queen's Own Hussars, 9th/12th Royal Lancers, The Black Watch and the Royal Army Medical Corps.

For many servicemen and women, there will be unique memories of seeing a grandmotherly outline of a much-loved Colonel-in-Chief arriving in a flowery hat and shimmery crossover dress, or gliding out from a 'spiffy' Air Force jet in high heels, incongruous alongside the polished boots of escorting officers. People remember her rolling walk as she inspected a line-up of straight-backed soldiers, took salutes and was greeted by salvos of artillery and squadrons of screaming jets.

'One for you, and one for me', she liked to say, presenting shamrock on St Patrick's Day to the Irish Guards, picking out sprigs from a wickerwork basket. It was a cheering sight, these guardsmen standing shoulders back, deadpan, as the Queen Mother, herself smothered in shamrock, pinned more greenery on stout shoulders.

In 1993, after a very cold windy ceremony, someone was foolish enough to suggest that perhaps the Queen Mother should give up the yearly pinning of shamrock. The fear was of an IRA assassin's bullet, to which the Queen Mother replied, rather sharply for her: 'Are you mad?' However, for the first time in many years she did not present shamrock in 1999. The battalion was in Germany and Cheltenham races coincided with the ceremony.

The Queen Mother had a way of bringing a light-heartedness to the most formal occasion. The Irish Guards reciprocated this sense of fun. When their mascot Cormac of Tara, an Irish wolfhound, refused to eat Good Boy chocolate drops offered by the Queen Mother, he was put on a charge. Under Section 69 of the Dog Act 1955, Cormac was found guilty of 'Conduct to the prejudice of good order and military discipline'. The Queen Mother sometimes enjoyed these little dog chocolates herself and was sad Cormac missed a treat.

Always fond of Northern Ireland, she remembered it from long before the Troubles. 'I have such happy memories of Hillsborough ... such lovely gardens.' Her sister Rose's husband, Lord Granville, had been Governor-General. Lady Granville, who died in 1967, had always been the favourite sister. These two Edwardians used to stroll round the Castle gardens, as far as the woodland, along rhododendron paths splashed pink, purple and scarlet, stopping to congratulate the gardeners. Another era, all rather different from the simmering, tense reality of 1988 when armed police with sniffer guard-dogs roamed the grounds, surrounded now by barbed wire against the terrorist, instead of a flowery hedge.

In June 1998 the Queen Mother had insisted on visiting the province. Ignoring advice from security experts she went to Enniskillen at a sensitive time, only months after a bomb had exploded killing eleven people and injuring sixteen during a Remembrance Day ceremony.

The ostensible reason for her visit was the opening of Castle Coole, Lord Belmore's home in Fermanagh which had been revamped by the National Trust. The Queen Mother knew that relatives of the bomb blast victims had been specially invited and was determined not to disappoint them. As she told Johnny Speight, creator of the outrageously racist character Alf Garnett in the TV series Till Death Us Do Part, who confessed at a Royal Command Performance he had been worried by bomb threats, 'I always ignore them and get on with my life.'

'We have thought about you so much,' she said gently when she met Mrs Joan Wilson, whose daughter Marie was killed in the blast and whose father Gordon Wilson held her hand as she lay dying.

'May God give them all courage and hope.' The Queen Mother, recalling the Remembrance Day disaster, spoke to the victims' families, 'You have all been so brave ... My heart goes out, as it did then.' The group brightened as she stayed on, refused to be hurried and, head on one side, listened to their sad stories.

It was not a dressy occasion. Mrs Wilson who, like many of the other women was not wearing a hat, just a simple cotton frock, thought the Queen Mother herself had set an example of bravery and courage by being with them on that day.

With more years in the service of the people than any other public figure in Britain, the Queen Mother did once confess to getting tired occasionally. 'I must admit that sometimes I feel something flow out of me.' It was not as effortless as she would have us believe. 'It is hard to know when to stop smiling.' Behind the apparent ease, there was a physical and mental toll, but the reward, she said, was always getting something back from the people, 'sympathy, goodwill, I don't know exactly and I feel strength again. In fact recharged. It is an exchange.'

What people remember about her especially are not so much the grand occasions, but the little human touches, like the aside to the Matron at the celebrated plastic surgery hospital at East Grinstead in Sussex. 'My feet are killing me,' the Queen Mother said after a long day on the wards and then, like any other woman, sat down for a moment and took off her shoes.

Her voice is usually heard murmuring 'thank you', 'how lovely' or 'how kind', but if she feels strongly about some injustice then there is no hesitation about making her views plain. Entering the fray surrounding National Health Service cuts she conveyed her disapproval in an abrasive letter from Clarence House, forcefully expressing her 'distress' about the threatened closure of a hospital she had opened in Merthyr Tydfil only a year earlier.

Britain did its best to show appreciation. The Queen Mother, the first woman to be made Warden of the Cinque Ports, was given a classical garden at Walmer Castle in Kent as a ninety-fifth birthday present by English Heritage. 'I have been given presents before but never a garden.' Specially designed, it represents stages in the Queen Mother's life, the Bury and Glamis by topiary pyramids and a small castle. Filled with herbs, a great deal of rosemary and all her favourite flowers including Buff Beauty and Nathalie Nypels roses, it may seem an extravagance since she visits Walmer only once a year, but it is also open to the public, a scented Queen Mother legacy.

There is a constancy about her and refreshing lack of snobbery. She dislikes pretentiousness. A friend said the Queen Mother was not easily irritated but could be acerbic if people were uppity or pompous. At the Pitlochry Festival Theatre, after a performance of J M Barrie's *The Admirable Crichton*, the cast was being presented. She stopped in front of a young player in the line-up of actors. 'His father, Ma'am,' the local worthy said ingratiatingly, 'is no less than Her Majesty's Ambassador to the Federation of Malaysia.' 'How very grand', the Queen Mother smiled, catching the actor's eye and almost winking at such Uriah Heepishness. She had never cared much for the last Viceroy of India's showy wife, so when she heard that Edwina Mountbatten had been buried at sea remarked 'poor dear Edwina, she always liked to make a splash'.

This was the way the Queen Mother coped with the unexpected too, never discomfited. Spotting some teenage boys in Windsor Great Park throwing stones at a car, she asked the chauffeur to stop and, stepping out of her Daimler NLT 1 said: 'I don't mind your throwing stones at me but what would the Americans think?' Surprisingly down to earth and not intimidated, she had simply taken all the fun out of this yobbish pastime.

The Queen Mother's admirable aplomb was often tested, but rarely more so than the evening when droplets of honey kept falling on her thinning grey hair through dinner at Hagley Hall near Stourbridge. Bees had swarmed in the rococo ceiling and were going about their apian tasks in a chandelier. If she was aware of a sugary crown, there was no sign of it.

Fortunately she is fond of honey. Every Christmas, a royal car comes to a stately halt outside The Hive, a honey shop near Clapham Junction. Under instructions ('no smelly soaps') a Clarence House steward buys a selection of presents, honeycombs, pure apple blossom or wildflower honey, beeswax candles, and reports back to the Queen Mother on her *protégé*, James Hamill and his bees.

Awarded a Queen Elizabeth scholarship by the Royal Warrant Holders to mark her ninetieth birthday, he spent the £6,000 grant studying bees throughout the world before setting up a honey shop in Northcote Road, not a very pastoral part of London. On his first visit to Clarence House, the Queen Mother talked knowledgeably and told him: 'We have had bees at one of our houses for years, but we would never dream of disturbing them.' Like most Americans with their passion for iced water, he picked one up from a silver tray. 'I gulped it down – only to find it was neat gin.' Every year he sends her a basket of goodies from the shop and was charmed by the pleasure she got from 'something as simple as a small wooden honey spoon'.

In January 1988 there was not much of a squeak out of the rest of the royal family, who were enjoying the traditional long Christmas break at Sandringham, stirring only for a pheasant shoot. Only the Queen Mother was out and off to present the Dambusters, No. 617 Squadron of the RAF, with new colours. In 1959 she gave them their original standard and now was determined to hand over its replacement personally.

The Queen Mother has that happy ability to look pleased whether in a formal royal family photograph, at a Golden Wedding party for the Queen at Guildhall, or as the country's perkiest pensioner having her first glimpse of a 'Meals on Wheels' free lunch in 1997. As President of the Women's Royal Voluntary Service, a service for the elderly and housebound, she invited them to drive one of their vans to the gates of Clarence House where she would inspect the dish of the day. However, when asked if she would try the roast beef and apple pie herself, she regretted that, alas, she had a long standing 'luncheon' engagement with the Canadian High Commissioner. There was no one better at gracefully detaching themselves. 'So kind ... Byee'.

There is always that charming questioning end to a sentence, never imposing an idea, rather a light suggestion: 'Don't you think?' On a visit to Winchester in 1986 to see the Domesday 900 exhibition she saw a model of Windsor Castle. 'Wasn't it nice,' she suggested with a slight smile, 'before Slough was there?'

Anything to do with the King can always strike a chord. Her response was warm and immediate when approached by Welsh villagers in Llangurig in 1997 for financial help towards two computers for the local school. Kindness shown to the Duke of York eighty years earlier when he was recovering from tuberculosis in this part of mid-Wales would stand the villagers in good stead.

Thanking her for her donation the headmaster, Ernest Jones, said he doubted if the Queen Mother knew very much about the Internet or the World Wide Web, but because of her generosity the twenty-nine pupils at this tiny primary school would now be able to join the Information Superhighway.

Standing on the balcony at Buckingham Palace for the VJ Anniversary Parade in 1995 and hearing the distant rumbling of a flypast, the Queen Mother looked up and fluttered her fingers at the sky. Watching her, someone said how remarkable her sight must be, but the Queen said: 'Don't be silly, Mummie hasn't been able to see a thing for forty years, she just instinctively knows what to do.'

CHAPTER 27

Drinky Poohs

'No outdoor games at all except dominoes.' The Queen Mother shares with Oscar Wilde a distaste for heartiness.

Lunch is a favourite sport, supper parties too. A stimulating conversationalist, the Queen Mother is a good listener with a readiness to be amused. Her regulars, sublimely unselfconscious assured raconteurs, old-style confident high Tories, excel in her company.

Teasingly, on asking Lord Carrington why the Conservative Party got rid of Mrs Thatcher – 'Well, frankly Ma'am, towards the end she became completely impossible' – the Queen Mother replied: 'Oh, then I think I should be thankful you're not responsible for me.'

Her London home is for serious entertaining: listening to politicians, tycoons, leaders in the arts and of course racing experts, she loves being in the know. Sir Claus Moser, formerly Chairman of Covent Garden, thought most of the men on her guest list were a bit in love with her. Those profiled too frequently at their stately homes with great colour photographs in glossy magazines were struck off.

One politician not in favour was the erudite Roy Jenkins when he headed the Social Democratic Party in 1981. 'I liked the old Labour Party,' the Queen Mother told the author A N Wilson, at a private dinner party, imitating Lord Jenkins of Hillhead's inability to pronounce his r's. She confided, 'I dislike this new socialist party of Woy's.' And with a touch of Edward Lear she added, 'Well you don't change socialist just by leaving off the end. I say it's a cheat to start something called the Social party.'

The Queen Mother's summer lunches at Clarence House were memorable if only for the beautiful presentation. Since eleven o'clock, the air would have been sniffed by liveried servants and, unless there was a force ten gale, up went the blue and white awning. Even if there were menacing clouds her hearty view was that 'Lunch is not a meal to be eaten indoors.'

If it is really warm, a green grotto dining room is created under the branches of a tree, a table laid with crisp white damask, crystal, incomparable silver and bowls of pink and white flowers. 'Is it all right to have a picnic like this?' the Queen Mother will ask, leading guests into the garden. 'It's only us.'

Pimms on the lawn followed by light, elegant food: a wealth of pale pink and green savoury mousses, a delicate soufflé, lobster croquettes served on gold and russet Chelsea porcelain, rare lamb, new potatoes and peas from Windsor – the Queen Mother sprinkles sugar on hers – then raspberries with Jersey cream or meringue with black cherries in liqueur.

Basking in this atmosphere of leisured elegance as the traffic surges by on the Mall, the Queen Mother might turn to a stressed executive and ask, 'Don't the fuschias remind you of freshly baked cherry pie?' with a whimsical enjoyment of a summer's day.

Footmen and butlers in black tailcoats, red waistcoats with gold trim and brass buttons replenish glasses, pouring from elaborate decanters shaped like leaping silver fish, or squirrels clutching silver acorns between their paws.

The only interruption to this pastoral idyll is the presence of the corgis. 'You'll find no pussy cats here,' the Queen Mother says advisedly as her four-legged pets explore the visitors' ankles. 'Oh do you mind them?' she asks and with smiling sycophancy nobody ever admits that they do. Unlike the Queen's corgis they do not wear special shoes as protection for their paws against the gravel at Buckingham Palace. Lawns at Clarence House are velvety, not rough.

The Queen Mother likes men about her who are clever and informed. Sir Woodrow Wyatt, opinionated and mischievous and who died in December 1997, had been a good Westminster source and was also useful for racing tips as Chairman of the Tote, though she knew he liked to be provocative. Lord St John of Fawsley, formerly Norman St John Stevas, was given a peerage for service to the arts and makes her laugh, although a member of the Household remarked: 'He was lunch; he never stayed.'

In touch and surprisingly modern, conversation at her table tends to be entertaining political gossip and current affairs. A discerning viewer, the Queen Mother worried about television presenters in war zones, particularly the BBC reporter Kate Adie whom she thought intrepid. 'Dear Kate, she always seems to be trudging through the mud or where there is some disaster or other.'

Competitive and informed, she likes to receive the best financial brains, graduates of Insead, the highly-charged business school in Paris, and to tune in to the latest gossip from the Euro Bourse. There has been a friendly rivalry between Clarence House and Buckingham Palace and there is nothing the Queen Mother likes better than casually mentioning an unexpected Stock Market percentage, information she might have carefully wheedled out of some City high-flyer.

To be invited to lunch or dinner in London is one thing but The Royal Lodge for the weekend is the ultimate accolade. Clarence House is usually duty entertaining, The Royal Lodge is for fun. Invitations come three weeks in advance and are rarely refused. Guests are never encouraged to arrive before six on a Saturday evening, a civilised time for any hostess. The Queen Mother likes to spend Saturday afternoons watching the racing. Weekends are altogether lighter; for best friends and 'old cosies'. Princess Margaret would complain of 'a lot of geriatrics' but always knew it would be most amusing company: artist Derek Hill, writer and broadcaster Ludovic Kennedy, Sir Alec Guinness, Sir John Gielgud and actress Maggie Smith. Popular couples have included Lord Gowrie and his blonde wife Neiti; also film director Bryan Forbes and his wife Nanette Newman, their easy Pinewood charm particularly acceptable because they had been married to each other for more than forty years.

Friends who enjoy 'church crawling', know about art, and enjoy the theatre and music included Sir Hugh and Lady

Casson, former President of the Royal Academy, Lady 'Mollie', Marchioness Salisbury, a dedicated gardener, and Hugh and Fortune, the Duke and Duchess of Grafton. These are the people who share the Queen Mother's birthday treats when she takes a small party to the ballet or theatre. The trouble is finding the right play, it has to be above reproach. If too *risqué* it is not that the Queen Mother would be shocked, but she finds it tedious when the audience turns round to watch her reaction. A safe, assured choice has been Peter Shaffer's play *Lettice and Lovage* and *The Phantom of the Opera* starring Michael Crawford: 'We all swooned,' a vintage Clarence House word, 'with excitement'.

There was no more sublime company with which to explore old churches than Sir John Betjeman, a great and humorous friend. When he died, the Queen Mother made sure Lady Elizabeth Cavendish, sister of the Duke of Devonshire and who had been the poet's companion, remained part of her Windsor weekend coterie.

Another Poet Laureate and a very different personality, the late Ted Hughes, was invited to Sandringham in the summer of 1997 and stayed with the Queen Mother in Scotland. Normally reclusive, wounded by the suicide of his wife Sylvia Plath and then his second wife, he found in the Queen Mother a kindred soul, who loved and knew about poetry. He wrote her long thank-you letters in his distinctive, narrative verse. When he died, the Queen Mother, leaning on Prince Charles' arm, attended an 'unusual service for an unusual man' in May 1999 at Westminster Abbey. Afterwards she visibly cheered up when Nobel Laureate Seamus Heaney made a fuss of her.

Houseguests at The Royal Lodge in summer are bombarded on arrival by the heavy scent of old-fashioned roses and carnations in their rooms. First sight of their hostess is at about eight o'clock on Saturday evening.

'Drinky poohs' for the Queen Mother might be gin and Dubonnet before lunch, or dry Martini before dinner. Sometimes as hostess she mixes them herself while quoting a line or two from Jane Austen, pursing her lips with pleasure if the drink is suitably potent and dry on the first sip.

Then she leads guests to the Gothic dining room, with its teal-green walls, a shade 'dear Bertie' liked so much. Special favourites are allowed to use his walking stick.

Over an excellent dinner, her skin radiating the luxury of leisurely scented baths, and relaxed, the Queen Mother enjoys sparkling, understated wit. If someone raises a subject which is taboo, such as sex or religion, she will suddenly have great difficulty working the pepper pot, 'wretched thing', and appear quite helpless, so that every man at the table wants to be the one to release the recalcitrant spice.

Guests all move up two places and women withdraw briefly, rejoining the men at around half past ten for a sing-song round the piano, or a game of Flip-Flop-Out or Racing Demon.

If conversation takes a turn the Queen Mother does not understand, her cry has always been 'Housemaids', a warning in Racing Demon if someone is not playing properly. The late Lord Home, who shared with her a love for Scotland, recalled the Queen Mother's deftness with cards. He always knew some coup was being delicately concealed when her hand fluttered at her throat.

In the old days at big parties it was not unusual to see the Queen Mother in tiara and spangled crinoline, with 'Bertie's' diamond brooch on an ample bosom, playing the bongo drums. She loves all sorts of music, classical, ballet, jazz and some of the modern composers. Sir Elton John was as likely to be playing the piano at The Royal Lodge as Rostropovich, the great Russian cellist. Partial to Victorian ballads she could recite 'The Shooting of Dan McGraw' nicely and once joined Nöel Coward in singing 'Follow the Van'.

The Queen Mother does enjoy over-the-top theatrical antics, like the 'shout of joy' given by waspish American writer Truman Capote when the summer pudding was brought in at a lunch given in her honour; Maggie Smith's eye-rolling as she read aloud after dinner; Sir Frederick Ashton's flamboyance as he swept the ground with an imaginary cloak murmuring 'Majesté' and kneeling at the Queen Mother's feet.

Once, partnered by the octogenarian Sir Frederick, they danced 'exotically', the Queen Mother using her chiffon sleeve as a yashmak, before sweeping her elderly guests along in a series of waltzes, tangos and paso dobles. Dowager Viscountess

Hambleden said afterwards she had 'never seen the eldest daughter in such glorious fits of laughter'. The Queen was amused. Ashton was treasured by the Queen Mother as an ideal guest with a finely honed, theatrical sense of occasion. He fitted in beautifully at The Royal Lodge weekends.

On Sundays women guests, encouraged to have breakfast in bed, are disappointed if they hoped to see the Queen Mother downstairs chatting over the kedgeree. But she does appreciate it if they accompany her to church. Lunch is usually a classic roast followed by a lively walk, perhaps to the Royal Mausoleum at Frogmore.

After the weekend, guests returning home on Monday find their clothes beautifully packed in tissue paper, their shoes and cars more highly polished than when they arrived.

It has not, however, been all crinolined evenings and Olde Ruritania. The Queen Mother also loves gardening, fishing – though the Queen has made her put her rods away – and racing.

The garden at Birkhall has been her joy. She can never quite make up her mind whether the charming eighteenth-century white house near Balmoral is a 'small big house', or a 'big small house'. Lived-in, comfortable and old-fashioned, Prince Charles took Camilla Parker-Bowles there for holidays. Landings are lined with *Spy* cartoons, most signed by the subjects, eleven long-case and carriage clocks stand in the dining room and by the television set there is a pile of *Fawlty Towers* videos.

'My mother was a dirt gardener,' the Queen Mother says, strolling in the garden which she created herself with apricot-coloured godetias, sweet peas and roses smelling of apples. Nasturtiums, she said, always reminded her of childhood. On either side of a long flight of steps, her monogram ER is often planted in white alyssum, dark blue lobelia and French marigolds. 'One of them will do for the Queen and the other for me.'

In the late afternoon, she likes to climb to the highest point of this old-fashioned garden where flowers and vegetables flourish alongside each other in the country style. She was joined sometimes by Prince Charles in the green gazebo, where both would enjoy spotting policemen disguised as ghillies prowling the heather. He inherited his love of organic gardening from his grandmother.

Scotland was for salmon fishing until a few years ago when the Queen persuaded her mother not to wade into the River Dee anymore, standing for hours in cold water. Once at Balmoral when there had been no sign of the Queen Mother by eight o'clock in the evening, search parties were sent out and they found her in her squashy felt hat dragging a salmon in the dark. Holding it up, she smiled: 'Sorry, but this is what has kept me.' Landing a twenty-pound salmon certainly earned the admiration of the ghillies. When a salmon fishbone lodged in her throat at dinner in 1982 and she began to choke, the Queen Mother called this 'the salmon's revenge'.

Norfolk is for walks on the beach and music festivals. The Queen Mother uses the royal family's small summer house on the edge of Lord Coke's estate at Holkham. She is an enthusiastic walker, unperturbed by the nudist beach antics on the coast road near King's Lynn. Picnicking on the beach at Holkham was never fancy. There were many cars, of course, and picnic baskets delivered by footmen, but otherwise it is a Formica table with plastic knives, forks and mugs and 'everyone diving in,' according to Lady Gowrie.

'To be present with her on a beach picnic is like having an oxygen tent along,' said one friend, who found it remarkable that when in the company of the Queen Mother 'you never saw a cross face or an uninterested expression.'

The trouble with owning horses, she used to say, was 'You get hooked; you never want to part with them.' National Hunt racing is still her passion. 'It's the danger – a bit of excitement.' Very rarely does she miss her beloved Cheltenham Gold Cup Festival; only 'flu would keep her away. Loving every minute, at the first meeting of the new century in March 2000 the Queen Mother could be seen in the Parade ring, leaning on two sticks, chatting easily with trainers and jockeys.

Behind the scenes, and with typical thoughtfulness, she had asked to meet the local Liberal Democrat MP Nigel Jones, recently traumatised by the death of his personal assistant from a sword attack. Invited to lunch with her in the swathed comfort of the Royal Box, he was able to talk about his feelings and the strain of the last few months.

The Queen Mother likes to catch up with the day's racing on a video re-run when she gets back to Clarence House. Once a hapless valet had videoed the wrong channel. There was no bad temper, just a question hovering lightly on the air. 'Might,' the Queen Mother asked gently, 'it be possible to find a copy?'

Edward Gillespie, Managing Director at Cheltenham was approached. Nothing was too much trouble where the Queen Mother was concerned. 'She does have that effect on people,' he recalled at the end of a long day.

In his account in *The Times* of this celebrated week in the racing calendar, Gillespie described Channel 4's willingness to provide another video, but how two hours had to be spent editing out the commentators' earthy asides on the original. Pity, the Queen Mother might well have enjoyed them.

Her racehorses, her 'darling boys', are the Queen Mother's special indulgence. Every week *Horse and Hound* and the *Racing Post* are brought to her sitting room on a silver salver by a footman. She even chose horsey language to reply to an inquiry about whether an old leg injury was better? Smiling, she replied: 'Still hanging on, they won't have to pin fire me yet,' a reference to a method used on horses of burning tissues to encourage new growth.

Her beloved 'boys' were the reason for her second hip replacement on 25th January 1998, when she slipped on her walking stick inspecting mares in foal in icy weather at the Royal Stud. Yet months after this gruelling surgery she was at Sandown to see her horse Norman Conqueror romping home in the *Horse and Hound* Grand Military Gold Cup, giving her 412th win and putting her in the record books. It was lucky the Queen loves horses too and helps pay her mother's racing bills.

Racing has been a very large part of her social life. Trainer Jeremy Tree once regretfully had to turn down an invitation to lunch, explaining: 'I'm awfully sorry but I've got Fred Astaire staying with me.' The Queen Mother replied: 'We shall expect you both at The Royal Lodge for lunch.' Fred Astaire was 'terrified', but when the legendary dancer got to Windsor, he had 'a marvellous time'. Another guest at the lunch recalled: 'The Queen and her mother both made a tremendous fuss of him.' Later a bemused Astaire, obviously bowled over by his hostess, told friends, 'Oh yes, and the little Queen was there too.'

The 'little' Queen once asked Michael Oswald who runs the stud at Sandringham, 'Why do you keep half of Mummie's mares at Sandringham and half at Wolferton?' He laughed. 'Well, if I didn't, Ma'am, one groom would think he hadn't had his fair share.' The Queen nodded. 'Yes, that is the effect Mummie seems to have on people.'

The stable lads always smile when they see the Queen Mother's Land Rover bumping gently along a muddy track at Sandringham. The electric step comes up and she gets out with a pocket full of carrots.

Whenever there was no news from Clarence House in the Court Circular, those solicitous for the Queen Mother hoped this meant that she was resting but would discover a week or so later that she had slipped out of the country on one of her 'jaunts abroad'. These are still important to her and she is far more European at heart than many of the royal family, loving France and Italy especially.

In 1992 she paid an informal visit to Andalusia. Over a jolly lunch with the Spanish King Juan Carlos, his wife Queen Sofia and the Domecq family, owners of the sherry-producing vineyards, her host the 8th Duke of Wellington explained that everywhere the Queen Mother went there were cries of 'guapa, guapa'. This, the Duke explained, meant 'pretty woman'.

Tuscany each May has long been a favourite destination, especially revisiting the Villa Capponi where she had such happy times as a little girl. But it was not until 1984 that, influenced by her friend John Julius Norwich, Lady Diana Cooper's son, she paid her first proper visit to Venice and shared his passionate commitment to saving *La Serenissima* from sinking into the sea. She had been once before, briefly, on the way to Belgrade in 1923.

'When we were York we saw it, but it was rather foggy,' the Queen Mother explained; 'Bertie and I were on our way to a christening. He was to be godfather to someone, but I've forgotten who.' The child Crown Prince Peter was forgotten, but not the place.

It was a grand arrival, sailing into the city in splendour on board the Royal Yacht *Britannia*. Predictably the Italians were charmed by her. Visits within the imperilled city were part work, part pleasure spent with friends in the arts sharing their concern for Venice, badly damaged by flooding in 1966.

The Italian security men were appalled that the Queen Mother should want to sail along the quieter canals where she might be vulnerable, but she got her way. 'I loved the stillness and the peace away from the noise of those motorboats. So restful.'

Entranced by Venice, waving, smiling, stepping delicately out of a black ceremonial gondola in high heels, she good humouredly bore being serenaded with 'Just One More Cornetto' and later explored the Byzantine cathedral on Torcello – though she confessed Durham was really her favourite.

These visits were not all beer and skittles. 'We did three churches and one or two big houses a day,' Sir Hugh Casson recalled of one private jaunt when the Queen Mother and a small group of special friends stayed at a hotel in Brittany.

In June 1989 she went to France twice, once to have lunch with Toulouse Lautrec's great-grandson and to explore the artist's house. Whether visiting the Hennessys or the Rothschilds in France, she would be entertained in the style she liked with memorable food and Veuve Clicquot or Krug, her special favourites. She speaks French well; when she and the Queen and Princess Margaret want a really good gossip this is the language they use.

The Queen Mother likes to tell a humorous story about herself. At a banquet in France for her ninetieth birthday, the French waitress asked her if she would like beef or lamb and she replied 'Boeuf', only to find the waitress bringing her gargantuan helpings of both. These restaurant visits could be hazardous. Once after an excellent lunch at the Prince de Ligne La Tremoilie's château at Serrant, the chef was sent for so that the royal visitor could thank him. When he arrived it was with his favourite ferret curled round his neck.

France was for châteaux and delectable soirées but was not so much fun for her after the death of her good friend Prince Jean-Louis de Faucigny-Lucinge, aged eighty-eight, in 1992. She missed this urbane companion who entertained so well, arranged epicurean delights and reminded her how they danced together in the 1920s before her marriage to the Duke of York.

Sometimes, the Queen Mother can be delightfully unworldly with a touch of the grand Edwardian – not unlike one Duke of Marlborough, who had always believed toothpaste arrived on a toothbrush until one day his valet was ill and he was mystified when it was missing; or the Twenties socialite Daisy Fellowes who stopped to admire some beautifully dressed, strange children, only to be told 'They are yours.'

A classic example was the treat masterminded by Prince Jean-Louis for the Queen Mother who wanted to be taken to 'just an ordinary French bistro' in the countryside. Needless to say a three-star Michelin restaurant in the Loire valley was chosen.

On the day, the Queen Mother thought it charming how nobody stared or made a fuss. 'How lovely,' she beamed, blissfully unaware of the massive planning that had gone on for months. No members of the public were allowed in the restaurant that day; instead the local Prefect had filled it with his policemen and their wives – the women with their short hair, poodles on leads and good grooming, their husbands florid in dark suits, and all appreciated the exceptional food.

'How easy it all was,' trilled the Queen Mother afterwards to Sir Pierson Dixon, the British Ambassador. 'You need not have worried ... Nobody bothered us at all.'

CHAPTER 28

Her Loving Net Spread Wide

Prince William symbolises new hope, a bright start to an updated 21st century monarchy. Serious and clever, he is as much loved by the Queen Mother as his father was at the same age. For his great-grandmother, William overcomes his shyness and lends a protective hand down church steps; she is always delighted to accept, when normally a million proffered arms are waved away. If he hurries (he was eighteen on 21st June 2000) she could be at his wedding.

As maternal head of the Family Firm, the Queen Mother sees in William the best qualities of his mother, the caring, the sense of fun, but also his father's thoughtfulness. Bright and a good all-rounder with twelve GCSE passes, he hopes to read History of Art at Durham or Edinburgh. The Prince has also expressed an interest in the University of East Anglia. This modern institution would be an unusual choice for an heir to the throne, especially since his father went to Cambridge. His choice of subject will be useful for getting to know the treasures in the royal galleries, but will it equip him for the career his father has in mind? Prince Charles would like him to join the Welsh Guards, where talk in the Mess is perhaps less about the detail of a Fra Angelico as the size of a steak dinner after manoeuvres.

Charles' eldest son is a determined character, however, and will not be dragooned prematurely into an army career or too many royal engagements. William knows his own mind and has made it plain that he wants to spend the next four years unencumbered by royal duties. During his student years, he says, he does not want too much bowing and curtseying or people calling him 'Sir', but it would be a reckless courtier who took this instruction too literally.

There was a little family concern when Prince William went through a phase of grumbling about his destiny, appearing keener to be Eton's Karaoke champion on field trips than a dutiful heir apparent. The Queen Mother, as always sagely comforting, suggested that it was only natural for a young man to feel like rejecting this fearsome future. George VI had been a reluctant king, but how quickly, she says, her husband restored the monarchy's iconic status after the debilitating effects of the Abdication.

Already a golden boy, William is an all-rounder, bright and athletic. He appears to have come through the trauma of his parents' divorce and his mother's death remarkably well-adjusted.

Recent talk of his father's secret wish to marry Mrs Parker-Bowles in Scotland coincided with a poll conducted by NOP for the Sunday Express which found that half the country wanted Prince William to succeed the present Queen, skipping a generation and leaving Prince Charles free to marry and pursue his interests in saving the planet.

Prince William would seem the perfect heir, but the House of Windsor has a habit of being unpredictable. While younger brother Prince Harry may now seem outwardly less suitable, if for some unforeseen reason he was forced to become King, he would follow in the footsteps of his great-grandfather George VI and great-great-grandfather George V, both younger brothers of the heir apparent.

Meanwhile the Queen Mother has watched with approval the carefully orchestrated programme for 'The Restoration' of Charles III, and the recovery of the Prince's image following the break-up of his marriage and the death of Diana, whom the country so admired. The Queen Mother's resolute disapproval of Mrs Parker-Bowles is about the only area of disagreement she has with Prince Charles. He would be wise to remember her unswerving resistance to the Duchess of Windsor when he next tries to get her to change her mind about accepting the 'woman he loves'.

These days Charles seems generally happier and more confident while doggedly trying to gain Mrs Parker-Bowles the respect and affection of a wife within the royal family. Hurt by the exclusion of his mistress from the Queen's party of 21st June at Windsor Castle, the most important royal family event for years, the Prince paraded Mrs Parker-Bowles at a public engagement in London's East End the night before. This significant gesture was designed to make up for any snub to his beloved.

The irony is that Camilla's ex-husband, Brigadier Andrew Parker-Bowles, a favourite with the Queen Mother, attended the party. Even the Duchess of York was there, although only invited for the dancing which seemed a bit half-hearted.

For a first foray in public life, Mrs Parker-Bowles coped well with the limelight in Shoreditch. Hardly a slinky figure in a baby pink Versace chiffon dress, the colour chosen by the Prince, its glitter fitted in perfectly with the rich European and American café society guests. What put Mrs Parker-Bowles head and shoulders above most of the other women was not her outfit or her newly highlighted hair, however, but her diamond necklace and earrings. It was the sort of jewellery a woman who behaves well receives from a royal admirer. These were not from Prince Charles, though, but gifts from Edward VII to his celebrated mistress, Mrs Keppel, now proudly displayed on the ample bosom of her great-granddaughter.

Such jewellery, a deliberate choice for the evening, was particularly eye-catching in Shoreditch where hecklers shouted some of their more disagreeable plans for the royal family and held up illustrations of a decapitated House of Windsor. In her bustling way, Mrs Parker-Bowles smiled gamely, hurrying on in with the Prince to drink champagne at the reception.

To confirm her standing as *maîtresse en titre*, she chose the wine for the evening. Food was served on black rubber tablecloths. The dinner celebrated the launch of a £6 million warehouse headquarters for the Prince's Architecture and the Urban Environment Foundation. This is one of his newest charity ventures. No longer under pressure from the Palace, he is not frightened to speak out about current issues and create new ground for the royal family who traditionally never express controversial opinions. Respecting the many religions in Britain today, he has declared that when he becomes King, he would like to be the 'defender of faiths' and not 'Defender of the Faith'.

Naturally philanthropic, the Prince embraces 'green' causes, has spoken out against genetically modified foods and brutalist architecture, and supports British beef. He has learnt a lesson about the value of compassion, something the Queen Mother has always known, and appears more at ease these days with himself and those he meets. He has always been viewed affectionately by the British people and hopes this will eventually include his mistress.

To add to his popularity Charles has become that modern phenomenon, a single parent. He has given up flamboyant polo, spends more time with his sons, and when the family appear together they are more like brothers. On a Spring 2000 Swiss skiing trip to Klosters, father and sons clowned around for the cameras, the princes' arms around their father, Prince Harry pretending to mess up Charles' hair over his bald spot.

A touching fatherly gesture was Charles' insistence that Prince William stay at Highgrove the night before his eighteenth birthday. Both father and son will have been aware of how proud Diana, Princess of Wales would have been of her strapping, good-looking son on the day of his coming of age. In order to wish him happy birthday before he rushed back to Eton to take A-level examinations, Charles wanted to see William and to watch him (metaphorically) unwrap his coming of age birthday present – a £2,000 Kawasaki 125cc motor bike.

Exams prevented William from attending the family party at Windsor on the night of his birthday, which was a great disappointment to the Queen and Queen Mother who are intensely proud of him and speak approvingly of his 'beautiful manners'. The Queen Mother believes Prince William will be a fine king and follow in her husband's dutiful footsteps. He will, though, thanks to his mother, know more about real life outside the castle walls than any of his predecessors and have emotional maturity, a hard-won spur of a turbulent childhood spent with warring but loving parents.

Since the death of Diana, Princess of Wales, the Prince has been spending more time at Windsor, growing close to the paternal influence, no longer torn by the child's agony of divided loyalties between mother and father. He and the Queen get on well together, and they share the same sense of humour and disdain for pomposity.

Surprisingly it was the Queen who agreed with William that he could postpone the use of his HRH title at least until he has graduated. In the meantime she will take him with her on some important royal engagements, an opportunity to bond with her agreeable grandson in a way she never could with Prince Charles.

For Prince William, an illuminating lesson about his heritage has unfolded in his lifetime. He has seen some crushing blows for the royal family, those narrowly averted crises, the ebb and flow of public opinion and, more encouraging of late, a surge of public warmth and renewed appreciation of the Queen.

No textbook could tell it better than the Queen. From her, William has absorbed his family history. Like a child's story, it begins with good Queen Victoria presiding over a model royal family, lucrative colonies and far-flung dominions; her son king Edward VII succeeds, not such a fine example, but much loved. He is followed by George V, upright and staunch, who restores the monarchy's impeccable aura. Then there is a nasty blip: enter the bad fairy. Mrs Simpson arrives from America and King Edward VIII abdicates; disaster threatens. The spell is broken until a brilliant recovery by George VI and his Queen, William's great-grandmother, a faultless Consort with personal charm and universal appeal.

Prince William is already aware of how important it is to choose the right wife; 'someone who knows the ropes', the Queen advises. She talks to him about her experience on coming to the throne in 1952. It has been a popular enough reign, even if his grandmother has in the past given an impression of being perched unattainably on a golden pedestal.

Then in 1981 along came a whirlwind in the shape of William's mother, Diana, Princess of Wales, who with youth and beauty and much more, would change things irrevocably for the royal family. The Princess had a mesmeric effect on people, with her extraordinary gift with the sick and the homeless. She also made sure her sons were not insulated in gilded cages. In addition, she was lovely to look at, had a natural gaiety and was a wonderful mother.

Her sudden death brought to the surface a simmering popular resentment against the royal family. The Princess had changed the public's perception of monarchy, and now it was criticised for a cold remoteness, for being out of touch and expensive. Towards the end of the century it was looking an endangered species but recovered, as it always has, to be on a sounder, warmer footing.

It is important, the Queen Mother feels, that her great-grandson should be aware of these tragic events and pitfalls but should look forward. If Prince Charles has his way, William will inherit a streamlined monarchy. Aware of social problems and what is on people's minds, Charles is openly political but has to keep his support for devolution in Scotland discrete. He wants to run a slimmed down 'People's Monarchy', although not quite like the Scandinavian bicycling royal families, because the British value pageantry too much.

When he is king, Charles plans to get rid of several royal homes and courtiers' grace and favour apartments which cost the taxpayer £20 million a year. The Royal Yacht *Britannia* has gone and it looks as if the Royal Train may be scrapped too, so perhaps King William V may need a bicycle after all. During his reign, royal daughters may receive the same rights to succession as their brothers; HRH titles for minor members of the royal family may have disappeared, and there will be altogether less bowing and scraping, fewer but more modern courtiers, less self-serving sycophancy.

Meanwhile William's training as heir to the throne goes on. The Queen Mother loves the fact that William is the first member of the royal family to go to Eton, her brother's old school, and is delighted he was elected to 'Pop', the ultimate accolade. During the 'eighties, when her good friend Lord Charteris was Provost, she would visit from Windsor and was 'marvellous with the young boys'. In 1999 this tall, cool, assured teenager was awarded Eton's Sword of Honour, about the highest honour for a first year cadet in the School's Combined Cadet Corps. In the holidays he has visited the House of Commons and enjoyed work experience at Spink, the Mayfair art dealers.

William is already a bit of a heartbreaker with a penchant for jazzy waistcoats, shades of his mother's fashion flair. He enjoys partying at country houses all over England. He shoots and dances well, enjoys cooking paella, swimming, rugby, football and water polo. All this was harmless enough until his recent introduction to the 'London scene' with its readily available Ecstasy, cocaine and other substances. His guide to the Chelsea and Soho nightspots has been Tom, Camilla Parker-Bowles' worldly son. Seven years older than Prince William, he works in public relations, that ubiquitous nineties job, and the Queen Mother's fear is that he might have had an enduringly bad influence on Prince William.

Prince Charles, who is Tom's godfather, is torn between being supportive of his mistress and being desperately anxious and protective of Prince William. He dreads the thought that William might end up with pinched nostrils, giggling helplessly at the Garter ceremony. Once again the name Parker-Bowles has sent a shiver of apprehension down the stiff spines of older Palace courtiers.

There was concern too that Prince Harry, outwardly uncomplicated, a daredevil on the ski slopes, still impressionable and also at Eton, might come under the influence of his glamorous older brother's mentor. But the two princes are too level-headed and have been through enough in life already to want to self-destruct with flaky habits. Drugs and illicit liaisons have always gone on in the royal family, but nowadays Sir Walter Bageshot dictum, 'Never let daylight in on the monarchy,' is no longer respected. While we can tolerate all sorts of wild entertainment and behaviour in Britain today, we are censorious about our royal family which must be seen to be above reproach.

William and Harry met Camilla Parker-Bowles by deliberate accident at St James' Palace and thought her pleasant enough. Soon afterwards, in January 1999, their father made a first public appearance with her at the Ritz in London. The Queen Mother thought it a dreadful idea and told Prince Charles he was making a spectacle of himself. When the presenter Jonathan Dimbleby asked a BBC Any Questions studio audience if they had been pleased about the couple's appearance together at the Ritz, only one hand was raised.

Meanwhile Charles remains oblivious to any residue of feeling against Mrs Parker-Bowles; they are very much a couple, hosting parties together at Buckingham Palace, taking holidays abroad. He expects a sceptical public to see the finer qualities of the woman with whom he is happy to breathe the same air. The Archbishop of Canterbury, Dr Carey, understands the Prince's dilemma and how he hopes that it may be possible for him to marry his divorced love. At private meetings however, Dr Carey has tactfully had to try and explain that remarriage in the Church of England could not be fully sanctioned.

Charles, though, like other royal princes over the centuries, listens to his advisers only when it suits him. And he has always had that hint of in-built princely arrogance which his late wife tried to defuse by teasing him, calling him 'Churlls'. She knew how blinkered from reality this troubled man could be.

Whatever Churlls' imperfections, in the Queen Mother's eyes he will always be 'numero uno' grandchild. The regard is mutual; he says, 'I can't tell you what the Queen Mother means to all of us.'

Of her six grandchildren, Prince Andrew, Duke of York, a serving naval officer with a passion for golf and blokeish jokes, might not be in as much harmony with her as Charles with his appreciation of art and classical music. He is, though, good-hearted and uncomplicated, and the Queen Mother admired his dignity during the humiliating breakdown of his marriage.

His children, the bright and lively Princess Beatrice and Princess Eugénie are, the Queen Mother says, 'dear sweet little girls' who may go to boarding school in Switzerland. And in the beginning she was fond of their mother, Sarah Ferguson, a jolly, red-haired former chalet girl whom Prince Andrew had married on 23rd July 1986. Quite quickly after the marriage however, the Queen Mother felt that the Duchess showed scant respect for her husband or the royal family as rumours spread of her cavorting with other men while her husband was away at sea.

In 1992 they separated. For the sake of her daughters, the estranged Duchess agreed to join the Queen, the Queen Mother and the rest of the royal family at Balmoral, though she thought of it as a granite prison. Nobody would ever forget the dreadful morning when any chance of reconciliation was wrecked by the appearance on the royal breakfast table, as the family toyed with their kippers, of tabloid newspaper pictures of a semi-naked Duchess of York. Paparazzi had snatched intimate shots of her by a swimming pool at a villa in St Tropez, having her toes sucked by her 'financial adviser', Johnny Bryan, a balding American. The Queen burst into tears. This set the seal for her on an 'annus horribilis' following the painful break-up of the Prince and Princess of Wales' marriage. Furthermore there had been the fire at Windsor Castle for which she was forced to foot the bill, the taxpayers having become disillusioned and unwilling to do so.

The Queen Mother was upset. She knew how rare it was for her impeccably sanguine daughter to show emotion and seethed at the discredit brought upon the York title, one she herself had enhanced. Later, the Duchess made the Queen Mother cringe again with the commercial promotion of cranberry juice and shopping malls in America to pay off her enormous debts. The Queen Mother was no stranger herself to the overdraft, but few people expected her to promote marshmallows or Goodboy chocolate drops.

There had, too, been earlier embarrassment when the Duchess' father, Major Ronald Ferguson, polo adviser to the royal family, was caught in a London massage parlour. The computer literate referred to him as CD Ron – Seedy Ron. The Duke and Duchess of York were divorced in 1996, the same year as the Prince and Princess of Wales.

Neither Mrs Parker-Bowles nor the Duchess of York were invited to Prince Edward's wedding to Sophie Rhys-Jones on 19th June 1999. The diplomatic reason was that, not having any rank, it would be difficult to accommodate them. Almost a year later this provided a useful explanation not to include Mrs Parker-Bowles at the glamorous Windsor Castle party, which had thirty-foot banks of peonies and delphiniums, garden flowers that the royal family love.

The Queen Mother had fully prepared for a summer of centenary celebrations, feverishly ordering new clothes and hats. Earlier in the day she appeared at Ascot in a fashionably strong shade of pink with a paler cartwheel hat. After a day's racing in high heels and a black-tie dinner, she occasionally looked a little tired. Then, as she was fêted by 700 invited guests including crowned and uncrowned heads from all over Europe, the band played *A Nightingale Sang in Berkeley Square*, one of her favourite wartime tunes, to round off an exceptionally happy day. However, much as he loves her a pained Prince Charles found it hard to accept that two of the women he loves most in the world could not be together at this party, so he toasted his grandmother's health but left early to drive back to St James' Palace, where Mrs Parker-Bowles was waiting.

The Duke of York and the Princess Royal, both divorced, understood his feelings, but Prince Edward, like his grandmother, could never forgive Mrs Parker-Bowles or Sarah Ferguson for what he sees as the damage done by these two women to the royal family's image.

The broken marriages of his three siblings had made Edward cautious, waiting for six years before marrying Sophie Rhys-Jones, a sporty thirty-four year old blonde. Thoroughly modern and owning her own public relations company, she became the Countess of Wessex on her wedding day, a title which did her business no harm.

The Queen Mother's bright eyes had rested approvingly on her from the start. As a result, the bride-to-be stayed at The Royal Lodge before her five o'clock wedding at St George's Chapel, Windsor, as did her parents Christopher and Mary Rhys-Jones. The newlyweds were lent the Queen Mother's beloved Birkhall in Scotland for their brief honeymoon. This was indeed full benediction.

Enjoying being involved with the wedding preparations, the Queen Mother was amused when Sophie Rhys-Jones complained of looking like a Latvian flight attendant in her engagement day photographs. The Queen looked happier at this wedding than at that of any of the other children and describes her latest daughter-in-law as 'easy, uncomplicated and intelligent'.

CHAPTER 29

Planning a Wonderful Journey

Born when Queen Victoria was still on the throne, the Queen Mother's life has spanned the entire twentieth century, but she has shown an engaging lack of curiosity about the importance of her place in history. Few could look back on a more fulfilled life. She was three when the first flying machine was launched, but lived long enough to see men go to the moon, babies conceived *in vitro* and the cloning of a middle-aged sheep called Dolly. Little surprises her anymore.

Unlike other Kings' widows, wheeled out only for grand occasions, Queen Elizabeth the Queen Mother remains a beloved national institution. We are aware of her high standards, humour and kindness, but have rarely heard her voice in public. Robust, cheerful and well-informed, she has known kings, presidents and emperors, and seen dynasties crumble. Politically alert, she saw colonial countries gain their independence but was sad to see the Empire decline. She enjoyed being the last Empress of India.

Her memories of Africa remain vivid, steeped in nostalgia for colonial days. There is sympathy for those 'good eggs' the white settlers, gradually becoming dispossessed in Rhodesia as she calls it – never Zimbabwe, which is a bit *too* African for her. Insistently she refers to 'Persia', long after her friend the Shah was overthrown, and never Iran as the mullahs decreed. Canada never disappointed, its wholesome and steady culture suited her ideals.

An old-fashioned Tory, she regretted the changes in the House of Lords when a Labour government saw off most of the hereditary peers and thought her old aristocratic friends admirably sanguine.

In a world of increasing violence with the threat of nuclear war, the spread of AIDS, ethnic unrest and fallible Presidents, the Queen Mother remained increasingly tolerant and pragmatic. Surprisingly unshockable, she was none the less distressed by the hurt done to the royal family in 1997 with the marriage breakdown of the Prince of Wales and the Duke of York. The frank revelations of her grandsons' voluble, disgruntled wives about life in the royal family was, to her, disloyal and distasteful. Philosophical as ever, she found comfort in a favourite prayer, 'All is well, all shall be well and all manner of thing shall be well', by the fourteenth-century anchorite Julian of Norwich.

A love of life and exceptional stamina made her unique amongst her contemporaries. Words like 'tired' or 'ill' were forbidden. Hating drugs, she could never be persuaded to take painkillers: homeopathic pills were pressed on rheumaticky friends thirty years younger.

Until quite recently the Queen Mother was fourth in the league of royal duties: still Colonel-in-Chief of several prestigious regiments, she also remains Patron of favoured organisations Dr Barnardo's, the Poultry Club, the National Trust, the Dachshund Club, the London Gardens Society and Master of the Bench of the Middle Temple.

Whether with Dunkirk veterans, fêted by the Worshipful Company of Grocers or offered an honorary citizen of Stalingrad for her help to the Russians during the war, or even wearing shamrock the size of a bird's nest when with the Irish Guards on St Patrick's Day, the Queen Mother has the same effect on people. When she has gone, they say to each other, 'Did you see her?' 'Isn't she wonderful? Would you believe she's as old as the century?' 'Ah, she's the best of the bunch.'

She is the darling of photographers. If they miss a shot or drop a roll of film, the Queen Mother notices and makes it easy for them to get another picture. It is hard to find an unkind photograph of her.

There is no vanity: flattering portraits were often returned. 'They are very nice,' she said, 'but I don't want people thinking I have come through my years on earth completely unscathed.'

Her recall remains impeccable. Unlike many old people she does not believe everything was better in the past but does relish 'delicious memories' of Richard Tauber and Dame Nellie Melba singing, Toscanini conducting, and watching Nijinsky and Pavlova dance at Covent Garden.

Her catholic circle of friends included the English composers Sir Benjamin Britten and Sir William Walton; artists Augustus John and Duncan Grant and several poets. Siegfried Sassoon eloquently captured for her that sense of loss in the 1914-18 war when she lost a brother in Flanders. Sir John Betjeman made her laugh, T S Eliot did not. Edith Sitwell comforted her and Ted Hughes charmed her.

A true Edwardian, she remembers hansom cabs with horses in summer bonnets; it seems only yesterday that a footman in velvet pantaloons anounced a telephone call with 'His Lordship is coming to the instrument, Your Majesty'. The feminist movement was not new to her – she was around for the suffragettes.

In the year of her Coronation, a saloon motorcar, good for race meetings, with leather upholstery, a mahogany dashboard and walnut drinks table cost about £285. The Queen Mother has very little experience of vinyl or of cars made by robots. For her a favourite memory was hearing the gentle 'whoa' as a coachman slowed down the horses outside her childhood home in Mayfair, as straw in the street deadened the sound of iron carriage wheels over the cobblestones.

She is a traditionalist and kept an old wind-up gramophone at The Royal Lodge. She cherished her shiny HMV records with a picture of a dog on the label. Not for her a neat high-tech black compact-disc player, nor has she ever felt the need for headphones.

The Times she enjoyed more in the days when 'gentlemen' wrote for the newspaper, and leader writers accustomed to a half bottle of claret with their work were occasionally found slumped over ancient typewriters with only one word, 'Consider', written.

The wireless and the piano have been enduring companions, whilst television is only selectively enjoyed. Those 'Yes Minister' and 'Call My Bluff' programmes were 'such fun'.

Achieving honours unknown for any other woman, even Florence Nightingale, the Queen Mother as Lady of the Garter,

Lady of the Thistle, first woman Chancellor of London University, secured an impregnable place in public affection. As Warden of the Cinque Ports, a post also held by Sir Robert Menzies and Sir Winston Churchill, she is entitled to 'all the flotsam and jetsam washed up between Shore Beacon in Essex and Redcliffe in Sussex'. The Queen Mother said simply: 'I feel both proud and humble to follow these great men.'

The daily postbag at Clarence House reflects her enduring popularity. A typical tribute was the special detour by a thirty-man detachment of the King's Troop, Royal Horse Artillery, early one morning. Solemnly they tethered their horses to the railings of King Edward VII hospital in London, and delivered a get-well card to the Queen Mother who was recovering from a hip replacement operation. Her appreciation as always was swift.

On every birthday well wishers surge forward along the Mall to sing 'Happy Birthday' and press posies of flowers and cards into her outstretched, chiffon covered arms, or even a Nebuchadnezzar of champagne. 'We'll polish this off,' she says and gives the impression of loving it all. Prince Charles always said that one of his grandmother's greatest gifts was an ability to 'enhance life for others through her own effervescent enthusiasm'.

As she got older the clamour of the birthday celebrations at Clarence House became more exhausting. Yet there was something jaunty and touching about the set of her head as she was driven back into her garden in a golf buggy festooned with ribbons and balloons; this was another triumph. She smiled and waved like a grand old actress. Only those close to her knew the true toll.

The Queen Mother faced her hundredth birthday celebrations with a mixture of pride and resigned gratitude. When she caught a slight chill in January 2000, she was amused by the intense speculation about her survival. A virulent 'flu was killing off her contemporaries, but they, unlike the Queen Mother, were not cosseted by a devoted Household and medical team, united in their efforts to protect the nation's treasure.

While one half of her Household was busy making elaborate birthday plans, the other had the delicate task of discreetly continuing with the funeral ceremonial. Cynics suggested that either the Thanksgiving service in St Paul's Cathedral on 11th July or the Horseguards Parade on 19th July might have to be adapted to fit the gloomier, unthinkable event. Friends and family never publicly recognise such a possibility. They tell you instead about the Queen Mother's continued love of dancing and how much she has been looking forward to the ball being given for her by the Queen in the Waterloo Chamber at Windsor Castle during Ascot week.

To the Queen Mother herself, the really important event is the Queen's Golden Jubilee, marking fifty years on the throne. The Queen fears to encourage celebrations of her accession, in case they might be too painful a reminder for her mother of George VI's death. She knows how her mother never stopped loving the King or missing him, and friends sometimes heard her say under her breath, 'Oh, if only Bertie could see this,' as they explored beautiful gardens or enjoyed old churches, ruined abbeys and Romanesque fonts.

Quietly religious, the Queen Mother has a light hearted spirituality. While she enjoys being spoilt by several generations of the royal family, she is a realist and with Scottish good sense faces the inevitable with far more equanimity than those around her.

She jokes with friends, 'One day, suddenly I will be down there', and a hand gaily points downwards, 'gone', quite gawn. She believes in a joyful after-life, so is truly optimistic.

Not at all gloomily, she visited Westminster Abbey to see how they were getting on with plans for her own funeral. The women at their needlework, delicately repairing antique embroidered robes, looked up in amazement to see her smiling but then shaking her head as she was shown the candles which would be used on the altar and round her coffin. 'Oh do you mind very much,' the Queen Mother asked, 'if I bring my own?' As if planning a wonderful journey.

It is perhaps almost forgotten now how hard the Queen Mother worked, particularly after the King's death. While he was alive, she was sheltered by the royal umbrella and made public appearances only as the monarch's wife. When George VI died, everyone expected her not to travel much further than Balmoral or occasionally to a French château; instead she surprised everyone.

For a woman to strike out alone in the fifties was brave enough, as a widow even more so. Thanks to Churchill's intervention the Queen Mother again made history, treading new ground by taking on arduous tours all over the world. Of course she had the support of her 'little family', as she called her Household, but the experience was fairly new to them too. Newly widowed, she took off for Bulawayo in Zimbabwe and then visited Uganda in 1953.

The wives of some of the tribal chiefs in these African countries were dismayed to find that the Queen Mother's affable Private Secretary, Sir Martin Gilliat, was not married. Constantly genial, he had invented a family for himself but a quite dysfunctional one, always in trouble. This earned instant sympathy from the dignitaries and their wives and the amusement of the Queen Mother.

The momentum of her overseas travels began to diminish in the early 1990s. Passionately committed to the Irish Guards, it was apt that a visit to them in Germany in 1992 proved to be her last official overseas engagement. The following year she saw them at Pirbright, Surrey; in March 2000 she distributed the traditional shamrock to them at Lancaster House in London.

1923   YUGOSLAVIA

The Duchess of York, with the Duke (late King George VI), visited Belgrade where they were sponsors at the christening of the heir to the throne, later to become King Peter II.

1924–25   EAST AFRICA

Visited Kenya, Uganda and the Sudan, with the Duke of York, where they spent the winter of 1924–25. It was mainly a private visit devoted to big game hunting.

1927   AUSTRALIA, NEW ZEALAND, WEST INDIES, MALTA AND GIBRALTAR

World tour, with the Duke of York, during which she opened the Federal Parliament of Australia in the new capital, Canberra. They visited every Australian state and toured New Zealand, and visited the West Indies, Panama, Polynesia, Mauritius, Malta and Gibraltar. The tour lasted from January to June.

1938   FRANCE

King George VI and Queen Elizabeth paid a State visit to Paris in July.

1939   CANADA AND UNITED STATES

With King George VI, embarked in May for a six-week tour covering Canada from coast to coast and a four-day visit to the United States where they were the guests of President Roosevelt in Washington and visited the World's Fair in New York.

1947   SOUTH AFRICA

Visited South Africa, with King George VI, Princess Elizabeth and Princess Margaret, in February. All the main towns were visited in the four months' tour which covered some 10,000 miles.

1953   SOUTHERN RHODESIA AND UGANDA

The Queen Mother visited Bulawayo, with Princess Margaret, where she opened the Central Africa Rhodes Centenary Exhibition on 3rd July. She also carried out a short tour in Southern Rhodesia and visited Entebbe in Uganda on her return journey.

1954   UNITED STATES AND CANADA

Visit to the United States and Canada during October and November, during which she attended the bicentennial ceremonies of Columbia University and received an honorary degree, and spent some days at the White House as the guest of President Eisenhower. Also visited Ottawa for five days.

1956   FRANCE

Made a short visit to Paris in March. While it was primarily a private visit, the Queen Mother opened the Franco-Scottish Exhibition.

1957   FRANCE, RHODESIA AND NYASALAND

Unveiled the Dunkirk war memorial in June. Made a three-week tour in the then Federation of Rhodesia and Nyasaland (now Zimbabwe, Zambia and Malawi) during which she was installed as first President of the University College of Rhodesia and Nyasaland (she resigned in 1970).

1958   NEW ZEALAND AND AUSTRALIA

Made a tour of New Zealand and Australia. The tour lasted from the end of January till March and in the course of the journey the Queen Mother flew round the world calling at Montreal, Vancouver, Honolulu and Fiji on the outward journey and Cocos, Mauritius, Uganda and Malta on the return.

1959   KENYA AND UGANDA

Made a tour of Kenya and Uganda lasting just over three weeks in February during which she travelled extensively.

ITALY AND FRANCE

Made a private visit to Rome in April, with Princess Margaret, as guest of the British Ambassador, followed by a private weekend visit to Paris.

1960   RHODESIA AND NYASALAND

In May visited the then Federation of Rhodesia and Nyasaland. The Queen Mother visited Salisbury, opened the Royal Show in Bulawayo and officially opened the Kariba Dam. The tour included an extensive visit to Northern Rhodesia and Nyasaland (now Zambia and Malawi respectively), where the Queen Mother spent some time in Zomba and in each of the three provinces.

1961   TUNISIA

Made a four-day visit in April during which she went from Tunis to La Marsa, saw the ruins of Carthage and the holy city of Kairouan, visited the Commonwealth war cemeteries at Medjez el Bab and Entidaville. After a visit to Monastir she sailed from the ancient port of Sousse.

1962   CANADA

Visited Montreal in June for the centenary celebration of the Black Watch (Royal Highland Regiment) of Canada, of which she is Colonel-in-Chief.

1964 WEST INDIES

Spent three weeks in the West Indies in March convalescing after an operation which had prevented her from visiting Australia and New Zealand as planned. During her stay she visited Jamaica, Antigua, Tortola, the British Virgin Islands, St Kitts and Nevis, Montserrat, Dominica, St Lucia, St Vincent, Grenada, Trinidad and Tobago, and Barbados.

1965 JAMAICA

Visited Jamaica for a week in February where she received the first honorary degree conferred by the University of the West Indies. She also visited Barbados.

CANADA

Visited Canada for five days in June in connection with the Jubilee celebrations of the Toronto Scottish Regiment.

FEDERAL REPUBLIC OF GERMANY

Made a four-day visit to regiments of BAOR in July.

1966 AUSTRALIA, FIJI AND NEW ZEALAND

Visited the Adelaide Festival of Arts and opened the new Flinders University in Adelaide: visited Perth, Canberra and the Snowy Mountains and Melbourne during her visit from 22nd March to 7th April. She paid a three-day visit to Fiji, and then toured New Zealand for three weeks from 16th April to 6th May. In Auckland she received an honorary doctorate of laws conferred by the University of Auckland.

1967 FRANCE

Paid a two-day visit to Northern France on 6th and 7th May, visiting Normandy, St Malo, Cherbourg, Arromanches, Brécy and Bayeux.

CANADA

Toured the Atlantic provinces of Canada for 13 days, from 10th to 23rd July. Visited New Brunswick, Nova Scotia, Prince Edward Island and Newfoundland.

1968 DENMARK

Attended the wedding, in February, of her goddaughter Princess Benedikte of Denmark, and Prince Richard zu Sayn-Wittgenstein-Berleburg.

1974 CANADA

Visited Canada for six days in June in connection with the presentation of new Colours to the Toronto Scottish Regiment in Toronto and to the Black Watch (Royal Highland Regiment) of Canada in Montreal.

1975   IRAN

Visited Iran for six days in April, including visits to Tehran, Shiraz, Persepolis and Isfahan.

CYPRUS

Paid a one-day visit to the Royal Air Force at Akrotiri.

1976   FRANCE

In October paid a four-day visit to Paris for the opening of the British Cultural Centre.

1978   FEDERAL REPUBLIC OF GERMANY

In November paid a two-day visit to regiments of which she is Colonel-in-Chief.

1979   CANADA

Paid a seven-day visit at the end of June and beginning of July to Halifax, Nova Scotia, and Toronto, Ontario.

1981   CANADA

Paid a seven-day visit at the beginning of July to the state of Ontario to attend the bicentennial celebrations at Niagara-on-the-Lake and to visit regiments of which she is Colonel-in-Chief.

1982   FRANCE

In May visited Paris for three days for the opening of the new wing of the Hertford British Hospital.

FEDERAL REPUBLIC OF GERMANY

For two days in July visited regiments of which she is Colonel-in-Chief.

1983   FEDERAL REPUBLIC OF GERMANY

Paid a two-day visit to the 1st Battalion the Irish Guards for St Patrick's Day (17th March).

NORWAY

Paid a three-day visit in July for the King of Norway's 80th birthday celebrations.

1984   FEDERAL REPUBLIC OF GERMANY

Paid a two-day visit in March to the British Military Hospital in Münster and to the 1st Battalion the Irish Guards on St Patrick's Day.

ITALY

Visited Venice for four days in October.

1985   FEDERAL REPUBLIC OF GERMANY

Made a one-day visit to the 1st Battalion the Irish Guards on St Patrick's Day.

1986   BELGIUM

One-day visit in June to the scene of the Battle of Waterloo.

1987   CANADA

In June spent four days in Montreal to celebrate the 125th anniversary of the Black Watch (Royal Highland Regiment) of Canada.

BERLIN

Visited Berlin for two days in July to commemorate the city's 750th anniversary. Attended celebrations to mark the 50th anniversary of becoming Colonel-in-Chief of the Black Watch (Royal Highland Regiment) and visited the British Military Hospital.

1988   ITALY

Visited Sicily for four days in June.

1989   CANADA

Paid a five-day visit to celebrate the 50th anniversary of her first tour of Canada.

1990   GERMANY

Visited Irish Guards and the 1st Battalion of Light Infantry, Berlin.

1991   GERMANY

One-day visit to Irish Guards.

FRANCE

6th May: S.O.E. memorial service at Valercay.

1992   GERMANY

Visited Irish Guards.

1993   GERMANY

Visited Irish Guards.

Chronology

1900   Elizabeth is born on *4th August*, second youngest of the huge Bowes-
         Lyon family.
         Flight of first Zeppelin.

1901   Death of Queen Victoria, succeeded by Edward VII.

1903   Suffragette movement begins.

1905   Einstein discovers Special Theory of Relativity.

1907   Labour Party formed and electric washing machine launched.

1909   Introduction of old-age pensions and (Ford) model T car invented.

1910   George V becomes King.

1911   Amundsen reaches South Pole.

1914   Start of First World War with assassination at Sarajevo.
         Glamis turned into a hospital.

1917   Russian Revolution and fall of Tsar Nicholas II.
         George V decides it is expedient to change the royal family's German
         name Saxe-Coburg-Gotha to Windsor.

1923   *26th April* Elizabeth's marriage to the Duke of York.
         First public appearances.

1923   *June* Duchess takes on first public engagement at RAF pageant
         in Hendon.

1924   First Labour government.

1926   *21st April* Birth of first child, Princess Elizabeth, at 17 Bruton Street.
         First pictures of the Princess with her mother.
         Television begins, but not for the masses.

1927   *27th January* The King insists the Duke and Duchess of York do a
         major tour of Australia and New Zealand, although it means
         leaving Princess Elizabeth at seven months old.
         After the tour, the Yorks move to 145 Piccadilly.
         Lindbergh flies the Atlantic.

1928   Women who are over 21 get the vote.
         Fleming discovers penicillin.

1929   Wall Street Crash and start of the Great Depression.

1930   *21st August* Princess Margaret born at Glamis.

1932   Mahatma Gandhi begins his campaigns for Indian independence and
         the Untouchables.

1934   Hitler creates Third Reich and instigates Night of the Long Knives.
         Stalinist purges in Russia.

1936   *20th January* King George V dies.
         Spanish Civil War begins.
         The new King, Edward VIII, seen publicly with Mrs Simpson.

1936   *December* The Abdication.
         Duke of York becomes King George VI.

1937   *15th February* George VI, the Queen and Princesses leave their family home (reluctantly) to move to Buckingham Palace.
12th May Coronation at Westminster Abbey.

1937   *June* Successful State visit to France.

1939   The King and Queen visit America, impress President Roosevelt and gain a valuable ally during the war.
Britain and France declare war on Germany. World War II begins.

1942   First nuclear reactor built.

1945   *8th May* VE Day Celebrations.

1946   The King, Queen and Princesses go to South Africa, last tour as a family.

1947   *20th November* Wedding of Princess Elizabeth and Prince Philip.

1948   *14th November* Birth of Prince Charles and the welfare state.

1950   *15th August* Princess Anne is born.
First successful kidney transplant carried out in America.

1951   *3rd May* King opens Festival of Britain.
2nd December National Day of Thanksgiving for improvement in King's health.

1952   *February* The King at Heathrow to see Princess Elizabeth and Prince Philip off on a five month tour of the Commonwealth.
5th February The King is dead.

1953   *2nd June* Queen's Coronation.
Discovery of DNA by Crick and Watson.
The Queen Mother wants to withdraw from the world and buys Castle of Mey: she is persuaded by Sir Winston Churchill to come back into public life.

1954   Queen Mother's first trip alone as a widow to America and Canada.

1955   Queen Mother is invited to be Chancellor of London University.
October Family crisis when Princess Margaret and Peter Townsend cannot marry.

1956   First commercial nuclear power station in Britain.

1957   Flight of Soviet Sputnik.

1959   Discovery of North Sea natural gas.

1960   Invention of lasers.
Princess Margaret and Lord Snowdon marry.
19th February Prince Andrew is born.
Vietnam war begins.
The pill becomes available.

1961   Berlin Wall goes up.
Manned space flight.

1963   President John F Kennedy is assassinated.

1964   The Queen Mother has her appendix removed.
20th March Prince Edward is born.
Word processor is invented.

1967   Dr Christian Barnard performs first heart transplant.

1969   First man on the moon.
        Concorde takes off.

1972   British miners' strike.
        Invention of CT body-scanners in England.

1975   Franco dies and the monarchy is restored in Spain.
        Apollo docks in space.

1978   Princess Margaret's marriage ends in divorce.
        First test-tube baby is born in the UK.

1979   Establishment of European Parliament and direct elections.

1979   Appointment of Margaret Thatcher, Britain's first woman Prime Minister.

1981   *29th July* Wedding of favourite grandson, Prince Charles, to Lady
        Diana Spencer.
        Space Shuttle Columbia leaves on first mission.

1982   *18th June* Prince William, a first great-grandson, is born.
        Britain and Argentina go to war over the Falklands.

1983   Compact Discs introduced.

1984   *15th September* Prince Harry born.

1985   The Queen Mother fulfils ambition with a flight on Concorde.

1988   The World Wide Web and Internet up and running.

1989   Berlin Wall comes down and Communism collapses in eastern
        Europe.

1993   Microsoft launches Windows operating system.

1994   Opening of Channel Tunnel linking France and England by rail.

1995   The Queen Mother has first hip replacement operation. Appears at
        Buckingham Palace for VJ Day Anniversary Parade.

1996   *28th August* Prince and Princess of Wales are divorced.

1997   *31st August* Death of Diana, Princess of Wales.

1998   Second hip replacement.

1999   *June* Queen opens first Scottish Parliament in 300 years.
        Dolly is the world's first cloned sheep.

1999   *11th May* Queen Mother unveils first memorial to 30,000 Londoners
        killed in the Blitz.

2000   *20th June* Prince Charles takes Mrs Parker-Bowles on a public
        engagement.
        21st June Prince William comes of age.
        The Queen hosts a party for 600 guests at Windsor Castle celebrating
        the Queen Mother's hundredth birthday, Princess Margaret's
        seventieth, Princess Anne's fiftieth (*15th August 1950*) and Prince
        Andrew's fortieth (*19th February 1960*).
        26th June Publication of the human genome.
        4th August The Queen Mother's 100th birthday.

F

G